Foreign Direct Investment in Latin America and the Caribbean 2025

UNITED NATIONS

ECLAC

The 2025 version of *Foreign Direct Investment in Latin America and the Caribbean* is the most recent edition of an annual series produced by the Unit on Investment and Corporate Strategies of the Division of Production, Productivity and Management of the Economic Commission for Latin America and the Caribbean (ECLAC). It was prepared by Martín Abeles, Tanner Boisjolie, Pablo Chauvet, Mauricio León, Andrea Laplane, Valentina Leiva, José Luis Lewinsohn and Orlando Reyes, and includes input from Willy Kracht and Nikolas Passos. Preparation of the document was coordinated by Cecilia Plottier and supervised by Marco Llinás. The databases were prepared by Leandro Cabello.

Comments and suggestions were received from José Manuel Salazar-Xirinachs, Javier Medina Vásquez, Vianka Aliaga, Jennifer Alvarado, Anahí Amar, Raquel Artecona, Martín Cherkasky, Ignacio Godoy, Sebastián Herreros, Valeria Jordán, Stephania Mageste, Jorge Mario Martínez, Nahuel Oddone, Nicolás Olave, Alejandro Patiño, Angela Penagos, Laura Poveda, Rafael Poveda, Sebastián Rovira, Amelia Santos Paulino, Astrit Sulstarova and Romain Zivy.

The document also includes inputs prepared with the support of the European Union-Latin America and the Caribbean Digital Alliance, a project financed by the European Union through the Global Gateway strategy.

Thanks are due to the government authorities and executives of companies consulted, for their inputs for the preparation of this document.

Any comments or suggestions concerning the contents of this document should be addressed to Cecilia Plottier (maria.plottier@cepal.org).

United Nations publication
ISBN: 978-92-1-003552-1 (print) • ISBN: 978-92-1-107357-7 (pdf) • ISBN: 978-92-1-107358-4 (ePub) • Sales No.: E.25.II.G.3
LC/PUB.2025/7-P/Rev.1 •Distribution: G •
Printed at United Nations, Santiago • S.2500611[E]

Explanatory notes:

Three dots indicate that data are not available or are not separately reported.
A dash indicates that the amount is nil or negligible.
A full stop is used to indicate decimals.
The word "dollars" refers to United States dollars, unless otherwise specified.
A slash between years (e.g. 2023/2024) indicates a 12-month period falling between the two years.
Individual figures and percentages in tables may not always add up to the corresponding total because of rounding.

This publication should be cited as: Economic Commission for Latin America and the Caribbean. (2025). *Foreign Direct Investment in Latin America and the Caribbean, 2025* (LC/PUB.2025/7-P/Rev.1).

Tables

Executive summary

A. Overview of foreign direct investment in Latin America and the Caribbean

This 2025 edition of *Foreign Direct Investment in Latin America and the Caribbean* comes against a backdrop of great global volatility and uncertainty, amid the tariff changes introduced by the United States, which have challenged the multilateral system and the rules-based order of the past 30 years.

In 2024, global FDI inflows amounted to US$ 1.50 trillion, up 3.7% from 2023. However, the major capital flows recorded in European financial centres are responsible for that growth; without them, global FDI inflows fell by 11.0%, and the outlook for 2025 is negative (United Nations Conference on Trade and Development [UNCTAD], 2025). FDI inflows in the United States grew, while those in China fell, and European countries recorded large fluctuations in financial centres and declines in major economies.

Investment project announcements declined globally relative to 2023. Total announced projects amounted to US$ 1.3 trillion, down by 6.5% year-on-year. The only regions bucking this trend were Latin America and the Caribbean and North America. Renewable energy continued to attract more announcements than any other sector for the sixth consecutive year (19.9% of the global total in 2024), despite a 30.7% drop in value. There was a significant increase in project announcements in the communications sector, explained mostly by an increase in the data processing, hosting and related services subsector. This boom was most prominent in Europe (48% of the global total in 2024) and in Asia and the Pacific (30% of the global total). Project announcements in the semiconductor industry also rose, reflecting rapid growth in demand for high-powered computer chips, a critical input for artificial intelligence applications. Most of this growth derived from investments made in the United States (61.7% of the sector's total).

Market- and technology-driven strategies, along with firms' efforts to position themselves in response to geopolitical circumstances and the consolidation of industrial policies in developed countries, shaped these geographical and sectoral trends.

Against this backdrop, FDI inflows in Latin America and the Caribbean amounted to US$ 188.962 billion in 2024, representing a 7.1% increase relative to 2023,[1] and accounting for 13.7% of gross fixed capital formation and 2.8% of GDP, lower than in the 2010s, when they represented 16.8% and 3.3%, respectively.[2]

However, analysis of the components supporting this growth shows that it was driven by transnational firms already operating in the region, owing mainly to increases in reinvested earnings, while equity inflows remain stagnant (see figure 1). Given that the equity inflows component includes new investments, its relative sluggishness is an indicator of new companies' limited interest in operating in the region.

In 2024, FDI inflows grew in Central America, Mexico and the Caribbean, while results in South American countries were mixed (see map 1). The largest boost came from increases in FDI to Brazil (by 13.8%) and Mexico (by 47.9%), which were the top two recipients of FDI, accounting for 38% and 24% of total inflows, respectively. Colombia, Chile and Argentina placed third, fourth and fifth, respectively, but all three recorded weaker FDI inflows than in 2023.

In 2024, manufacturing inflows increased and services inflows decreased, bringing the two sectors' shares of FDI closer to par (43.6% and 40.4%, respectively).[3] Nearly half the countries that provide information

1 The data on FDI inflows and outflows included in this report derive from countries' official statistics, according to the asset and liability criterion of the *Balance of Payments and International Investment Position Manual: Sixth edition (BPM6)* (International Monetary Fund [IMF], 2009). These data therefore differ from those presented in line with the directional criterion of the *Balance of Payments Manual: Fifth edition (BPM5)* (IMF, 1993), which fundamentally affects figures for Brazil and Mexico. The application of distinct methodologies explains the different result for Latin America and the Caribbean presented by UNCTAD (2025).

2 The regional overview for both indicators is mixed. Percentages represent average values.

3 To date, the countries with FDI inflow data disaggregated by sector for 2024 are Argentina, Brazil, Colombia, Costa Rica, the Dominican Republic, Ecuador, El Salvador, Guatemala, Guyana, Honduras, Mexico, Nicaragua, the Plurinational State of Bolivia and Trinidad and Tobago, which account for a combined 88% of FDI inflows. Data for Brazil are not included in the reinvested earnings component, and sectoral data for Costa Rica and Mexico are computed using the approach established by Balance of Payments Manual: Fifth Edition. As a result, the sum of the sectoral totals is not equal to total inflows.

disaggregated by sector recorded decreased services inflows, which in 2024 especially affected Brazil, Argentina and Ecuador. In contrast, Colombia, the Dominican Republic, Guatemala, Honduras, Mexico and Nicaragua all received increased inflows to the services sector. Manufacturing inflows trended in the opposite direction, increasing in the region's major destination countries. This growth could be indicative of shifting patterns in investment localization and a reconfiguration of global value chains. Lastly, natural resources had the smallest share of inflows (16% of the regional total). Nearly all countries saw declining investment in this sector, except Argentina, where a 44% increase carried the sector's share of the total to 39%, and Guyana, where inflows to the sector —up 43% on the back of expanded hydrocarbon production— accounted for 98% of total inflows.

Figure 1
Latin America and the Caribbean (25 countries):[a] FDI inflows, by component, 2010–2024
(Billions of dollars)

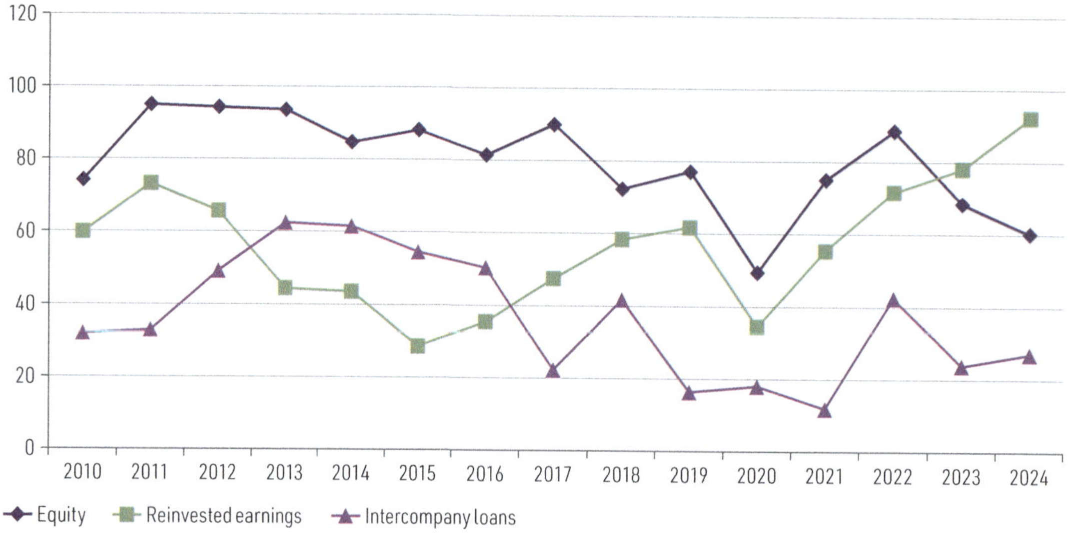

Source: Economic Commission for Latin America and the Caribbean, on the basis of official figures as at 30 June 2025.
[a] Includes the countries with 2024 data by component available: Antigua and Barbuda, Argentina, Bahamas, Brazil, Chile, Colombia, Costa Rica, Dominica, Dominican Republic, Ecuador, Grenada, Guatemala, Honduras, Mexico, Nicaragua, Panama, Paraguay, Peru, Plurinational State of Bolivia, Saint Kitts and Nevis, Saint Lucia, Saint Vincent and the Grenadines, Suriname, Trinidad and Tobago and Uruguay.

In 2024, there were 326 cross-border mergers and acquisitions in the region, down by 13.3% from 2023. Of the top 20 transactions of 2024, the largest involved services firms, including in real estate and financial services, commerce, electricity, gas and water, and telecommunications, as well as hydrocarbon production and mining.

Data for countries reporting the origin of FDI inflows in 2024 show that the United States has held its position as the region's largest investor, accounting for 38% of invested value. The relative share of investment from the European Union (excluding Luxembourg and the Kingdom of the Netherlands) fell to 15% of the regional total in 2024, the lowest figure since 2012. Investment originating from Latin America and the Caribbean represented 12% of FDI inflows, making it the third-largest region of origin. Meanwhile, investments originating from China and Hong Kong, China have generally represented a small proportion of FDI inflows reported in balance-of-payments statistics and, in 2024, Chinese FDI accounted for just 2% of total inflows.[4]

[4] Efforts to trace the origin of FDI through national accounts data are hampered by the fact that these data only identify the immediate source of capital, which may differ from the location of the investing entity. As a result, countries such as Luxembourg and the Kingdom of the Netherlands tend to be overrepresented, given that because of their tax regimes, they are often used by multinational companies to invest in third countries. Investors from China tend to be underrepresented as the immediate source of capital in comparison with their position as its final owner, given that many of their investments are made through third countries. Furthermore, since 2010, investments by Chinese companies have mainly been in the form of purchases of assets already owned by foreign companies, so they have not been reflected in the balance of payments (ECLAC, 2021). Many of the activities of Chinese companies in the region are linked to concessions and construction contracts, which are not FDI.

Map 1
Latin America and the Caribbean (selected countries and subregions): FDI inflows, 2023 and 2024
(Billions of dollars)

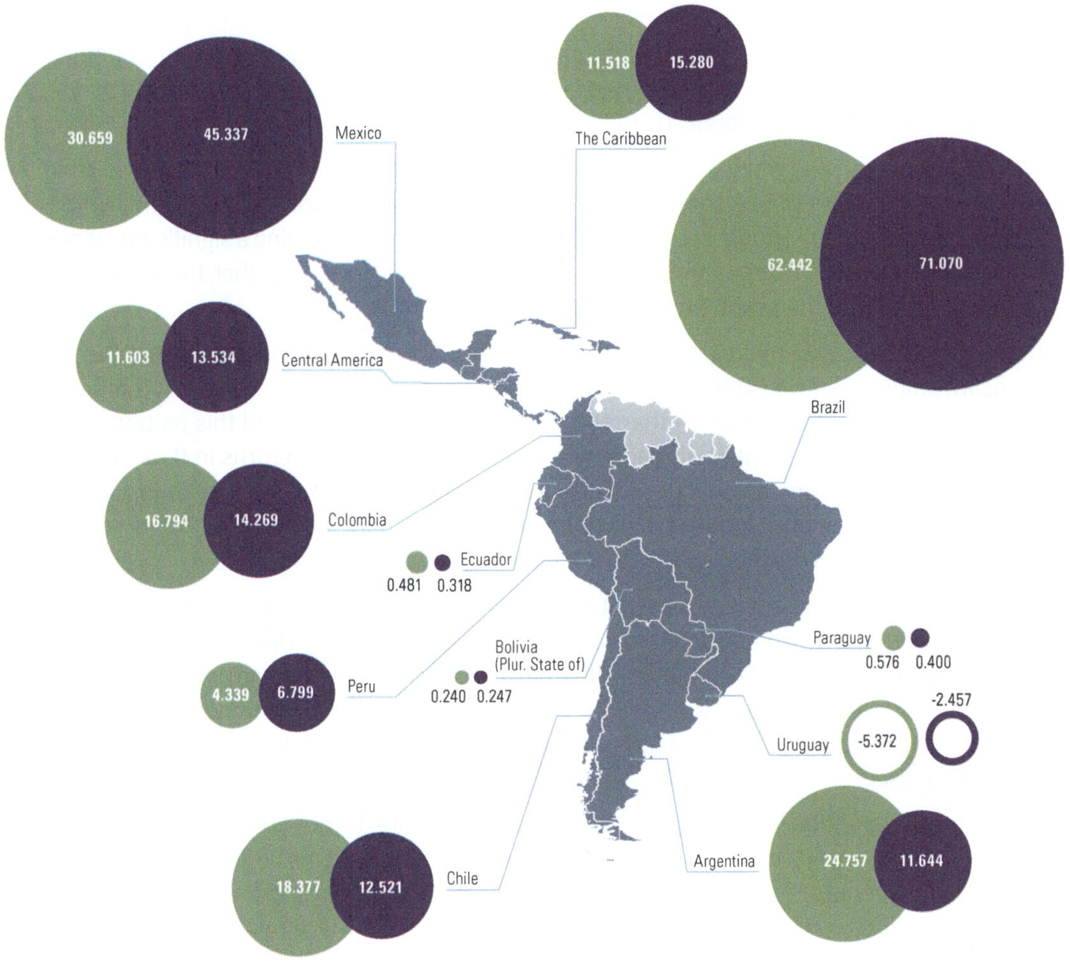

Source: Economic Commission for Latin America and the Caribbean, on the basis of official figures as at 30 June 2025.

The value of projects announced in the region in 2024 surged by 40% relative to 2023, to US$ 168.2 billion, setting a record for the region. This growth is attributable to a considerable increase in hydrocarbon projects, which accounted for 38% of the value of announced projects in 2024, with megaprojects in liquefied natural gas in Argentina and Mexico, and oil exploitation in Guyana. This differs from the global trend of communications, renewable energies and the semiconductor industry accounting for the bulk of FDI announcements in 2024. Despite this growth in non-renewable energy, opportunities in renewable energy continued to attract foreign investors, although the value of announced projects was 13% lower than in 2023, representing the second-highest total to date and more than double the sector average over the previous decade. Brazil accounted for the largest number of these announcements, followed by Peru and Chile. The communications sector also underwent a significant shift in 2024, with announced projects 71% higher than in 2023, owing primarily to planned investments in data processing centres. Brazil, Mexico and Colombia attracted the sector's biggest projects in 2024. The metals and minerals sector, meanwhile, recorded sharp declines in both the number and the value of projects announced.

More innovation-intensive sectors, such as technology-intensive manufacturing, account for a smaller share of announcements, reflecting a decrease from 20% of the region's total announced investment in the 2010s to 15% between 2020 and 2024. In addition, some of the goods production sectors that have been the greatest beneficiaries of project announcements have strong export ties with the United States, which may make them vulnerable to escalating trade restrictions. For example, 69% of automotive sector exports were destined for the United States market in 2023, while that sector accounted for 9% of total announced FDI in the region between 2020 and 2024.

FDI outflows from the region grew in 2024 to US$ 53.033 billion, up 47% over 2023. Brazil was the largest outward investor (46% of the total), despite a slight drop in outward FDI (3%), while investments from Mexico showed the strongest growth, Colombia ranked third following a significant increase in outflows, and outward investment from Chile and Argentina was lower. Together, these five countries accounted for 91% of the region's total FDI outflows.

These figures show that the region is a net recipient of FDI, and that just a few countries invest significant amounts abroad. However, taking a more medium-term view, investment outflows from the region were 15% higher in 2024 than the average for the 2010s. Should this pattern continue, trans-Latin companies' activities abroad could begin to bring greater returns in their countries of origin, not only in the form of foreign-exchange income from the repatriation of earnings generated abroad, but also in the opportunities that could arise to open markets, create distribution networks for other companies in the region, and thus, enable regional integration.

In concluding, this document indicates that the region still needs to improve its policies to attract FDI and coordinate them with productive development policies to increase FDI inflows into the region, as well as its impact on recipient economies. Although trends across countries are mixed, equity inflows for the region reflect the second-lowest figure since 2010, investment announcements grew thanks to major investments in hydrocarbons, and the share of renewable energy and technology-intensive sectors decreased.

One important condition is that FDI should be viewed as a strategic tool of productive development policy (ECLAC, 2024a, 2024c). This perspective is helpful in identifying the best instruments and tools for attracting and maximizing the impact of investment in countries and their territories, and the most effective institutional governance mechanisms for productive development and FDI attraction.

This document includes a non-exhaustive list of guidelines for action aimed at helping countries and their territories to improve their technical, operational, political and prospective (TOPP) capabilities to attract FDI and generate positive productive development outcomes. The technical capabilities to be developed involve: (i) strengthening the capacity of institutions responsible for attracting and managing FDI; (ii) aligning FDI management policies and productive development policies, (iii) designing tools that foster positive FDI impact, (iv) evaluating the use of fiscal and financial incentives and regularly monitoring their results, (v) identifying priority sectors and markets in FDI management strategies, (vi) strengthening the training of human talent for productive development, (vii) strengthening aftercare services and monitoring, and (viii) creating spaces for sharing good practices in Latin America and the Caribbean. Operational capabilities include: (i) allocating resources for FDI management policies, (ii) establishing information systems to monitor FDI and transnational corporate activities, (iii) implement investment facilitation tools and (iv) ensuring monitoring and evaluation of FDI management policies. Political capabilities involve: (i) establishing institutional mechanisms for effective coordination, (ii) incorporating FDI management in governance frameworks at the highest level and (iii) fostering multi-stakeholder participation in designing and adopting FDI attraction policies. Lastly, prospective capacities include: (i) building desirable future scenarios and (ii) encouraging the diversification of FDI by origin.

B. Foreign direct investment in mining and the potential of critical minerals in Latin America and the Caribbean

Humanity is facing an unprecedented environmental crisis. In this context, the energy transition is urgently needed to mitigate the adverse effects of climate change and promote sustainable development. Clean energy technologies, such as solar panels, wind turbines and electric batteries, are more mineral-intensive than conventional fossil fuel-based technologies.

Critical or strategic minerals are defined as those essential to the energy transition and to fostering productive, inclusive and sustainable development in the region's countries with high geological potential. According to this definition, the main critical minerals found in the region are aluminium (bauxite and alumina), cobalt, copper, graphite, lithium, nickel and rare earth elements.

Against this backdrop, Latin America and the Caribbean has emerged as a region of increasing interest, given its high levels of reserves and production of some critical minerals, especially lithium and copper, making it an attractive destination for FDI in the sector. The relative scarcity of these minerals, combined with geopolitical competition, creates both new opportunities and substantial challenges for the region. Historically, the region has not fully leveraged its natural resource endowment. Given its natural competitive advantages, the region could capitalize on its strategic position to strengthen the alignment of policies for FDI attraction and for productive development in the sector.

Critical minerals for the energy transition are geographically concentrated in a limited number of regions, including Latin America and the Caribbean. Chile holds 31.3% of the world's lithium reserves and Argentina has 13.3%. Chile accounts for 19.4% of global reserves of copper, Peru has 10.2% and Mexico holds 5.4%. Brazil possesses 26.5% of the world's graphite reserves and is the second-largest holder of global reserves of rare earth elements, with a 23% share.

Ownership of a significant share of global mineral reserves does not necessarily translate into a high share of production. The region is the world's leading producer of mined copper, accounting for 38% of global production. It is also the second-largest global producer of lithium, with a 33% share. However, it produces a much smaller or marginal share of other critical minerals, such as rare earth elements.

The growth in global demand for critical minerals is driven by decarbonization agreements and the deployment of technologies enabling the transition to low-carbon energy. In Latin America and the Caribbean, this stronger demand has not translated into a larger share of global production. Although production of copper, lithium, bauxite, alumina and graphite increased between 2000 and 2024, the region lost global market share to other regions.

Regional exports of critical minerals expanded markedly over the same period, from US$ 29 billion to US$ 102 billion. However, this represents only slight growth in the region's share in the global critical minerals market, driven primarily by copper and lithium exports. The increased production and export of critical minerals from Latin America and the Caribbean has not been accompanied by greater diversification of the export basket, as raw materials continue to represent a substantial share of the region's exports. For instance, between 2019 and 2023, 62% of the region's critical mineral exports consisted of unprocessed products or those having undergone only basic refining.

Mining investment in Latin America and the Caribbean has been driven by both domestic and foreign capital, with their respective shares fluctuating over time. The share of foreign capital has been growing since the 1990s. FDI has played a fundamental role in the development of mining in several countries of the region.

Official data from 11 countries of the region indicate that so far this century, FDI inflows in the mining sector of Latin America and the Caribbean have largely followed the trend in international mineral prices. FDI inflows to the region's mining sector have rebounded in recent years, totalling

US$ 19.8 billion in 2023, but are still below the peak recorded in 2012. Indeed, the US$ 9.9 billion annual average in the period 2019–2023 was 20% lower than the 2005–2009 average and 53% lower than the 2010–2014 average. Latin America and the Caribbean is falling behind other regions in terms of its capacity to attract capital.

According to project announcements, the value of global FDI in mining in the past two decades surpassed US$ 1.166 trillion, with 36% concentration in Asia and 21% in Latin America and the Caribbean. The Latin American and Caribbean share of the global total contracted, from 24% in the first decade of analysis (2005–2014) to 19% in the second (2015–2024), reflecting the region's diminished role relative to other parts of the world.

Between 2005 and 2024, there were 1,152 project announcements in the minerals and metals sectors in Latin America and the Caribbean, totalling US$ 230.065 billion (see figure 2). Critical minerals accounted for 23.5% of the number and 41.6% of the value of these announcements. Copper is the top mineral of interest to investors in the region, with the highest concentration of announcements occurring in Chile and Peru. More recently, there has been growing interest in lithium and, to a lesser extent, nickel. Since 2016, lithium-related FDI announcements have increased more than ninefold compared to the previous decade, concentrated mainly in Argentina.

Figure 2
Latin America and the Caribbean: FDI project announcements in critical minerals, 2005–2024
(Billions of dollars)

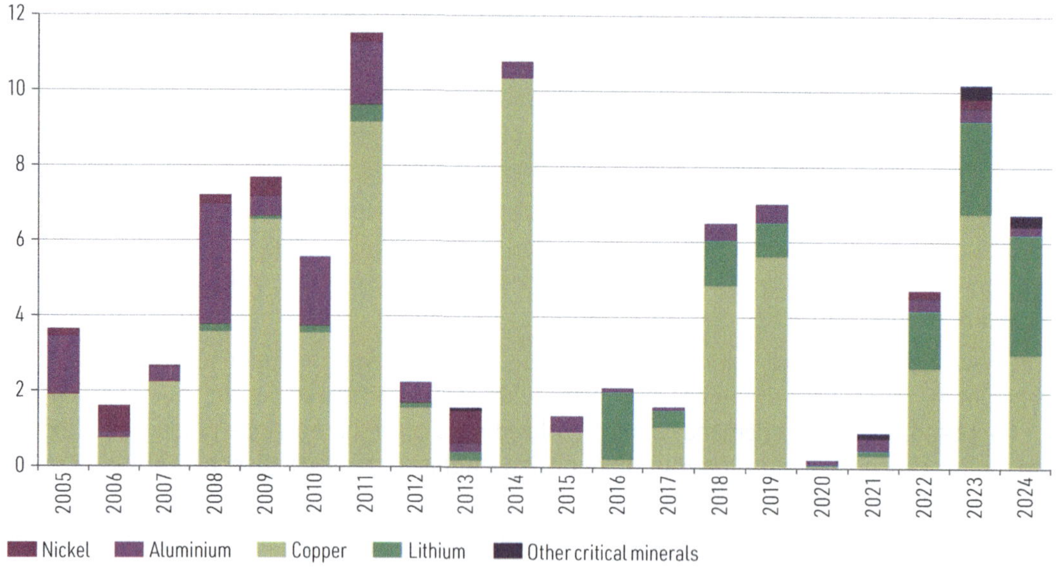

Source: Economic Commission for Latin America and the Caribbean, on the basis of Financial Times. fDi Markets. https://www.fdimarkets.com/

Note: FDI project announcements in critical minerals correspond to the subset of announcements in the minerals and metals sectors (as defined in the source) that pertain to minerals designated as "critical". The aluminium category includes announcements pertaining to bauxite, alumina and aluminium, and the "other critical minerals" category includes those pertaining to cobalt, graphite and rare earth metals.

Not many countries have been able to attract investment in mining and develop new productive and technological capacities at the same time. Some countries have focused on developing extraction technologies, others on supplier development and still others on downstream value addition. Australia and Canada are notable for the important role that their productive development policies have played in capacity absorption and development at all three strategic levels. Both countries have established a wide variety of incentives to attract mining investments geared towards primary activities, with backward and, to a lesser extent, forward linkages.

In Latin America and the Caribbean, investments in the mining sector are concentrated mainly in extractive activities. Investment attraction policies are primarily based on tax incentives and, in general, do not include local content, supplier development or technology transfer commitments. What few productive development policies there are in the mining sector have focused on lithium.

Chile, for example, has implemented a mixed public-private model based on its National Lithium Strategy, which aims to support the industry's sustainable development, recognizing in that pursuit an opportunity to generate productive linkages and advance technological development.

Although FDI in mining has historically been substantial in Latin American and Caribbean countries with a mining tradition, it has declined over the past 20 years. Still, the region remains a global leader in terms of reserves, production and exports of critical minerals, in particular copper and lithium. These minerals offer an unprecedented opportunity to attract new FDI and simultaneously implement productive development policies.

To take advantage of this opportunity, it is essential to strengthen what ECLAC has termed the technical, operational, political and prospective (TOPP) capabilities of the State institutions involved in this arena. Sectoral FDI attraction policies must be coordinated with productive development policies; better coordination in their design and implementation can significantly amplify their impact in the countries of the region, so that their socioeconomic effects are not confined to extractive activities but instead ripple outward.

Today, Latin America and the Caribbean is ideally positioned to adopt these policies as part of a strengthened productive development strategy to capitalize on its strategic critical mineral reserves. Only with sustained efforts in this direction will the region be able to extract maximum benefit from the exploitation of its strategic wealth in these minerals.

C. Digital transformation and foreign direct investment: trends, challenges and opportunities for Latin America and the Caribbean

The digital transformation has become a key driver of development in the twenty-first century. Artificial intelligence, cloud computing, big data analytics, the Internet of things, blockchain technology and other advanced technologies are increasingly consequential, bringing disruptive change to production, service provision, consumption and business models. These technologies also have the potential to boost productivity, efficiency and resilience in various sectors, improve quality of life and enhance environmental sustainability and social inclusion. In this context, digital technologies must be effectively adopted and supported by adequate governance to minimize their associated risks while leveraging their full potential (ECLAC, 2025), especially to address the three development traps facing the region: low capacity for growth; high inequality and low social mobility and cohesion; and weak institutional capacities and ineffective governance (ECLAC, 2024a).

Digitalization is redefining transnational corporate strategies and driving increased FDI flows, which can be an important source of financing to boost digital progress in developing countries to support their productive transformation. However, achieving this is only possible if FDI is complemented by the receiving economy's absorptive capacity, which is determined by macroeconomic, institutional and governance factors and the existence of a solid innovation ecosystem, backed by learning capacities and policies that foster its development, including FDI promotion, regulation and management policies and productive development policies (ECLAC, 2024b). In the digital sphere, key elements include the presence of infrastructure, appropriate regulation and human talent and skills.

The global landscape of FDI for the digital transformation is evolving rapidly. In recent years, investment in semiconductors and data centres has ballooned, especially in the form of large-scale project announcements, spurred on by technological, economic and geopolitical factors. The rise of artificial intelligence, fifth-generation mobile networks, cloud computing and other technologies that involve large-scale data processing has caused global demand for advanced chips to soar. More powerful and resilient infrastructure will be required to sustain the accelerating digitalization of the productive sectors and the rise in digital service provision, translating into a greater need for computing capacity and data centres. Semiconductor production and data centres have thus become assets with strategic value for technological leadership, digital sovereignty and national security, leading many governments to designate them as priority sectors and put in place incentives and regulations in their favour, reshaping investment patterns in the process and restructuring production worldwide.

However, regions and countries have not benefited equally from this trend, and existing gaps could widen further if governments do not take proactive measures. Developed countries have attracted more investment in digital projects than the developing countries group, in which approximately 80% of announcements between 2020 and 2024 were concentrated in just 10 recipient economies (UNCTAD, 2025). From 2005 to 2024, Asia and the Pacific, Western Europe and North America were the main destinations for FDI announcements, while Latin America and the Caribbean accounted for 7% of the announcements' total value. Despite its progress in digitalization, the region continues to present significant gaps in technological adoption and local conditions, which play a part in limiting its share of global FDI flows linked to the digital transformation. Mexico and Brazil accounted for 32% and 29%, respectively, of the cumulative value of project announcements destined for the region in the period 2005–2024; combined with Argentina, Chile and Colombia, they accounted for 80% of the total.

In Latin America and the Caribbean, by sector, communications has been the leading recipient of project announcements in terms of value, reflecting its function of providing connectivity and its central role in supporting critical infrastructure for artificial intelligence, such as data centres and high-speed networks. The software and information technology services sector, meanwhile, leads in number of announcements, accounting for more than half (52%) the total number, in addition to being a significant source of quality jobs.

With regard to the origin of regional FDI inflows, the United States and the countries of the European Union were the main investors. China also figured prominently, especially in 2024, when it increased its FDI announcements in digital technologies by 72% year-on-year. Technological change has also heralded the arrival of technology giants in the region (see figure 3), especially those involved in data processing and cloud services. This reflects an ongoing reconfiguration of the digital industry, one that calls for more complex and multi-sectoral regulatory frameworks.

In order to strengthen the region's position in an increasingly challenging and evolving market, sound and coordinated strategies and comprehensive policies must be implemented and sustained over time. This has not gone unnoticed by investment promotion agencies and institutions, which are being called to perform a strategic function. Internationally, these agencies are incorporating digital transformation into their priorities by designing strategies and initiatives to attract digital FDI. In this regard, the global landscape is quite uneven, as countries and regions are in different stages of development as regards the digital economy, institutional frameworks for investment promotion, and the reorientation of FDI attraction practices towards digital sectors (UNCTAD, 2017; Economic and Social Commission for Asia and the Pacific [ESCAP], 2023).

To understand the role of these agencies in supporting investment in the region's digital transformation and how their strategies and activities are linked to digital and productive development policies, primary data were collected beginning in March 2025 through an online questionnaire circulated to the region's national investment promotion agencies (or to institutions that performed this function in the past). The following 10 countries responded: Argentina, Brazil, Chile, Colombia, Costa Rica, Dominican Republic, Guyana, Panama, Peru and Uruguay.

Figure 3
Latin America and the Caribbean: value of FDI project announcements related to digital technologies, by investing firm and destination country, 2015–2024
(Billions of dollars)

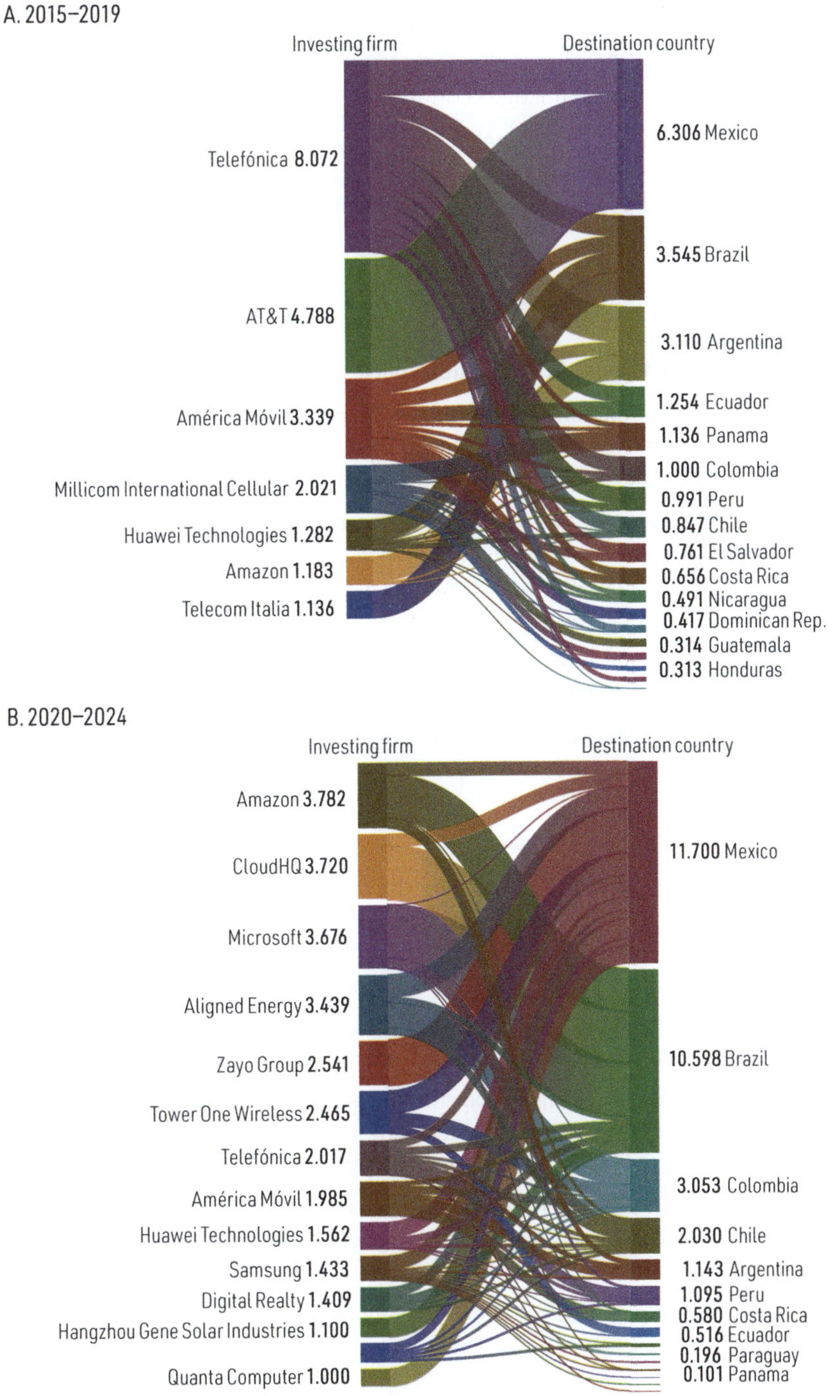

Source: Economic Commission for Latin America and the Caribbean, on the basis of *Financial Times*. fDi Markets. https://www.fdimarkets.com/

Note: The sectors included are communications, software and information technology services, semiconductors, electronic components, consumer electronics, and business machines and equipment. Also included are parent companies that announced investment projects worth more than US$ 1 billion in countries of the region and recipient countries with announcements worth more than US$ 300 million in 2015-2019 and more than US$ 100 million in 2020-2024.

An analysis of the results, complemented by secondary sources, made it possible to identify similarities and differences in institutional strategies and capacities for the promotion, attraction and facilitation of FDI in key sectors for the digital transformation, in addition to linkages with other policies and governance mechanisms.

The results underscored that aligning investment promotion strategies with digital and productive development policies is key for more coherent and effective action. However, in Latin America and the Caribbean, institutional coordination and linkages continue to face persistent obstacles.

Against this backdrop, 10 (non-exhaustive) policy guidelines are proposed below to support progress in attracting and leveraging investments that are aligned and integrated with the digital policies and productive development of countries and their territories (see box 1).

Box 1

Guidelines for formulating and strengthening FDI attraction policies in the digital sphere

1. Carry out a detailed analysis of current capacities, investment gaps and potential to attract investment, with emphasis on infrastructure, digital industries and digitalization of traditional sectors. This should be the basis for subsequent strategic decisions and should be reviewed periodically.
2. Develop a national strategy with a vision for the country and for the future that explicitly incorporates the role of FDI. This vision should guide both investment promotion agencies and productive sectors, ensuring coherence between national and sectoral objectives, such as those defined in the framework of cluster initiatives.
3. Ensure effective linkages between digital, productive development and investment policies through governance mechanisms that promote an integrated and complementary approach.
4. Promote collaboration among national and subnational public bodies, through coordination mechanisms with clear functions (consultative, deliberative, executive) that ensure the effective implementation of investment attraction strategy.
5. Direct FDI attraction efforts towards strategic niches previously identified in the analysis phase, prioritizing projects with high potential impact (on employment, innovation, added value and the environment) over the volume of investment.
6. Assess the incorporation of requirements or incentives that channel FDI towards long-term objectives, such as the creation of quality employment, technology transfer, productive linkages and environmental sustainability.
7. Design and implement monitoring and evaluation systems to measure the impact of FDI on strategic objectives, using investment quality indicators that are comparable and aligned with national priorities.
8. Provide funding for the development of the technical, operational, political and prospective capabilities of the institutions responsible for attracting investment, promoting the incorporation of expertise, the effective use of digital technologies, continuous learning and strategic intelligence.
9. Strengthen the structural and institutional factors that determine the location of FDI and the positive impacts thereof, including digital infrastructure, human talent, regulatory frameworks and productive linkages (e.g. through cluster initiatives).
10. Foster regional-level dialogue and joint efforts to address common regulatory, investment and digitalization challenges.

Source: Economic Commission for Latin America and the Caribbean.

Bibliography

Economic and Social Commission for Asia and the Pacific. (2023). *Policy Guidebook on Attracting and Promoting FDI in the Digital Economy* (ST/ESCAP/3075).

Economic Commission for Latin America and the Caribbean. (2021). *Foreign Direct Investment in Latin America and the Caribbean, 2021* (LC/PUB.2021/8-P).

Economic Commission for Latin America and the Caribbean. (2024a). *Development Traps in Latin America and the Caribbean: Vital Transformations and How to Manage Them. Summary* (LC/SES.40/4).

Economic Commission for Latin America and the Caribbean. (2024b). *Foreign Direct Investment in Latin America and the Caribbean, 2024* (LC/PUB.2024/8-P).

Economic Commission for Latin America and the Caribbean. (2024c). *Panorama of Productive Development Policies in Latin America and the Caribbean, 2024* (LC/PUB.2024/15-P/Rev.1).

Economic Commission for Latin America and the Caribbean. (2025). *Overcoming Development Traps in Latin America and the Caribbean in the Digital Age: The Transformative Potential of Digital Technologies and Artificial Intelligence* (LC/CMSI.9/3/Rev.1).

International Monetary Fund. (1993). *Balance of Payments Manual: Fifth edition.*

International Monetary Fund. (2009). *Balance of Payments and International Investment Position Manual: Sixth edition (BPM6).*

United Nations Conference on Trade and Development. (2017). *World Investment Report 2017: Investment and the Digital Economy.*

United Nations Conference on Trade and Development. (2025). *World Investment Report 2025: International investment in the digital economy.*

CHAPTER

I

Overview of foreign direct investment in Latin America and the Caribbean

Introduction

This year, 2025, marks the thirtieth edition of *Foreign Direct Investment in Latin America and the Caribbean*. Since its beginnings, this publication has reported on the main trends in the activities of transnational corporations in Latin America and the Caribbean. Originally, it focused on compiling and analysing balance-of-payments statistics and reported on the external accounts at a time when the countries of the region were beginning to open their economies up to transnational firms. Thereafter, the analyses have been adapted to the emerging realities and needs of the countries and, now, the 2025 edition comes against an international backdrop of great volatility and uncertainty, amid the tariff changes introduced by the United States, which have challenged the multilateral system and the rules-based order of the past 30 years.

This edition focuses on the trend in investments during 2024. Although the events of the first quarter of 2025 could not have been foreseen, shifts were already occurring in the geographical and sectoral loci of foreign direct investment (FDI), not only because of market- and technology-driven strategies, but also because of firms' efforts to position themselves in response to geopolitical circumstances and the consolidation of productive development policies in developed countries. In 2024, FDI inflows to the United States continued to grow, inflows to China declined along with those to other Asian countries, and European economies saw large fluctuations in financial centres and declines in major economies. In this scenario, FDI inflows to Latin America and the Caribbean rose. However, analysis of the components underpinning this growth shows it has been driven by transnational companies already operating in the region, while equity inflows remain stagnant. Accordingly, the region still needs to improve its policies to attract FDI and link them with its productive development policies, so that the activities of transnational companies in the region can contribute to productive, inclusive and sustainable development.

Section A discusses trends at the international level, particularly investment announcements, which support a more granular sectoral approach than balance-of-payments figures. Section B looks at the main trends in inward FDI in the region, with analysis of balance-of-payments statistics, major cross-border mergers and acquisitions, and FDI announcements. Section C considers outward FDI from the region, while section D offers recommendations and conclusions. Section E gives a detailed analysis of FDI inflows and announcements for each country in the region with the available data.

A. Foreign direct investment globally

FDI inflows have performed unevenly across regions. In 2024, global FDI inflows totalled US$ 1.50 trillion, up 3.7% from 2023 (United Nations Conference on Trade and Development [UNCTAD], 2025). However, the major capital flows recorded in European financial centres are responsible for that growth; without them, global FDI inflows fell by 11.0% (UNCTAD, 2025). In North America, inflows increased: the United States was by far the largest recipient market (18.0% of the total), with an increase of 19.6%, and Canada's inflows were also up (see table I.1). Most European countries, conversely, received less investment than in 2023. France was the only European country in the top 10 recipients globally, even with a decrease in inflows, as also occurred in other leading FDI recipients in Europe, such as Germany, Italy, Poland, Spain and Sweden (not shown in table). In Asia, China's FDI inflows dropped for the second year running, accounting for 8% of the world total. India also received less FDI, although the drop was very slight (-2.0%), while Indonesia received 13.0% more than the previous year. Egypt's inclusion in the top destinations was largely the result of progress on the construction of an urban development megaproject, in partnership with the Government of the United Arab Emirates (UNCTAD, 2025).

Table I.1
World (top 10 extraregional destinations):[a] FDI inflows, 2020–2024
(Billions of dollars and percentages)

	2020	2021	2022	2023	2024	Relative change, 2023-2024 *(Percentages)*	2024 share *(Percentages)*
United States	93.373	386.097	316.895	233.106	278.848	19.6	18
Singapore	71.550	130.955	142.128	135.104	143.352	6.1	10
Hong Kong (China)	134.710	140.186	109.685	122.947	126.181	2.6	8
China	149.342	180.957	189.132	163.253	116.238	-28.8	8
Luxembourg	-3.358	24.809	-316.383	-9.279	105.987	1 242.2	7
Canada	25.594	61.450	45.827	46.525	64.096	37.8	4
Australia	16.420	27.021	65.943	30.577	53.454	74.8	4
Egypt	5.852	5.122	11.400	9.841	46.578	373.3	3
United Arab Emirates	19.884	20.667	22.737	30.688	45.632	48.7	3
France	11.359	32.663	76.520	42.284	33.736	-20.2	2
World	**868.563**	**1 676.523**	**1 389.526**	**1 454.976**	**1 508.803**	**3.7**	

Source: Economic Commission for Latin America and the Caribbean, on the basis of United Nations Conference on Trade and Development. (2025). *World Investment Report 2025: International Investment in the Digital Economy* (UNCTAD/WIR/2025).
[a] Brazil and Mexico were excluded from the top 10, as they will be analysed in section I.B.

For a fuller picture, there follows an analysis of how FDI project announcements have evolved. This information represents the expression of investment intentions by transnational corporations. Accordingly, it is unclear whether and when these investments will ultimately materialize, and if so, what their final amount will be. The information given here is therefore not comparable with balance-of-payments statistics. Rather, it is an analysis of recent trajectories of FDI announcements, which provides an insight into the main sectoral trends and the principal destinations and origins of intended investments. This is extremely useful information for policymakers seeking to attract investment to boost productive development. This caveat applies to all analyses of investment announcements throughout this report.

1. Shifting regional trends in FDI project announcements

Investment project announcements declined globally relative to 2023. Total announced projects amounted to US$ 1.3 trillion, down 6.5% year-on-year. The most pronounced falls in value were in the Middle East (48%) and Africa (41%), with declines of 15% in both Europe and Asia and the Pacific (see figure I.1). The only regions bucking this trend were Latin America and the Caribbean, which registered an increase of 40%, buoyed by record-breaking megaproject announcements in Argentina, Mexico and Guyana, and North America (up 56%, driven largely by a 74% upswing in the United States).

Figure I.1
Global: FDI project announcements, by destination region, 2005–2024
(Billions of dollars)

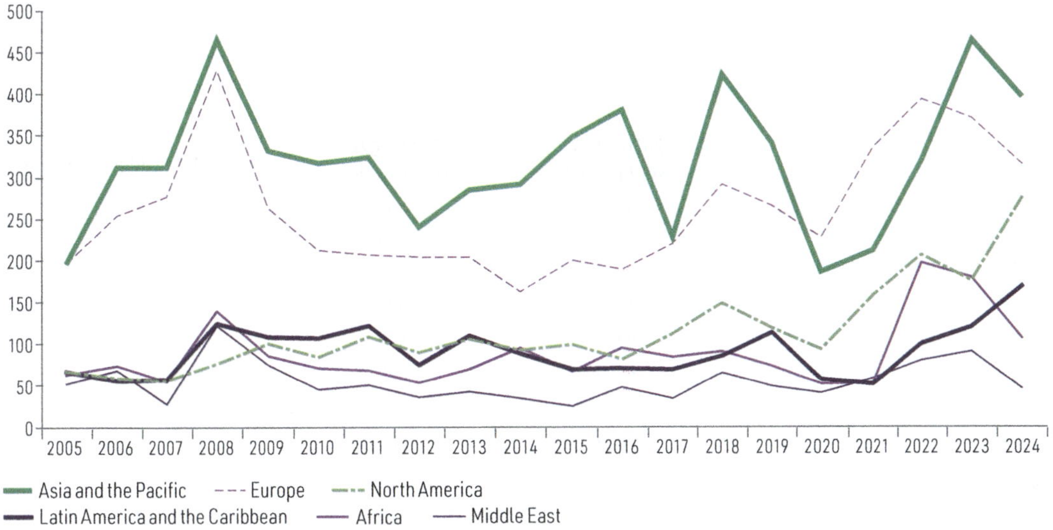

Source: Economic Commission for Latin America and the Caribbean, on the basis of *Financial Times*. fDi Markets. https://www.fdimarkets.com/.

As has been the case for most of the twenty-first century, Asia and the Pacific was the top destination for FDI project announcements in value terms in 2024, accounting for 30% of the global total, followed by Europe (24%), North America (21%), Latin America and the Caribbean (13%), Africa (8%) and the Middle East (4%).

Although it remains in third place, North America —long an attractive investment destination— has seen the largest relative growth in project announcement value this decade, with a few sectors standing out as drivers of this growth. Project announcements in the semiconductor sector, for example, grew from an average of US$ 2.3 billion per year in the 2010s to US$ 28.9 billion in the 2020s. The electronic components sector registered a similar expansion, from US$ 2.2 billion to US$ 24.4 billion per year over the same period. The renewable energy sector has also contributed significantly to the increase in FDI attracted to North America, accounting for an average of US$ 22.1 billion in annual announcements since 2020, compared with an average of US$ 8.8 billion in the 2010s.

Each of these three sectors has been the focus of concerted industrial policy efforts in the United States to secure the country's lead in industries of growing strategic importance, particularly against a backdrop of intensifying competition with China. Between 2020 and 2022, the United States launched a wave of industrial policy initiatives backed by more than US$ 500 billion in funding. These included the Creating Helpful Incentives to Produce Semiconductors (CHIPS) and Science Act of 2022, which aimed to boost domestic semiconductor research and manufacturing; Executive Order No. 14017 on America's Supply Chains, an initiative to ensure resilience by prioritizing domestic production capacity for semiconductors, batteries, critical minerals and pharmaceuticals; the Infrastructure Investment and Jobs Act of 2021, which included a focus on clean energy infrastructure; and the Inflation Reduction Act of 2022, which extended additional support for clean energy programmes.

These policies draw on a wide range of mechanisms, including workforce education initiatives, loans, guaranteed contracts and tax incentives. They also seek to facilitate the engagement of stakeholders with a view to building strong innovation ecosystems and bolstering target industries in the United States (Bonvillian, 2024). Although investment decisions are influenced by a number of factors and it is still too early to fully assess the long-term impact of these policies, the rapid increase in projects in the semiconductor, electronic components, and renewable energy sectors may be an indicator of the efficacy of such efforts.

Conversely, there has been a sharp decline in projects undertaken in China. Since 2020, average FDI project announcements in China have fallen 58% compared with 2010–2019, and this across all major sectors (see table I.2).

Table I.2
China: top 10 sectors of FDI project announcements, annual averages for 2010–2024
(Billions of dollars and percentage change)

Sector	2010-2019 average value	2020-2024 average value	Percentage change in average
Real estate	10.399	2.356	-77
Automotive OEM (original equipment manufacturing)	9.579	3.519	-63
Chemicals	7.957	3.320	-58
Semiconductors	6.628	2.628	-60
Transportation and warehousing	6.344	4.628	-27
Electronic components	6.205	3.268	-47
Financial services	5.968	2.896	-52
Food and beverages	3.566	1.482	-58
Auto parts	3.011	1.065	-65
Consumer products	2.801	1.635	-42

Source: Economic Commission for Latin America and the Caribbean, on the basis of *Financial Times*. fDi Markets. https://www.fdimarkets.com/.

Despite the sharp decline in project announcements in China, the overall stability of announced project value for the Asia-Pacific region can be attributed to increased investor interest in other major economies (see figure I.2). Since 2020, India has emerged as the top destination in the region and Australia has also seen a marked increase in the average annual value of project announcements.

Figure I.2
Asia and the Pacific (10 countries): FDI project announcements, by destination country, annual averages for 2010–2019 and 2020–2024
(Billions of dollars)

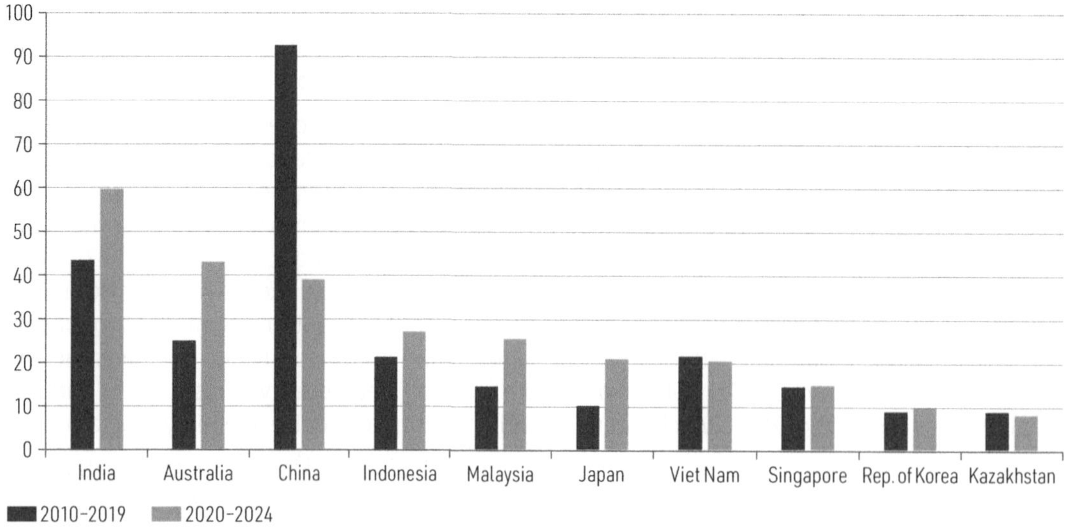

Source: Economic Commission for Latin America and the Caribbean, on the basis of Financial Times. fDi Markets. https://www.fdimarkets.com/.

2. Sectors driving investor interest in 2024

Despite a 30.7% decrease in the announced value of projects relative to 2023, the renewable energy sector continued to attract more announcements than any other for the sixth consecutive year (19.9% of the global total in 2024) (see figure I.3). Announced renewable energy project values declined in nearly all regions, with particularly steep drops in the Middle East (-77.7%), Africa (-62.2%) and Europe (-27.2%). North America was the only region where the value of such projects increased, up 17.6% from 2023.

Figure I.3
Global: FDI project announcements, by sector, 2010–2024
(Billions of dollars)

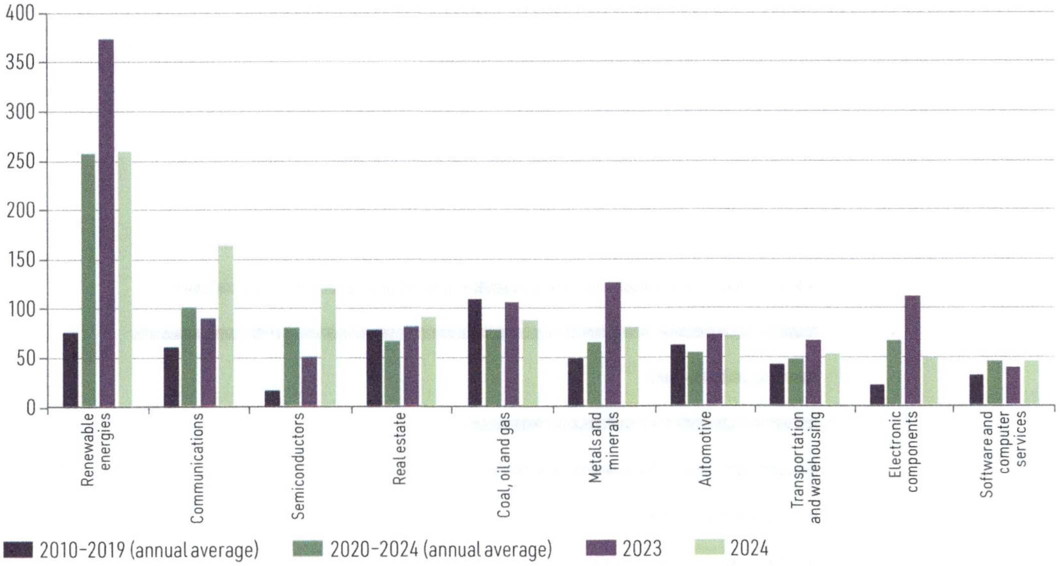

Source: Economic Commission for Latin America and the Caribbean, on the basis of *Financial Times*. fDi Markets. https://www.fdimarkets.com/.

There was a significant increase in project announcements in the communications sector, explained mostly by an increase in the data processing, hosting and related services subsector (89% of the total). This boom was most prominent in Europe, where the value of projects in the subsector surged by 209% (to US$ 69.2 billion), accounting for 48% of the global total in 2024. In Asia and the Pacific, investment announcements in the subsector rose by 53.9% to US$ 43.2 billion, bringing the region's share to 30% of the global total. Large relative increases were also registered in North America (233.8%), the Middle East (127.8%) and Latin America and the Caribbean (42.2%), although these regions accounted for significantly smaller shares of the global total. Chapter III of this report analyses FDI in digital economy sectors in Latin America and the Caribbean, and provides valuable insights into the drivers of these investments in the region and related challenges and opportunities.

Globally, the primary force behind the increased investor interest in data processing, hosting and related services was a massive upswing in investment intentions by United States-based companies. Other significant origins of investment in the subsector included Singapore and China.

Project announcements in the semiconductor industry amounted to US$ 119.8 billion in 2024, a 138.8% increase on the 2023 figure. This reflects rapid growth in demand for high-powered computer chips, a critical input for artificial intelligence applications. Most of this growth can be attributed to investments made in the United States, which was the destination for US$ 73.9 billion worth of semiconductor projects —nearly 30 times the 2023 amount—, representing 61.7% of the global total announced for 2024. Other major destinations for semiconductor projects were Asia and the Pacific (US$ 32.2 billion) and Europe (US$ 13 billion), which accounted for 27% and 11%, respectively, of the value of announced projects, albeit with little variation compared with 2023. In 2024, the largest investors in the sector were based in Taiwan Province of China, the Republic of Korea and the United Arab Emirates, collectively accounting for 82% of the value of the year's announced projects.[1]

3. Project announcements by origin

Overall, the United States returned to its position as the largest country of origin of FDI project announcements globally in 2024, after being surpassed by China in 2023 (see figure I.4). Companies based in the United States announced US$ 223.4 billion in projects, a figure 10% higher than the previous year. Although China remained the second largest origin of FDI project announcements with a total value of US$ 93.3 billion, the value of projects announced by Chinese firms fell by 56.6% relative to the 2023 peak.

Figure I.4
Top 10 economies of origin of FDI project announcements worldwide, 2023 and 2024
(Billions of dollars)

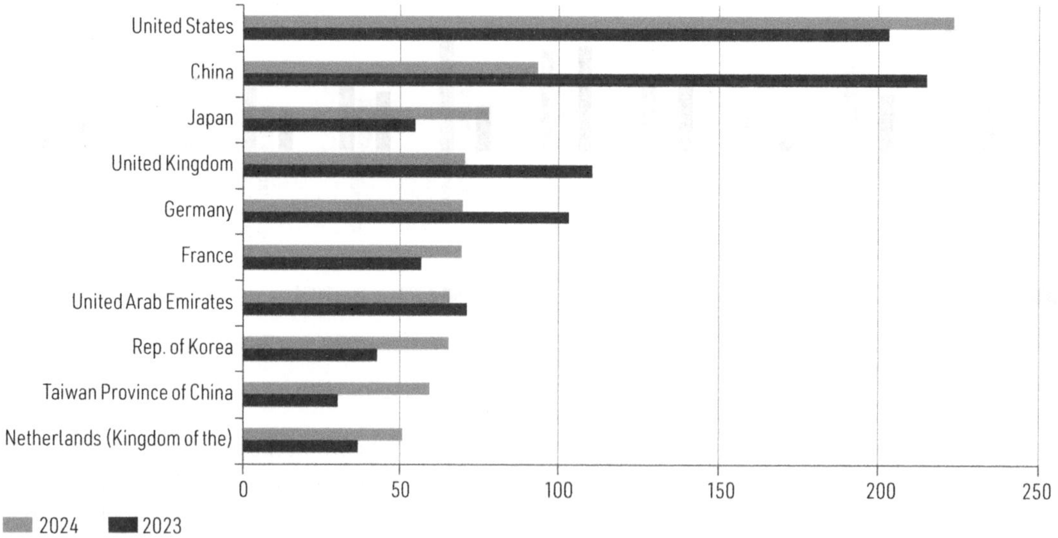

Source: Economic Commission for Latin America and the Caribbean, on the basis of *Financial Times*. fDi Markets. https://www.fdimarkets.com/.

Looking at the longer-term trends, since 2020 there have been notable shifts in terms of the top economies of origin for FDI project announcements (see table I.3). While the top three remained unchanged (United States, China and Germany), the relative gaps between them have widened: while average annual project announcements originating in the United States have increased by 39%, international project announcements by Chinese and German companies have grown in value by 19.3% and 16.4%, respectively.

[1] All figures in this section have been verified on the basis of data from fDi Markets as at 26 February 2025.

Table I.3
Top 10 economies of origin of FDI project announcements worldwide, annual averages for 2010–2019 and 2020–2024
(Billions of dollars)

A. 2010-2019

	Economy	Value
1	United States	150.2
2	China	78.2
3	Germany	64.6
4	Japan	58.2
5	United Kingdom	50.1
6	France	47.2
7	Republic of Korea	30.1
8	Spain	25.7
9	Netherlands (Kingdom of the)	22.7
10	Canada	22.1

B. 2020-2024

	Economy	Value
1	United States	208.8
2	China	93.4
3	Germany	75.2
4	United Kingdom	70.9
5	France	58.1
6	Japan	51.8
7	United Arab Emirates	51.0
8	Republic of Korea	48.1
9	Taiwan Province of China	39.4
10	Singapore	33.1

Source: Economic Commission for Latin America and the Caribbean, on the basis of *Financial Times*. fDi Markets. https://www.fdimarkets.com/.

In the case of Taiwan Province of China, average annual investment announcements since 2020 have grown by 155% compared with 2010–2019, driven primarily by international semiconductor projects. Singapore has also seen substantial growth in overseas project announcements, as Singaporean firms have increased annual investment intentions by 50%. Lastly, the United Arab Emirates has emerged as a considerable source of FDI project announcements in the first half of the 2020s. Companies based in the United Arab Emirates have been particularly active in the renewable energy and real estate sectors, which have accounted for 71% of all announcements originating from the country in this period. This has come amid broader efforts to diversify the country's economy, with green energy being a key part of this strategy (United Arab Emirates, 2023). State-linked companies have been particularly active in recent years and investments in solar, wind and green hydrogen projects have positioned the United Arab Emirates as an increasingly influential investor in the global energy transition (*Financial Times*, 2023).

B. Overview of Latin America and the Caribbean

The purpose of analysing FDI inflows is to identify trends in the regional investment patterns of transnational corporations, as their activity has the potential to contribute to growth, productive transformation and employment in Latin America and the Caribbean.

However, these statistics offer only a partial view of such investments; therefore, the study is complemented with data that more directly reflect transnational corporate activity, such as cross-border mergers and acquisitions and FDI project announcements. These data enable more precise approximations at the sectoral level and offer a better understanding of the origins of capital flows (see section I.A for a discussion of the analytical utility and limitations of FDI project announcements).

Cross-border mergers and acquisitions, which include the purchase of assets located in the region, can be divided into two types according to their impact on the balance of payments: acquisitions of domestic firms, which are likely to generate a capital inflow,[2] and acquisitions of foreign firms, which do not necessarily generate a capital inflow for the country in which the asset is located.

Both types of transaction are analysed throughout this report, because they offer a glimpse into which sectors are most attractive to foreign capital and which countries and businesses are most active in the region.

1. Trends by component and destination

In 2024, FDI inflows in Latin America and the Caribbean reached US$ 188.962 billion, representing a 7.1% increase relative to 2023 (see figure I.5)[3] and accounting for 13.7% of gross fixed capital formation and 2.8% of GDP.[4] This reflects a reduction in FDI as a share of both total investments and the overall economy compared to the 2010s, when FDI inflows accounted for 16.8% of gross fixed capital formation and 3.3% of GDP. The region accounted for 12.5% of the total value of FDI inflows worldwide, which is similar to the 2023 figure (12.1%). This percentage is greater than the region's share in global trade in 2023 (6% of goods exports and 3.2% of services exports).

The analysis of FDI by component attributes the growth recorded in 2024 to an increase in reinvested earnings. The three components of FDI identified in the balance of payments are equity, reinvested earnings and intercompany loans. The equity inflows component, which includes greenfield FDI and cross-border mergers and acquisitions of domestic companies, is the most telling indicator of new foreign firms' interest in investing in the region. Reinvested earnings and intercompany loans, on the other hand, represent investments by companies that are already operating in the region and therefore do not indicate the arrival of new investors. Regarding intercompany loans in particular, data suggest that some companies act as financial intermediaries, absorbing liquidity from international capital markets to invest it both domestically and abroad in order to take advantage of interest rate differentials (De Camino, Pérez Caldentey and Vera, 2023). As a result, intercompany loans cannot be unreservedly qualified as productive flows.

---

2 It is possible for transactions involving complex financial details to have no impact at all, even if the acquired firm is domestic.

3 FDI inflow and outflow data used in this report are drawn from official statistics provided by the countries and presented according to asset and liability criteria as defined in International Monetary Fund. (2009). *Balance of Payments and International Investment Position Manual: Sixth Edition (BPM6)*. These data differ from the figures presented according to the directional criteria defined in International Monetary Fund. (2009). *Balance of Payments and International Investment Position Manual: Fifth Edition (BPM5)*, fundamentally affecting the figures provided for Brazil and Mexico. The difference in methodologies explains the discrepancy between the regional total presented in this report and that presented in UNCTAD (2025).

4 The regional overview for both indicators is mixed. Percentages represent average values.

Figure I.5
Latin America and the Caribbean (29 countries):[a] FDI inflows, 2010–2024
(Billions of dollars and percentages of GDP)

Source: Economic Commission for Latin America and the Caribbean, on the basis of official figures as at 30 June 2025.
Note: Except in the case of Peru, information was obtained according to the criteria established by International Monetary Fund. (2009). *Balance of Payments and International Investment Position Manual: Sixth Edition (BPM6)*.
[a] Antigua and Barbuda, Argentina, Bahamas (The), Belize, Brazil, Chile, Colombia, Costa Rica, Dominica, Dominican Republic, Ecuador, El Salvador, Grenada, Guatemala, Guyana, Honduras, Jamaica, Mexico, Nicaragua, Panama, Paraguay, Peru, Plurinational State of Bolivia, Saint Kitts and Nevis, Saint Lucia, Saint Vincent and the Grenadines, Suriname, Trinidad and Tobago and Uruguay.

In 2024, reinvested earnings increased by 18%, accounting for 52% of the region's total inflows (see figure I.6), the component's highest share since 2010. The second-largest component was equity inflows, amounting to 34% of the total despite a 12% decrease that marked a second consecutive year of declines. Moreover, between 2020 and 2024, annual equity inflows totalled US$ 68.066 billion, which is 20% lower than the value recorded for the 2010s. Intercompany loans, meanwhile, grew by 14% year-on-year to account for 15% of total inflows in 2024.

Figure I.6
Latin America and the Caribbean (25 countries):[a] FDI inflows, by component, 2010–2024
(Billions of dollars)

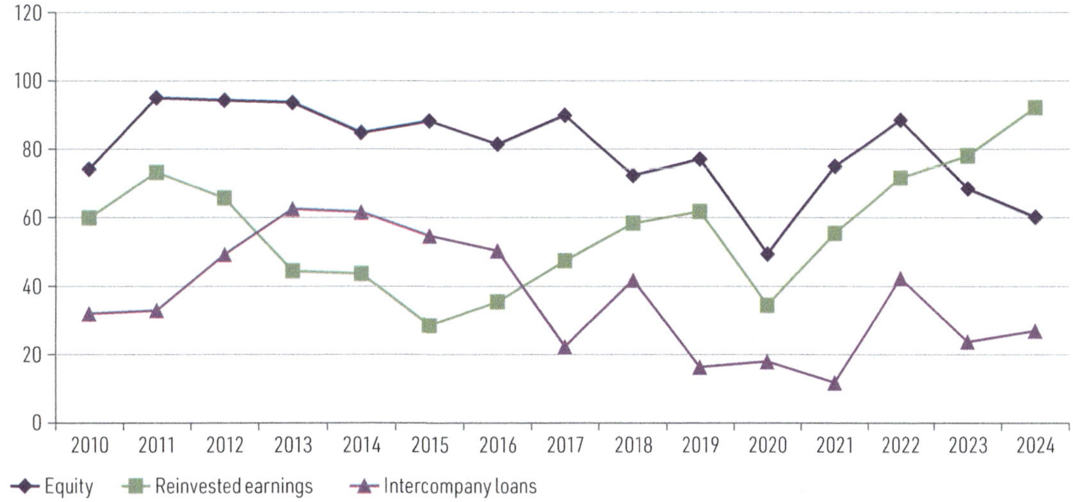

Source: Economic Commission for Latin America and the Caribbean, on the basis of official figures as at 30 June 2025.
[a] Includes the countries with data disaggregated by component available for 2024: Antigua and Barbuda, Argentina, Bahamas (The), Brazil, Chile, Colombia, Costa Rica, Dominica, Dominican Republic, Ecuador, Grenada, Guatemala, Honduras, Mexico, Nicaragua, Panama, Paraguay, Peru, Plurinational State of Bolivia, Saint Kitts and Nevis, Saint Lucia, Saint Vincent and the Grenadines, Suriname, Trinidad and Tobago and Uruguay.

With regard to the destination of FDI, most countries received more investments in 2024 than in 2023 (see table I.4). The largest boost came from increases in FDI to Brazil (by 13.8%) and Mexico (by 47.9%), which were the top two recipients and, together, accounted for 61.6% of the region's total inflows. They were followed by Colombia, Chile and Argentina, although all three countries recorded decreased inflows relative to 2023.

Table I.4
Latin America and the Caribbean (32 countries): FDI inflows, by destination country and subregion, 2010–2024
(Billions of dollars and percentages)

Country or subregion	2010-2019[a]	2020	2021	2022	2023	2024	Absolute change, 2023-2024	Relative change, 2023-2024 *(Percentages)*	Share of total regional FDI, 2024 *(Percentages)*
South America	**134.256**	**65.141**	**91.737**	**147.411**	**122.633**	**114.812**	**-7.822**	**-6.4**	**60.8**
Argentina	9.729	4.884	6.658	15.206	24.757	11.644	-13.112	-53.0	6.2
Bolivia (Plurinational State of)	665	-1	584	6	240	247	7	2.9	0.1
Brazil	79.559	38.270	46.441	74.606	62.442	71.070	8.628	13.8	37.6
Chile	17.556	11.447	15.177	18.772	18.377	12.521	-5.856	-31.9	6.6
Colombia	13.296	7.459	9.561	17.182	16.794	14.269	-2.525	-15.0	7.6
Ecuador	797	1.119	650	882	481	318	-163	-34.0	0.2
Paraguay	634	326	358	745	576	400	-176	-30.6	0.2
Peru	7.636	663	7.142	11.201	4.339	6.799	2.460	56.7	3.6
Uruguay	2.430	973	5.165	8.810	-5.372	-2.457	2.915	-54.3	-1.3
Venezuela (Bolivarian Republic of)	1.955	...	...	...	...	...	...	...	...
Mexico	**32.811**	**31.538**	**35.460**	**39.136**	**30.659**	**45.337**	**14.677**	**47.9**	**24.0**
Central America	**10.519**	**1.556**	**10.640**	**9.801**	**11.603**	**13.534**	**1.931**	**16.6**	**7.2**
Costa Rica	2.802	2.103	3.593	3.673	4.687	5.298	611	13.0	2.8
El Salvador	406	24	386	172	718	640	-79	-11.0	0.3
Guatemala	1.156	935	3.462	1.442	1.611	1.694	84	5.2	0.9
Honduras	1.155	224	800	759	1.085	1.309	224	20.6	0.7
Nicaragua	858	747	1.047	1.287	1.114	1.352	238	21.4	0.7
Panama	4.143	-2.477	1.353	2.467	2.387	3.240	853	35.7	1.7
The Caribbean[b]	**5.953**	**7.107**	**8.463**	**9.270**	**11.518**	**15.280**	**3.761**	**32.7**	**8.1**
Antigua and Barbuda	115	77	290	313	328	308	-20	-6.2	0.2
Bahamas	1.311	435	383	531	322	241	-82	-25.4	0.1
Barbados	349	262	237	0	0	0	0	...	0.0
Belize	97	76	125	141	16	128	112	697.4	0.1
Dominica	39	22	28	17	48	49	2	3.5	0.0
Dominican Republic	2.538	2.560	3.197	4.099	4.390	4.523	133	3.0	2.4
Grenada	115	136	152	163	220	269	49	22.2	0.1
Guyana	454	2.074	4.468	4.393	7.198	10.401	3.203	44.5	5.5
Haiti	149	25	51	39	0	0	0	...	0.0

Country or subregion	2010-2019[a]	2020	2021	2022	2023	2024	Absolute change, 2023-2024	Relative change, 2023-2024 *(Percentages)*	Share of total regional FDI, 2024 *(Percentages)*
Jamaica	617	265	320	319	377	165	-212	-56.3	0.1
Saint Kitts and Nevis	104	6	19	53	31	22	-9	-29.3	0.0
Saint Lucia	99	48	91	59	123	180	56	45.5	0.1
Saint Vincent and the Grenadines	105	65	168	65	74	74	0	-0.6	0.0
Suriname	123	1	-133	-9	-53	-38	16	-29.3	0.0
Trinidad and Tobago	-262	1.056	-935	-914	-1.555	-1.041	515	-33.1	-0.6
Total[b]	**183.540**	**105.342**	**146.300**	**205.618**	**176.414**	**188.962**	**12.548**	**7.1**	**100.0**

Source: Economic Commission for Latin America and the Caribbean, on the basis of official figures as at 30 June 2025.
Note: Except in the case of Peru, information was obtained according to the criteria established by International Monetary Fund. (2009). *Balance of Payments and International Investment Position Manual: Sixth Edition (BPM6)*.
[a] Simple averages.
[b] For the purpose of calculating absolute and relative change, countries for which 2024 data were unavailable were not included in the 2023 totals and subtotals.

The analysis of inflows by destination country reveals disparities in the region, not only in terms of magnitude and trends but also with regard to the relative weight of FDI inflows in countries' GDP. Average FDI inflows for the period 2021–2024 did not exceed 6% of GDP in the top five destination countries of 2024. Of that group, Chile and Colombia had the highest FDI as a share of GDP (5.1% and 4.0%, respectively) (see figure I.7). At the other end of the spectrum, Guyana —the sixth-largest FDI destination thanks to hydrocarbon production— had FDI inflows amounting to 42.6% of GDP in the same period.

Figure I.7
Latin America and the Caribbean (29 countries): FDI inflows, by destination country (2023 and 2024) and average share of GDP (2021–2024)
(Billions of dollars and percentages)

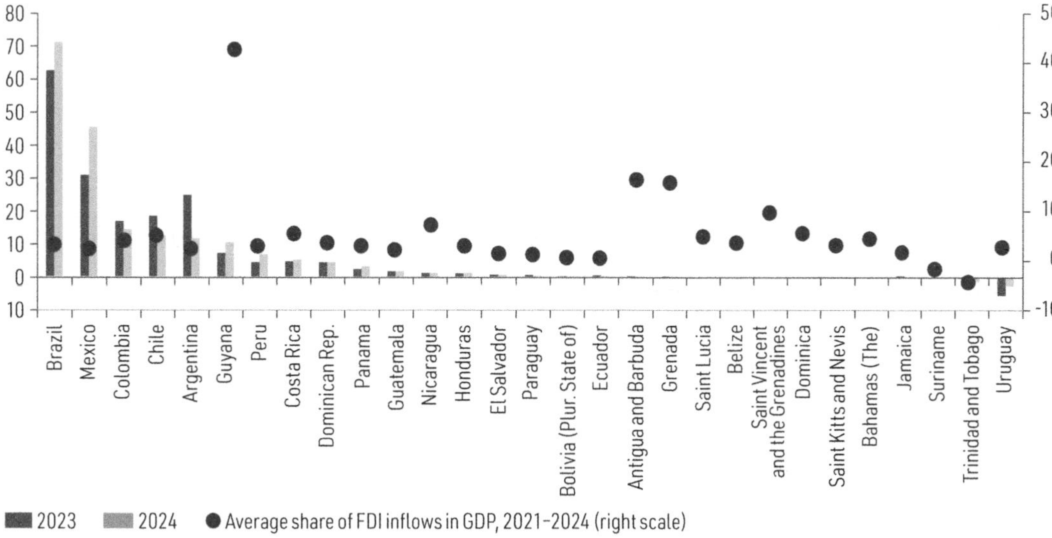

Source: Economic Commission for Latin America and the Caribbean, on the basis of official figures as at 30 June 2025.

2. FDI inflows by sector

From a productive development standpoint, identifying the sectors that are the largest FDI recipients is important for evaluating the extent to which investments contribute to diversification and technological sophistication, the energy transition, employment and the digital transformation in the countries of the region.

Official balance-of-payments statistics enable only a limited analysis, as few countries publish FDI inflows disaggregated by sector, and the general level of disaggregation is very broad. This allows only three major categories to be compared: services, manufacturing and natural resources. Therefore, to obtain a more detailed sectoral perspective, the analysis also includes cross-border mergers and acquisitions and, in the following subsection, project announcements.

(a) Balance-of-payments data

Post-pandemic, the sectoral composition of FDI inflows changed relative to the 2010s, with services gaining a more prominent share (see figure I.8). However, this trend shifted in 2024, when a decrease in services inflows and an increase in manufacturing inflows brought the two sectors' shares of FDI closer to par (43.6% and 40.4%, respectively).[5]

Figure I.8
Latin America and the Caribbean (14 countries):[a] sectoral distribution of FDI inflows, 2010–2024
(Percentages)

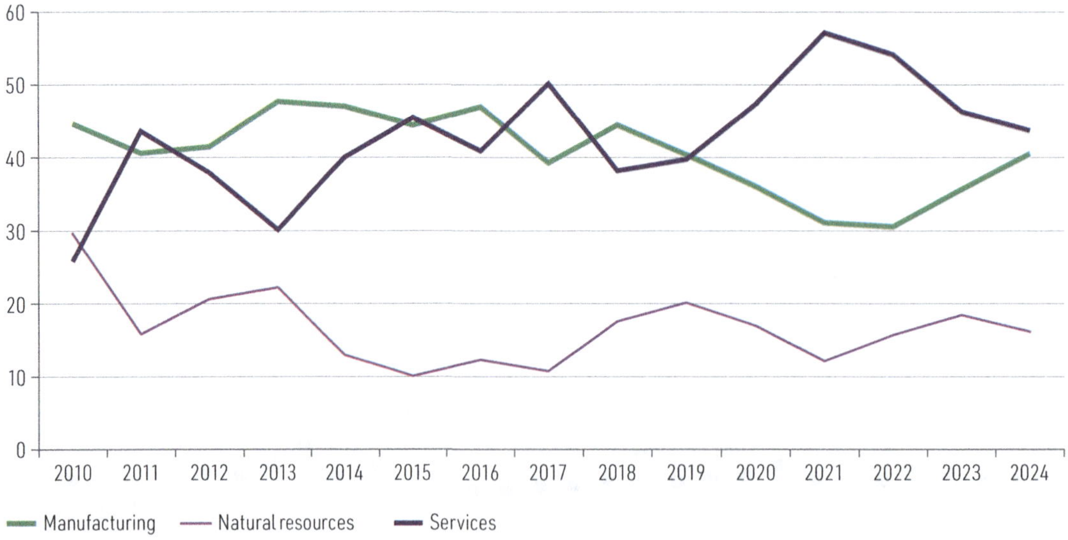

Source: Economic Commission for Latin America and the Caribbean, on the basis of official figures as at 30 June 2025.
Note: The information for Brazil does not include the reinvested earnings component. Sectoral data for Costa Rica and Mexico were computed using the approach established by International Monetary Fund. (1993). *Balance of Payments and International Investment Position Manual: Fifth Edition (BPM5)*.

[a] Countries with sectoral data available for 2024: Argentina, Brazil, Colombia, Costa Rica, Dominican Republic, Ecuador, El Salvador, Guatemala, Guyana, Honduras, Mexico, Nicaragua, the Plurinational State of Bolivia and Trinidad and Tobago.

[5] To date, the countries with FDI inflow data disaggregated by sector for 2024 are Argentina, Brazil, Colombia, Costa Rica, the Dominican Republic, Ecuador, El Salvador, Guatemala, Guyana, Honduras, Mexico, Nicaragua and the Plurinational State of Bolivia and Trinidad and Tobago, which account for a combined 88% of FDI inflows. Data for Brazil are not included in the reinvested earnings component, and sectoral data for Costa Rica and Mexico are computed using the approach established by *Balance of Payments and International Investment Position Manual: Fifth Edition (BPM5)*. As a result, the sum of the sectoral totals is not equal to total inflows.

Nearly half the countries that provide information disaggregated by sector recorded decreased services inflows. In 2024, this especially affected Brazil (24%), Argentina (60%) and Ecuador (66%), where services accounted for 43%, 45% and 25% of the respective countries' total inflows. In contrast, Colombia, the Dominican Republic, Guatemala, Honduras, Mexico and Nicaragua all received increased inflows to the services sector. In Colombia, the sector accounted for 59% of FDI inflows, and in the Dominican Republic, 89%.

Manufacturing inflows trended in the opposite direction, increasing in the region's major destination countries. This growth could be indicative of shifting patterns in investment localization and a reconfiguration of global value chains. In Brazil, manufacturing FDI increased by 49% to account for 57% of inflows, compared to 35% in 2023. Mexico's manufacturing inflows increased by 10% (53% of total inflows), and Costa Rica's inflows to the manufacturing sector grew more than the other sectors (+35%), accounting for 68% of the total.

Lastly, natural resources had the smallest share of regional inflows at just 16% (down from 18% in 2023). Nearly all countries saw declining investment in this sector, except Argentina, where a 44% increase carried the sector's share of the total to 39%, and Guyana, where inflows to the sector —up 43% on the back of expanded hydrocarbon production— accounted for 98% of total inflows.

(b) Cross-border mergers and acquisitions

In 2024, there were 326 cross-border mergers and acquisitions in the region, down 13.3% from 2023. The manufacturing, mining and quarrying, financial and insurance, and real estate sectors garnered the most interest from foreign investors (see figure I.9). The manufacturing sector and the financial and insurance sector were particularly resilient, registering hardly any year-on-year change in the number of transactions despite a decline in the overall figure.

Figure I.9
Latin America and the Caribbean: cross-border mergers and acquisitions, by sector, 2024
(Number and percentages of total)

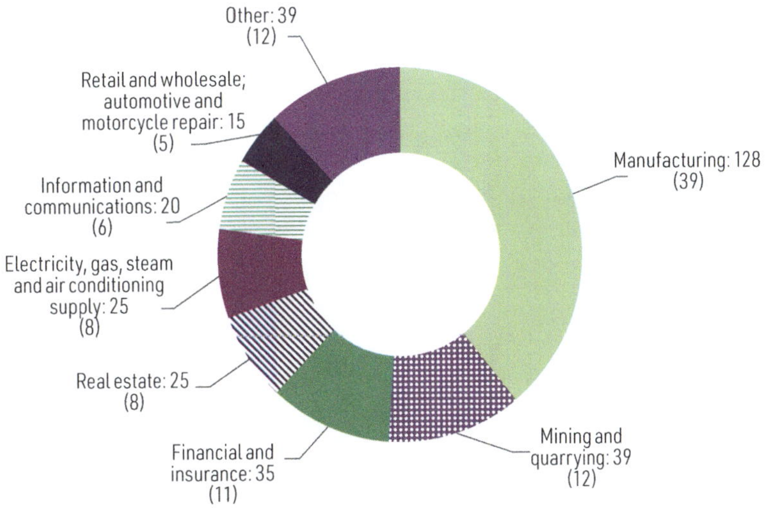

Source: Economic Commission for Latin America and the Caribbean, on the basis of Bloomberg.

Of the top 20 transactions of 2024, the largest involved services firms, including in real estate and financial services, commerce, electricity, gas and water, and telecommunications, as well as hydrocarbon production and mining (see figure I.5).

Table I.5
Latin America and the Caribbean: top 20 cross-border mergers and acquisitions, 2024
(Percentages and millions of dollars)

Firm	Country of origin	Assets acquired	Country of assets	Sector	Percentage	Value
Manara Minerals Investment Company	Saudi Arabia	Vale Base Metals Limited	Brazil	Mining and quarrying	10	2 500
Prologis, Inc.	United States	PLA Administradora Industrial S. de R. L. de C. V. (Terrafina)	Mexico	Real estate activities	77	1 701
HDI International	Germany	Liberty Seguros S.A.	Chile, Colombia and Ecuador	Financial and insurance activities	100	1 587
BP PLC	United Kingdom	BP Bunge Bioenergia	Brazil	Manufacturing	50	1 400
Actis LLP	United Kingdom	Enel Generación Perú S. A. A. y Compañía Energética Veracruz S. A. C.	Peru	Electricity, gas and water supply	87	1 300
Grupo Calleja	El Salvador	Almacenes Éxito S.A.	Colombia	Commerce	87	1 175
Visa Inc.	United States	Pismo Soluções Tecnológicas Ltda.	Brazil	Financial and insurance activities	100	1 000
Plaza S. A.	Chile	Open Plaza S. A.	Peru	Real estate activities	100	848
ITOCHU Corporation	Japan	CSN Mineração S. A.	Brazil	Mining and quarrying	11	779
Caisse de dépôt et placement du Québec	Canada	Transportadora Associada de Gás S. A.	Brazil	Oil and gas supply	15	641
EPAM Systems, Inc.	United States	NEORIS N. V.	Argentina, Brazil, Chile, Colombia, Ecuador, Mexico and Peru	Financial and insurance activities	100	630
Actis LLP	United Kingdom	EDP S. A.	Brazil	Electricity, gas and water supply	100	540
Atlas Investissement S. A. S.	France	Millicom International Cellular S.A.	Bolivia (Plurinational State of), Colombia, Costa Rica, El Salvador, Guatemala, Honduras, Nicaragua, Panama and Paraguay	Information and communications	11	496
Mill Point Capital LLC	United States	Imbera S. A. de C. V. and Grupo Torrey S. A. de C. V.	Mexico	Manufacturing	100	447
EIG Global Energy Partners LLC	United States	Ocyan Participações S. A.	Brazil	Professional, scientific and technical activities	100	390
Actis LLP	United Kingdom	EDP Transmissão Aliança SC S. A.	Brazil	Electricity, gas and water supply	90	383
Mitsui & Co., Ltd.	Japan	Industrial Pesquera Santa Priscila S. A.	Ecuador	Agriculture, forestry and fisheries	20	360
China Nonferrous Metal Mining Co. Ltd.	China	Mineração Taboca S. A.	Brazil	Mining and quarrying	100	340
Westlawn Americas Offshore LLC	United States	Brava Energia (Atlanta and Oliva fields)	Brazil	Oil and gas	20	309
Zijin Mining Group Co., Ltd.	China	Pan American Silver, La Arena copper and gold mine	Peru	Mining and quarrying	100	245

Source: Economic Commission for Latin America and the Caribbean, on the basis of Bloomberg.

While this specialization is not dissimilar to that of the 2010s, there are some transactions that hint at the possible diversification and sophistication of FDI. One factor generating business opportunities is the digital transformation (see chapter III, which addresses the possibilities and challenges facing the region regarding the use of FDI for the digital transformation). The US$ 1 billion acquisition by United States firm Visa of Brazilian start-up Pismo Soluções Tecnológicas Ltda., which offers cloud-based banking services and payment solutions, is an interesting development for local entrepreneurs. The sale of NEORIS NV, a high technology consulting firm with talent hubs in several countries, by Mexican construction materials firm Cemex (founder) and the fund Advent International to EPAM Systems in the United States for US$ 630 million is a sign of openness to new sectors on the part of traditional sector firms. Another generator of opportunities is the energy transition; for example, in 2024, BP PLC of the United Kingdom acquired a 50% holding interest in the Brazilian biofuel joint venture BP Bunge Bionergia.

3. Foreign direct investment by country of origin

(a) FDI inflows

Efforts to track the origin of FDI through national accounts data are complicated by the fact that only the immediate origin of capital is identified, and this may differ from the location of the entity making the investment. Consequently, countries such as Luxembourg and the Kingdom of the Netherlands are frequently overrepresented because, owing to their tax systems, they are often used by multinational corporations to invest in third countries. A further limitation in the region is that this information is reported by very few countries.[6]

Data for countries reporting the origin of FDI inflows in 2024 show that the United States has solidified its position as the region's largest investor, accounting for 38% of invested value, compared with 34% in 2023 (see figure I.10). The share of investment from the United States was largest in Guyana, totalling US$ 10.1 billion and representing 97% of Guyana's total inflows. United States firms' investment in Mexico grew substantially, from US$ 13.7 billion to US$ 16.5 billion, although the relative share in Mexico's inflows declined from 45% to 38% of the total.

The relative share of investment from the European Union (excluding Luxembourg and the Kingdom of the Netherlands) fell to 15% of the regional total in 2024, the lowest figure since 2012. Among European Union countries, Spain was the largest investor in 2024, accounting for 40% of the aggregate total, despite the 48% decline year-on-year in investment from Spanish companies in the countries reporting data. Germany was another significant source, accounting for 29% of European Union investment. Meanwhile, inflows from French investors plunged by 72%.

Investment originating from Latin America and the Caribbean represented 12.4% of FDI inflows to the countries reporting data, up from 11.6% in 2023. The countries of the region accounting for the largest share of the regional total were Brazil (21%), Chile (20%) and Panama (18%). Total investment from Brazil and Argentina, the largest investors in 2023, fell substantially, by 33% and 51%, respectively.

---

6 To date, the countries with FDI inflow data disaggregated by origin for 2024 are Argentina, Brazil, Colombia, Costa Rica, the Dominican Republic, Ecuador, El Salvador, Guatemala, Guyana, Honduras, Mexico, Nicaragua, the Plurinational State of Bolivia and Trinidad and Tobago, which represent over 80% of total FDI inflows in 2024.

Figure I.10
Latin America and the Caribbean (14 countries):[a] distribution of FDI inflows, by origin, 2015–2024
(Percentages)

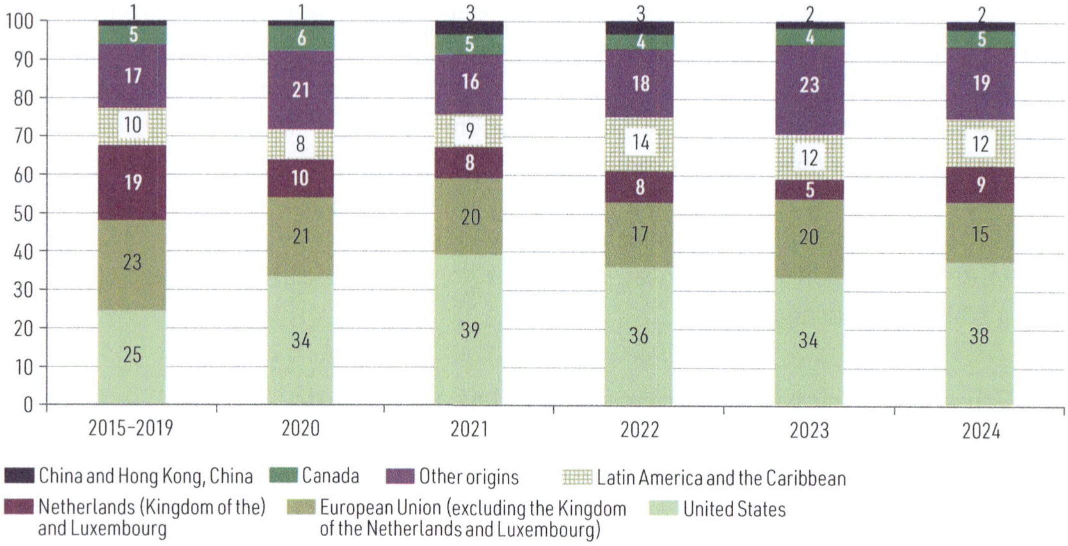

Source: Economic Commission for Latin America and the Caribbean, on the basis of official figures as at 30 June 2025.
Note: The information for Brazil does not include the reinvested earnings component. Data for Costa Rica and Mexico were computed using the approach in International Monetary Fund. (1993). *Balance of Payments Manual: Fifth Edition*.
[a] Argentina, Brazil, Colombia, Costa Rica, Dominican Republic, Ecuador, El Salvador, Guatemala, Guyana, Honduras, Mexico, Nicaragua, the Plurinational State of Bolivia and Trinidad and Tobago.

At the regional level, investments originating from China and Hong Kong, China[7] have generally represented a small proportion of FDI inflows reported in balance of payments statistics. In 2024, in the Latin American and Caribbean countries reporting data on origins, Chinese FDI accounted for just 2% of total inflows. Investment originating from the Chinese market represents a relatively small share of official FDI figures for most countries, but Ecuador was a significant exception. In 2024, China-based entities stepped up their investments in the country by 58%, bringing in US$ 111 million, or 35% of the country's total inflows.

Using complementary data sources, such as the methodology employed in the *Monitor of Chinese OFDI in Latin America and the Caribbean 2025* to track investments made by Chinese companies, the share of Chinese investment in the region was estimated at 4.85% in 2024, confirming the downward trend since 2020 (Dussel Peters 2025; Economic Commission for Latin America and the Caribbean [ECLAC], 2025).

(b) Cross-border mergers and acquisitions

In terms of cross-border mergers and acquisitions targeting assets in the region, the United States remained the primary country of origin, accounting for 112 of the 326 deals recorded in 2024, or 34% of the total. Firms based in the United States carried out some of the year's largest transactions and were behind 6 of the 20 largest deals (see table I.5).

[7] Investors from China tend to be underrepresented as the immediate source of capital in comparison to their position as its final owner. Conversely, tax havens or countries such as Luxembourg and the Kingdom of the Netherlands, with financial markets that make them favourable for cross-border investments by companies from other countries, are overrepresented. Furthermore, since 2010, investments by Chinese companies have mainly been in the form of purchases of assets already owned by foreign companies, so they have not been reflected in the balance of payments (ECLAC, 2021).

In 2024, European Union countries carried out 66 operations, or 20% of the total mergers and acquisitions, making the bloc the second-largest origin. Within this group, four countries accounted for almost 75% of the total: France (17), Spain (15), Italy (9) and Germany (7). However, despite the large number of transactions by European Union firms, they were involved in only 2 of the 20 largest deals.

A longer-term analysis shows that the average annual number of mergers and acquisitions originating from major countries of origin peaked between 2010 and 2014 and has since declined. Although the average number of transactions for most major sources continued to decline in the period 2015–2019 and again in 2020–2024, there were a few notable exceptions: the average number of annual transactions by companies from the United States, Canada and Australia increased by 3%, 15% and 13%, respectively (see figure I.11).

Figure I.11
Latin America and the Caribbean: cross-border mergers and acquisitions, by origin, annual averages for 2005–2024
(Number of transactions)

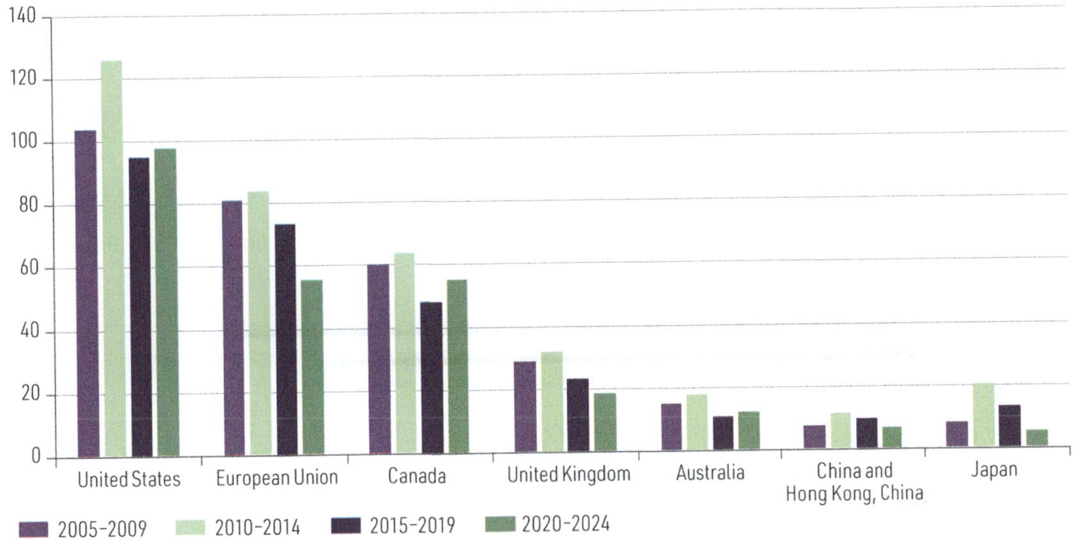

Source: Economic Commission for Latin America and the Caribbean, on the basis of Bloomberg.

4. FDI project announcements

(a) 2024 overview

The value of projects announced in the region in 2024 surged by 40% relative to 2023, to US$ 168.2 billion, setting a record for the region and marking the third consecutive annual increase following the sharp decline prompted by the coronavirus disease (COVID-19) pandemic in 2020 (see figure I.12).

In terms of value, Brazil, Mexico, Argentina and Guyana accounted for the largest share of projects announced in the region in 2024 (82%), with each recording significant increases relative to 2023 (see figure I.13).

Figure I.12
Latin America and the Caribbean: FDI project announcements, 2005–2024
(Billions of dollars and number of projects)

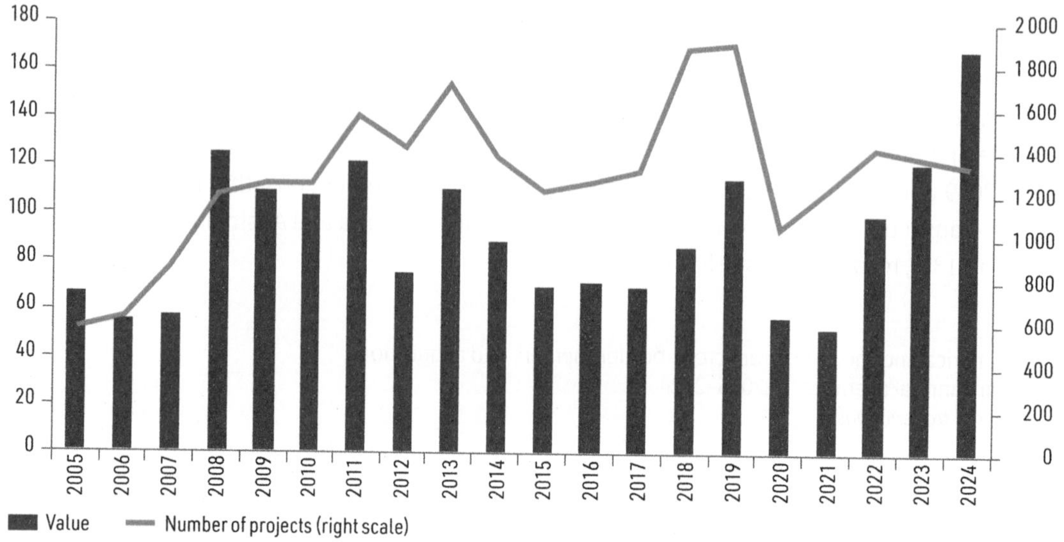

Source: Economic Commission for Latin America and the Caribbean, on the basis of *Financial Times*. fDi Markets. https://www.fdimarkets.com/.

Figure I.13
Latin America and the Caribbean: FDI project announcements, main destination countries, 2023 and 2024
(Billions of dollars)

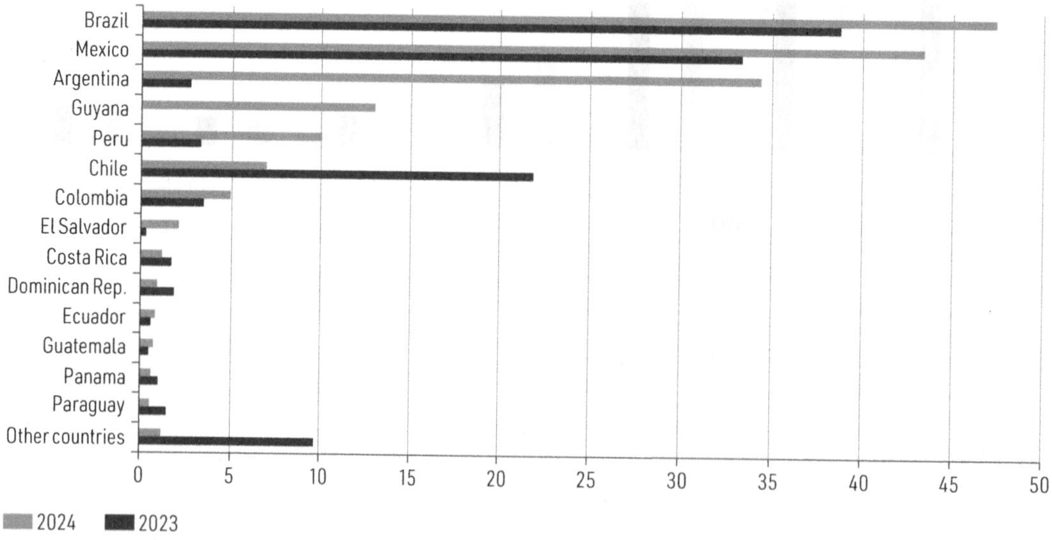

Source: Economic Commission for Latin America and the Caribbean, on the basis of *Financial Times*. fDi Markets. https://www.fdimarkets.com/.

For the second consecutive year, Brazil was the region's top destination for FDI projects announced in 2024, with a 22% increase over 2023. Although multiple megaprojects were announced in the country, no single one accounted for the lion's share of the total. The renewable energy sector was the main driver of growth, accounting for 38% of total announced value. Within this sector, green hydrogen projects predominated, with multiple announcements made for the Pecém Industrial and Port Complex and the Port of Açu. Brazil was also the destination of megaprojects announced in the telecommunications and forestry products sectors.

Mexico also recorded significant growth (30%) in FDI projects announced relative to 2023, driven largely by a record-breaking megaproject. United States-based Mexico Pacific, which is developing the Saguaro Energía LNG Facility and the Sierra Madre Pipeline, announced additional investments of US$ 15 billion in projects in northern Mexico. This sum, combined with the company's previous investments of US$ 15 billion in Mexico, makes Mexico Pacific the largest private investor in the country's history (*El Financiero*, 2024a). The new project accounted for 35% of investments announced in Mexico.

The value of projects announced in Argentina jumped relative to 2023, fuelled by an agreement between YPF and Shell PLC to develop a liquefied natural gas (LNG) project in the province of Río Negro (YPF, 2024). With an expected investment of US$ 30 billion (*La Nación*, 2024), the project will be the largest in the region since at least 2005. It accounted for 87% of the value of projects announced in Argentina in 2024, the highest annual total recorded for the country.

In Guyana, ExxonMobil announced an expansion of its activities through the US$ 12.7 billion Whiptail offshore development (ExxonMobil, 2024). This project is the company's sixth in the Stabroek block and accounted for nearly 100% of the value of projects announced in Guyana in 2024.

(b) Analysis by sector

The sectoral composition of FDI projects announced in 2024 shifted dramatically towards coal, oil and gas, which accounted for 38% of announced project value (see figure I.14). This surge was driven largely by the megaprojects of Shell, Mexico Pacific and ExxonMobil referenced in section 4.a, in addition to significant announcements in Brazil's Santos and Pelotas basins by TotalEnergies and CNOOC Limited.

Figure I.14
Latin America and the Caribbean: FDI project announcements, by sector, 2024
(Percentages of total value)

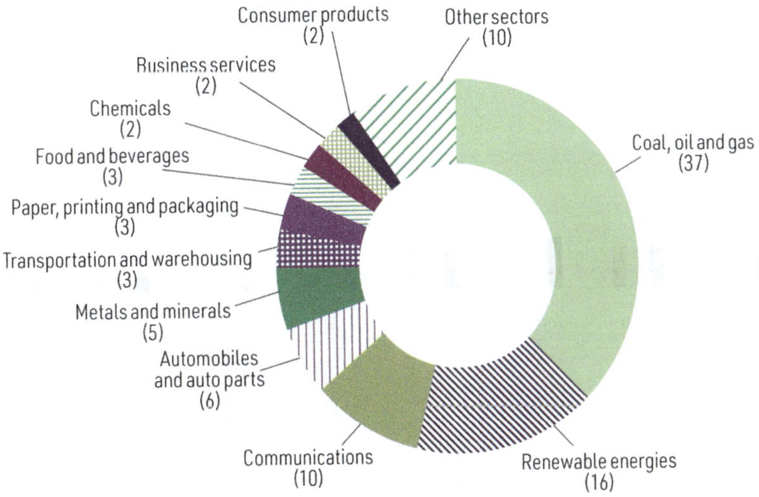

Source: Economic Commission for Latin America and the Caribbean, on the basis of *Financial Times*. fDi Markets. https://www.fdimarkets.com/.

Opportunities in renewable energy continued to attract significant attention from foreign investors, accounting for US$ 27.5 billion of announced project value. Although this amount is 13% lower than in 2023, it is the second-highest total to date and more than double the sector average over the previous decade. Announcements in Brazil, involving mainly green hydrogen and ammonia projects, represented 66% of project value for the region's renewable energy sector. Other major projects in the region included South Africa-based Phelan Green Energy's US$ 2.4 billion green ammonia project in

Arequipa, Peru, and a partnership between Chile's H2 Green Mining and United States-based Ohmium International to develop green hydrogen projects to decarbonize mining operations (Phelan Green Energy, 2024; Ohmium International, 2024).

The communications sector also underwent a significant shift in 2024, with announced projects totalling US$ 16.7 billion, 71% higher than in 2023, owing primarily to planned investments of US$ 11.3 billion in data processing centres. Brazil attracted the largest projects in this subsector, which notably included a US$ 2.6 billion investment in cloud and artificial intelligence infrastructure by Microsoft and plans by Amazon to invest US$ 1.8 billion to expand data centre operations in the country (Microsoft, 2024; Reuters, 2024). Major data centre projects were also announced in Mexico and Colombia, amounting to US$ 3.4 billion and US$ 1.6 billion, respectively.

The metals and minerals sector, meanwhile, recorded sharp declines in both the number and the value of projects announced (30% and 43%, respectively), from the recent highs of 2023. This drop in value was attributable mainly to a US$ 4.5 billion decrease in the projects announced in Mexico and a US$ 2.8 billion drop in the projects announced in Chile. Still, project announcements for the sector did strengthen in some countries within the region, such as Peru, which recorded an increase of 35.4% in value, buoyed by the US$ 2 billion expansion of the Antamina copper and zinc mine (Antamina, 2024).

There has been a discernible shift in the sectoral composition of project announcements in 2020–2024 compared with the 2010 decade (see figure I.15). The massive increase in the value of projects announced in the coal, oil and gas sector and the renewable energy sector has been the most striking.

Figure I.15
Latin America and the Caribbean: FDI project announcements, by sector, 2010–2024
(Billions of dollars)

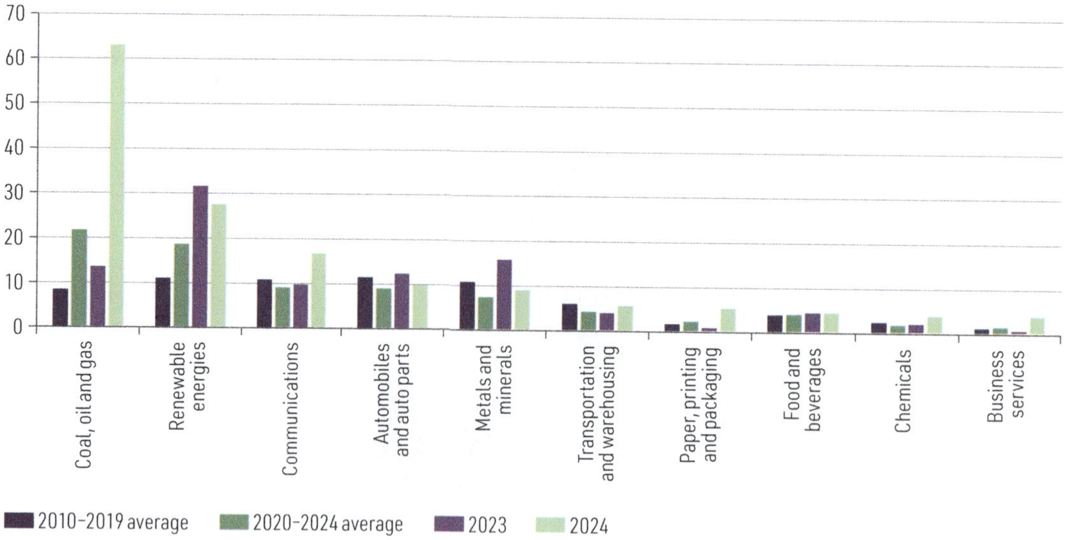

Source: Economic Commission for Latin America and the Caribbean, on the basis of *Financial Times*. fDi Markets. https://www.fdimarkets.com/.

Average annual project values declined for most other sectors. The automobiles and auto parts sector, for example, attracted the most investment in the 2010–2019 period, but its annual average fell by 22% in 2020–2024. Notwithstanding the strong performance of communications in 2024, the sector's average annual investment announcements since 2020 have contracted by 16% compared with the 2010s. The region's metals and minerals sector, historically among the most attractive for international investors, also recorded a 31.3% decrease in average annual project announcements (chapter II of this report analyses challenges and opportunities in attracting investments and fostering productive development for strategic minerals in the region).

(c) Analysis by country of origin

The United States, the United Kingdom, and China accounted for the most announcements in the region in 2024, with 55% of the total (see figure I.16). The value of projects announced by companies based in the United States soared by 179% relative to 2023, with these investors involved in 4 of the 15 largest projects in the region in 2024, including major oil and gas projects and data centre investments. The United Kingdom remained the second-largest investor in 2024, with announcements dominated by Shell PLC's involvement in the previously mentioned LNG project in Argentina.

Figure I.16
Latin America and the Caribbean: FDI project announcements, by main country of origin, 2023 and 2024
(Billions of dollars)

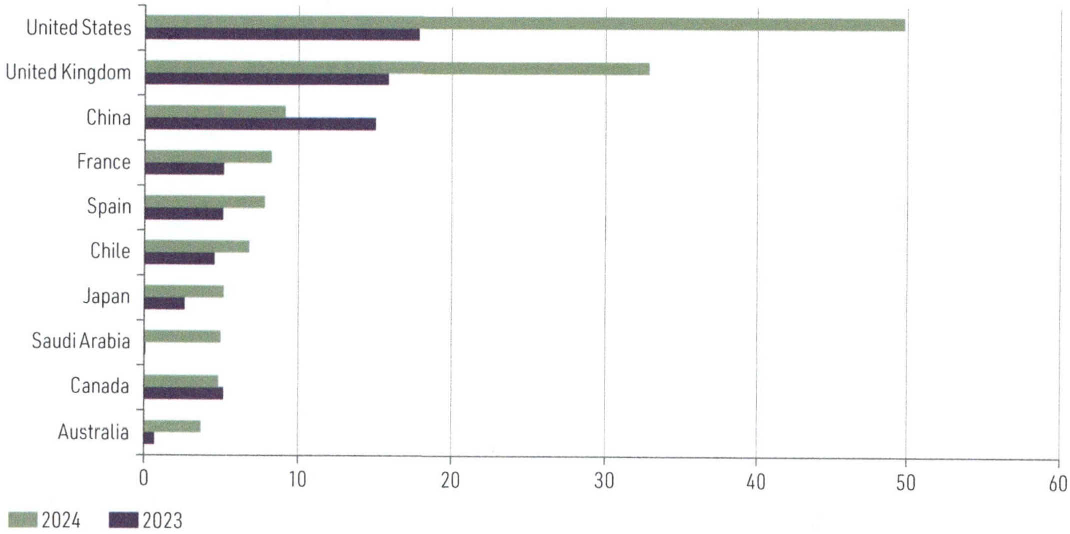

Source: Economic Commission for Latin America and the Caribbean, on the basis of *Financial Times*. fDi Markets. https://www.fdimarkets.com/.

Although announced investment from China was 39% lower than in 2023, it was still much higher than the 2010–2023 average of US$ 5.8 billion. Despite the year-on-year decline in terms of value, Chinese companies announced 102 projects in 2024, the second-highest total since 2005. This included 25 projects in the automotive sector, 16 in communications and 23 in other technology-intensive sectors such as industrial equipment and electronic components. The region's largest investment originating from China in 2024 was CNOOC Limited's announcement of four concession contracts for exploration in Brazil's Pelotas Basin through its local subsidiary (CNOOC Limited, 2024). Mexico, meanwhile, was the primary destination of Chinese investment, accounting for 42 projects collectively valued at US$ 5.2 billion, or 57% of the total value of Chinese announcements in the region in 2024. This confirms a long-term trend: between 2010 and 2019, Chinese firms announced an average of US$ 1.4 billion in projects in Mexico annually, and between 2020 and 2024, the figure increased to US$ 3.5 billion, making the country the largest destination by far for Chinese investments in the region.

French companies announced US$ 8.2 billion in projects in the region, a 61% increase over 2023. The largest of these was a green hydrogen and ammonia project by the energy group Voltalia in

Brazil through its local subsidiary, valued at US$ 3 billion (Pecém Industrial and Port Complex, 2024). Further investment announcements in energy also contributed to the high total for France, including oil development by TotalEnergies in Brazil's Atapu and Sépia oilfields and a collaboration between ENGIE and the Nuevo León Renewable Energy Agency to promote biomethane projects in the Mexican State (TotalEnergies, 2024; Mexico Business News, 2024b).

Although Germany is regularly one of the largest sources of investment in the region, the value of projects announced by German companies in 2024 dropped by 65%. Meanwhile, Saudi Arabia emerged as a major investor in the region through investments announced by Fotowatio Renewable Ventures, a fully owned subsidiary of Abdul Latif Jameel based in Spain.

An analysis of long-term trends in projects announced by the top investors in Latin America and the Caribbean reveals that the annual value of project announcements in the region has risen significantly since the COVID-19 pandemic for most countries of origin (see figure I.17). The European Union is an exception. Among European Union investors in Latin America, Spanish firms have recorded the biggest drop in average annual value of announced projects (55%) when comparing 2020–2024 with the preceding decade. Over the same period, the average annual value of investments announced by firms from Germany, Italy and the Kingdom of the Netherlands also declined, by 19%, 17% and 13%, respectively. Nonetheless, these downward trends were partly offset by large increases for firms based in France (20%), Denmark (32%), and Sweden (289%).

Figure I.17
Latin America and the Caribbean: FDI project announcements, by selected countries and country groupings, 2005–2024
(Billions of dollars)

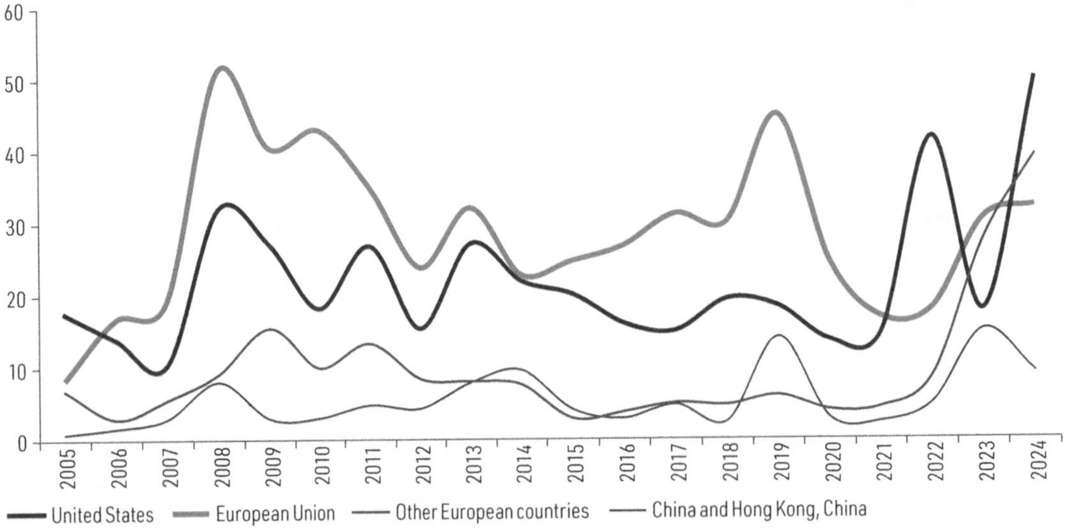

Source: Economic Commission for Latin America and the Caribbean, on the basis of *Financial Times*. fDi Markets. https://www.fdimarkets.com/.

By contrast, Chinese companies have announced investments averaging US$ 6.8 billion per year since 2020, compared with US$ 5.7 billion from 2010 to 2019 (an increase of roughly 20%). Announced investments in Latin American and Caribbean markets by United States-based companies has also increased substantially, averaging US$ 27.6 billion per year between 2020 and 2024, compared with US$ 19.8 billion in the previous decade (a 39% increase).

European countries outside the European Union, meanwhile, have announced average investments of US$ 16.7 billion per year since 2020, an increase of 143% compared with US$ 6.9 billion in the 2010s. This trend has been observed across major non-European Union economies, with notable increases for Switzerland (19%), the United Kingdom (184%), and Norway (463%).

(d) Project announcements by technology intensity

Although FDI can be a catalyst for advancing productive development in emerging economies, not all investments are equally beneficial in this regard. The extent to which investments foster capacity development, technology transfer and innovation, key elements in enhancing productivity and prospects for growth, varies depending on the destination sector. Although tracking how much a given investment promotes such outcomes is challenging, sectoral classification schemes can facilitate such analysis.

To that end, project announcements in the region were classified into five groups. The first three include manufacturing sectors categorized according to the intensity of input use, on the basis of the classification proposed by Katz and Stumpo (2001). The remaining two groups include services sectors classified according to contributions to innovation and capacity development, highlighting the importance of digital and communications services and financial and professional services for productive development. Table I.6 outlines the sector groupings used in this analysis and their relevant characteristics for productive transformation.

Table I.6
Classification of FDI project announcements: groups, descriptions and characteristics

Group	Description and relevant sectors	Characteristics
Natural resource-intensive	Processing or transformation of locally available resources (including food and beverages, wood and paper products, and basic metals)	Barring certain subsectors, tend to exhibit relatively low technological complexity, with productivity improvements stemming from efficient deployment of equipment rather than sustained technological innovation
Labour-intensive	Reliance on low-cost, low-skilled labour (including sectors such as textiles, footwear and furniture)	Are often highly vulnerable to international competition and make relatively limited contributions to technological upgrading and long-term productivity growth
Engineering-intensive	Intensive use of technological and knowledge inputs, and their more complex design, engineering and production processes (examples include the machinery, electronics, and automotive sectors)	Require qualified human capital and drive innovation and integration with global value chains. Key drivers of productivity growth because of their heightened innovation capacity
Digital and communications services	Encompassing sectors such as software development, information technology services, data processing, telecommunications and digital infrastructure	Highly dynamic, reliant on knowledge inputs, technology and skilled labour, and characterized by rapid innovation cycles. Often make outsized contributions to productive transformation by enhancing connectivity, automation and digitalization throughout the economy
Financial and professional services	Including sectors such as banking, insurance, engineering, legal services, accounting and other knowledge-intensive business services	High human capital intensity and dependence on firm reputation. Contribute to productive transformation by offering institutional and technical support for investment, innovation and business development

Source: Economic Commission for Latin America and the Caribbean, on the basis of Katz, J. and Stumpo, G. (2001). Sectoral regimes, productivity and international competitiveness. *CEPAL Review* (75) (LC/G.2150-P). Economic Commission for Latin America and the Caribbean.

Projects in these groups account for just over half of the value of all FDI projects announced since 2010, although this proportion has shrunk in recent years amid a shift towards megaprojects in oil and gas and renewable energy (see figure I.18A), which tend to be dependent on global price cycles and generate more limited spillovers to other sectors, as productivity gains are often tied to imported capital equipment and external expertise.

Figure I.18
Latin America and the Caribbean: project announcement trends, by aggregated sector, 2010–2024

A. Value of announcements, averages for 2010-2019 and 2020-2024
(Percentages of total)

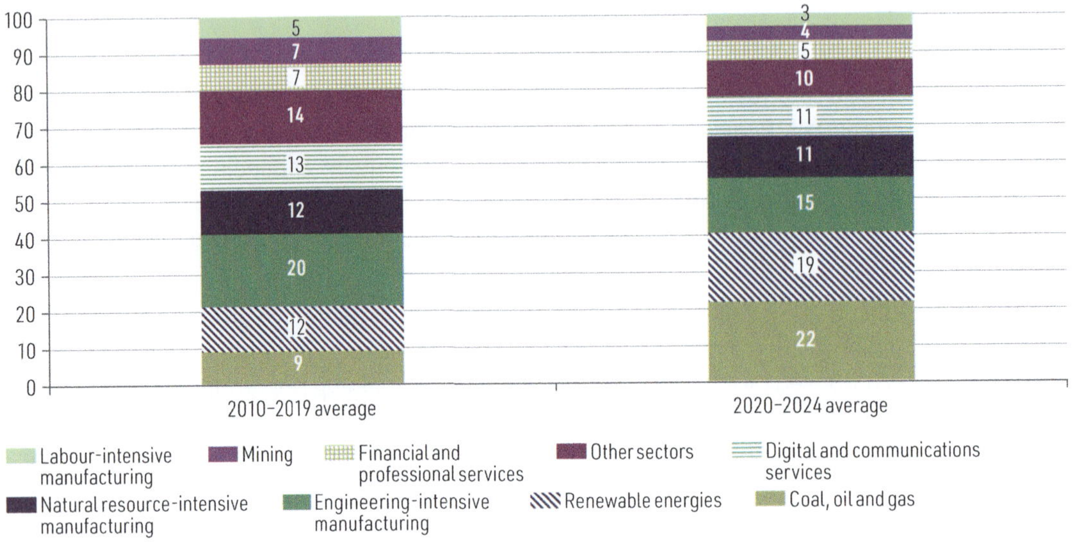

B. Value of announcements in selected aggregated sectors, 2010-2024
(Billions of dollars)

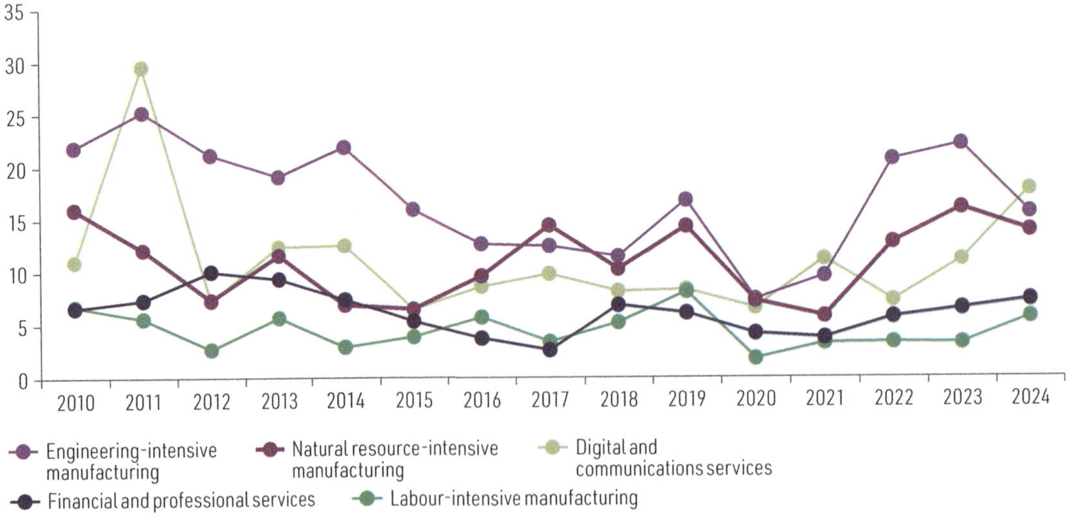

Source: Economic Commission for Latin America and the Caribbean, on the basis of *Financial Times*. fDi Markets. https://www.fdimarkets.com/.

Accordingly, the regional investment profile has gradually moved away from sectors associated with innovation, workforce capability enhancement and long-term productivity growth, although in some sectors, such as digital and communications services and financial services, the value of project announcements increased (see figure I.19B). In 2010–2019, the average combined share of project value directed towards digital and communications services and engineering-intensive manufacturing stood at 33%; since 2020, that figure has fallen to 26%. The share of financial and professional services, meanwhile, has fallen from 7% to 5% of the total value of announcements over the same periods. These declines suggest a missed opportunity to harness FDI as a driver of productive development.

Amid the increasing weight of energy megaprojects in FDI in the region, these trends underscore the importance of monitoring not only the volume of such inflows, but also the technological and innovative capacities of destination sectors if the region is to use FDI as a catalyst for productive transformation. Policymakers should consider incorporating strategies to attract FDI into productive development policies (ECLAC, 2024a) to ensure that Latin America and the Caribbean is a competitive destination for investment in sectors with stronger productivity linkages and innovation potential.

(e) Potential impact of United States tariffs on project announcements

The region's proximity to the United States has shaped FDI inflows in several of its countries, as investors have sought to leverage geographical proximity to the United States market (*nearshoring*) and what they perceived as its relative safety from potential trade barriers associated with geopolitical tensions (*friendshoring*). This subsection analyses the potential impacts on FDI inflows of confirmed and potential changes to the tariff and trade policies of the United States, by categorizing the region's exports of goods to the United States according to sectoral classifications used to analyse FDI project announcements.[8]

To illustrate the role of exports to the United States market in shaping FDI inflows, table I.7 lists the top 10 sectors for exports to the United States by value. Collectively, these sectors accounted for more than US$ 245 billion of the value of projects announced between 2020 and 2024, or 49% of the total. The United States accounts for more than half of all exports for six of these sectors, particularly manufacturing sectors. For example, of the US$ 178 billion in exports of the automotive sector (representing 12% of total exports), 69% were destined for the United States market. That country plays a similarly dominant role in the region's exports of electronic components, industrial equipment, business machines and medical devices.

Table I.7
Latin America and the Caribbean: top 10 sectors for exports to the United States, 2023, and FDI project announcements, 2020–2024
(Billions of dollars and percentages)

Sector	United States export value, 2023	World export value, 2023	Percentage of exports to United States, 2023	Announced project value, 2020-2024
Automobiles and auto parts	123.769	178.290	69	44.884
Food and beverages	83.087	359.219	23	19.844
Coal, oil and gas	55.361	180.498	31	108.121
Electronic components	52.510	67.695	78	5.578
Industrial equipment	49.542	73.520	67	6.982
Metals and minerals	36.283	195.132	19	36.653
Business machines and equipment	29.797	35.793	83	2.119
Consumer products	24.531	67.936	36	15.179
Textiles	18.557	34.653	54	2.556
Medical devices	18.318	28.118	65	3.133

Source: Economic Commission for Latin America and the Caribbean, on the basis of *Financial Times*. fDi Markets. https://www.fdimarkets.com/ and the Observatory of Economic Complexity. https://oec.world/en.

Given the important role of the United States as an export destination, changes to that country's tariff and trade policies can be expected to weigh on investment decisions in the medium to long run. This may be particularly true for investors from the United States, who have announced nearly

8 This analysis is based on the "industry sector" classification used by fDi Markets to categorize investment project announcements, and on the correspondence between this system and the Harmonized System Codes for the region's 2023 exports.

US$ 138 billion worth of projects in the region since 2020. Of this amount, the largest share (53%) went to services sectors not accounted for in this analysis. Among tradable goods, United States investors have concentrated on coal, oil and gas and metals and minerals (US$ 50 billion in announcements since 2020), while sectors producing manufactured goods accounted for US$ 34 billion.

United States-based investors play a particularly active role in sectors with strong exports to that country, in some cases dominating investment flows. For instance, these investors accounted for 78% of project announcements in the engines and turbines sector (for which 68% of exports go to the United States) and 64% of announced value in the medical devices sector (with the United States receiving 65% of those exports).

In several other sectors, while the United States is the main export destination, investors from that country account for a smaller share of total project announcements, as firms from other regions invest to compete in supply chains oriented towards the United States market. For example, while the United States market receives 83% of business machines and equipment and 81% of consumer electronics exported from the region, United States-based investors accounted for 19% and 14% of announced investment in those sectors, respectively, between 2020 and 2024. In the automotive sector, the United States purchases 69% of exports from the region, while accounting for 21% of announced project value (see table I.8).

Table I.8
Latin America and the Caribbean: top 10 sectors for FDI project announcements from United States and China, 2020–2024
(Billions of dollars and percentages)

United States			China		
Sector	Announced project value, 2020–2024	Percentage of total announced project value	Sector	Announced project value, 2020–2024	Percentage of total announced project value
Coal, oil and gas	47.503	44	Automobiles and auto parts	10.265	23
Automobiles and auto parts	9.557	21	Metals and minerals	3.867	11
Food and beverages	7.823	39	Chemicals	1.935	23
Consumer products	3.236	21	Electronic components	1.870	34
Metals and minerals	2.833	8	Rubber	1.464	37
Medical devices	1.998	64	Consumer products	1.345	9
Industrial equipment	1.704	24	Coal, oil and gas	1.299	1
Paper, printing and packaging	1.504	13	Industrial equipment	664	10
Chemicals	1.390	16	Ceramics and glass	615	23
Ceramics and glass	1.350	51	Non-automotive transport OEM (original equipment manufacturing)	573	35

Source: Economic Commission for Latin America and the Caribbean, on the basis of *Financial Times*. fDi Markets. https://www.fdimarkets.com/.

Investors from China are heavily represented in sectors that export primarily to the United States. Of the US$ 34 billion in projects announced in the region by Chinese investors between 2020 and 2024, 75% went towards sectors producing exportable goods, including US$ 20 billion in manufacturing sectors.

Although Chinese investors represent just 7% of project announcements in the region since 2020, they have a heavy presence in some of the sectors most tied to the United States market. For example, in the automotive sector, Chinese firms accounted for 23% of announced investment between 2020 and 2024, surpassing the share of United States-based investors. Chinese firms were also the largest source of announcements in the electronic components sector, accounting for 34% of announced project value between 2020 and 2024. In consumer electronics, meanwhile, where 81% of exports go to the United States market, Chinese investors accounted for 14% of announced project value.

In conjunction with the 20% increase in Chinese FDI announcements between 2020 and 2024 compared with 2010–2019, these examples indicate that Chinese firms have increased their interest in the region as a hedge against the perceived risks of geopolitical tensions to their access to the United States market. Given the impact of United States tariff measures on the sectors receiving Chinese investment, this may pose a further risk for the region's relative attractiveness to foreign investors. As these examples illustrate, changes to tariff policies may influence future supply chain decisions. Given that sectors associated with exportable goods have accounted for nearly 60% of announced investment value since 2020, it is critical for the region to develop strategies to maintain its attractiveness to international investors. As stated by Salazar-Xirinachs (2025), governments in the region should avoid reactive measures that could increase uncertainty and should articulate a "two-pronged strategy that distinguishes between short-term stabilization and long-term transformation".

In the short term, such strategies might include sector-specific measures for those industries most at risk from tariff volatility. In the longer term, concerted efforts to diversify trade partnerships and reduce dependence on the United States market are the best hedge against this volatility. Seeking alternative export markets in blocs such as the European Union may provide an opportunity, as might boosting and diversifying trade with emerging economies such as China and India. Such efforts may be further bolstered by strengthening economic integration within the region to enhance its international competitiveness, including by facilitating intraregional trade, harmonizing regulations, creating logistics corridors and developing regional value chains (Salazar-Xirinachs, 2025).

C. Foreign direct investment outflows from the region

FDI outflows from the region increased in 2024, totalling US$ 53.033 billion, 47% higher than in 2023 (see table I.9). Brazil was the largest outward investor (46% of the total), despite a slight drop in outward FDI (3%), while investments from Mexico showed the strongest growth, and came to US$ 13.031 billion in 2024. Colombia ranked third following a significant increase in outflows, while outward investment from Chile and Argentina was lower. Together, these five countries accounted for 92% of the region's total FDI outflows.

Table I.9
Latin America and the Caribbean (selected countries): FDI outflows, 2010–2019 and 2020–2024
(Billions of dollars and percentages)

	2010-2019[a]	2020	2021	2022	2023	2024	Absolute change 2023-2024	Relative change 2023-2024 *(Percentages)*	Share of total regional FDI in 2024 *(Percentages)*
Brazil	14.518	-3.467	16.239	33.355	25.148	24.319	-830	-3	45.9
Mexico	11.209	5.033	-150	17.343	755	13.301	12.546	1.662	25.1
Colombia	4.555	1.733	3.181	3.384	1.269	4.576	3.307	261	8.6
Chile	10.324	6.398	14.573	14.055	8.765	3.592	-5.173	-59	6.8
Argentina	1.338	1.177	1.544	2.090	3.023	2.757	-267	-9	5.2
Other countries	4.308	250	7.357	8.251	-2.915	4.488	7.403	-254	8.5
Latin America and the Caribbean	**46.253**	**11.125**	**42.744**	**78.477**	**36.045**	**53.033**	**16.987**	**47**	**100.0**

Source: Economic Commission for Latin America and the Caribbean (ECLAC), on the basis of official figures as at 30 June 2025.
Note: Except in the case of Guyana and Peru, information was computed in accordance with International Monetary Fund (IMF), *Balance of Payments and International Investment Position Manual: Sixth Edition (BPM6)*, Washington, D.C., 2009.
[a] Simple averages.

These figures show that the region is a net recipient of capital in the form of FDI, and that just a few countries invest significant amounts abroad. However, taking a more medium-term view, investment outflows from the region were 15% higher in 2024 than the average for the 2010s. Should this pattern continue, trans-Latin companies' activities abroad could begin to bring greater returns in their countries of origin, not only in the form of foreign-exchange income from the repatriation of profits generated abroad, but also in the opportunities that could arise to open markets and create distribution networks for other companies in the region.

The amounts involved in FDI announcements by trans-Latins are small by comparison with balance-of-payments capital movements. In 2024, 295 projects were announced, amounting to US$ 13.6 billion (27% below the 2023 peak). The intended projects also belong to just a few sectors (see figure I.19): Paper, printing and packaging (34%), food and beverages (15%) and consumer products (12%) accounted for 60% of the total amount announced in 2024. The investment announced by Chile's CPMC to build a new US$ 4.6 billion plant in Brazil was the biggest of the year. The food and beverage sector has also seen significant growth in recent years, with announcements of over US$ 2 billion in 2024. Mexican companies were particularly active, with announcements from Grupo PiSA, Grupo Bimbo and Arca Continental. Within the consumer products sector, much of the growth reflected projects linked to the expansion of MercadoLibre of Argentina and Falabella of Chile.

Figure I.19
FDI announcements by Latin American and Caribbean firms, by sector
(Millions of dollars)

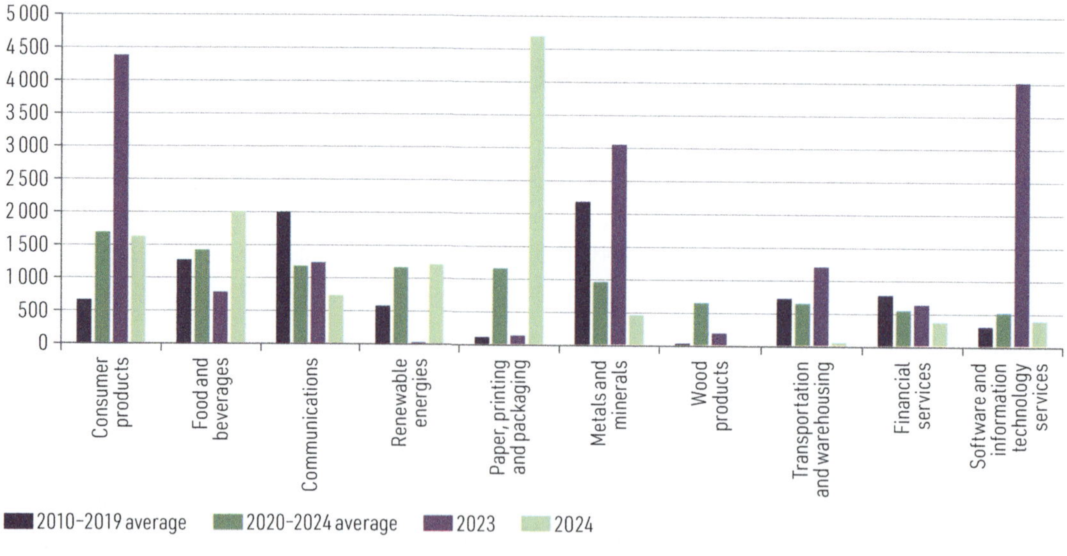

Source: Economic Commission for Latin America and the Caribbean, on the basis of *Financial Times*, fDi Markets. https://www.fdimarkets.com/.

Trans-Latins have preferred to invest within the region. In 2024, the region accounted for 72% of FDI projects announced, by value, with North America in second place (see figure I.20). Brazil was a particularly attractive market for trans-Latins, accounting for 49% of announcements by value.

Figure I.20
FDI announcements by Latin American and Caribbean firms, by destination region, 2024
(Percentages by value)

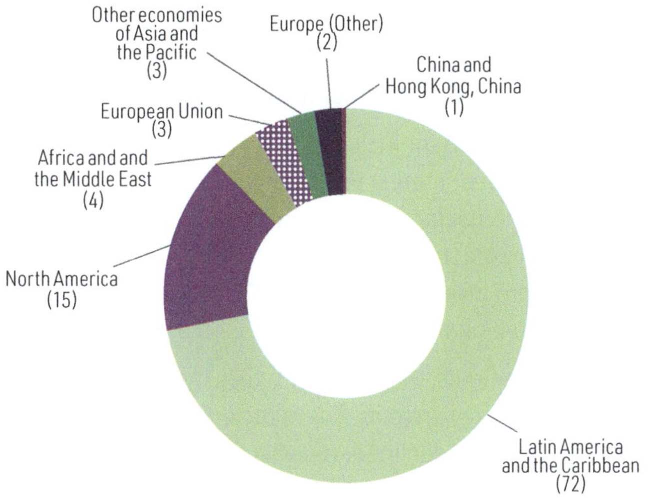

Source: Economic Commission for Latin America and the Caribbean, on the basis of *Financial Times*. fDi Markets. https://www.fdimarkets.com/.

D. Conclusions and recommendations

The purpose of this study is to provide comparable and up-to-date information to the public, private and academic sectors and to civil society about transnational corporations' activities in Latin America and the Caribbean, including on trends, major sectors and origins. To that end, it analyses FDI flows recorded in balance-of-payments statistics, identifies and examines the major cross-border mergers and acquisitions carried out in the region and considers FDI project announcements. This section presents countries and territories with recommended measures to attract more FDI and extract the maximum possible benefits from transnational corporations' activities while mitigating their possible negative effects.

Figures for 2024 show that FDI inflows have increased year-on-year but there is still considerable room for improvement if FDI is to meaningfully contribute to the achievement of more productive, inclusive and sustainable development. In terms of value, FDI grew in most countries, mainly on the back of an increase in reinvested earnings. Equity inflows, however, fell, for the second consecutive year, hitting their second-lowest level since 2010, only above that seen in 2020. The increase in reinvested earnings signals a desire on the part of firms already operating in the region to expand their activities in the countries where they are already present, reflecting their confidence in local markets. Nevertheless, stagnant equity inflows are a worrying sign for productive development investments.

One possible factor behind growth in reinvested earnings is the relative macroeconomic stability that most of the countries of the region are currently enjoying, with overall declines in inflation bringing the median rate to 3.4% in 2024, close to the target range established by many central banks in Latin America and the Caribbean (ECLAC, 2024b). Meanwhile, although average regional growth remained low (2.3% in 2024), Brazil —the region's largest recipient of FDI— recorded growth of 3.4%, which may have encouraged greater investment in the country. In Mexico, rising investment in the manufacturing industry helped to cement its key position in North American value chains. Manufacturing capacities were also one of Costa Rica's major selling points, where FDI inflows increased for the fourth year running thanks to the implementation of a long-term national strategy with institutional backing that identifies transnational corporate activity as a key pillar of development.

Given that the equity inflows component includes new investments, its relative sluggishness is an indicator of new companies' limited interest in operating in the region, which could be attributed to any number of internal or external factors. External factors include the high level of uncertainty regarding global economic prospects and the intensifying geopolitical conflicts that dissuade transnational corporations' from investing abroad (OECD, 2025). This situation puts a damper on global investment and affects regional FDI.

With regard to project announcements, there was growth in hydrocarbon production and, recently, declining values for renewable energy projects. The relative weight of the more innovation-intensive sectors in announcements has also declined, despite a recent increase in telecommunications investments driven by data centre projects. In addition, some of the goods production sectors that have been the greatest beneficiaries of project announcements have strong export ties with the United States, which may make them vulnerable to escalating trade restrictions.

There are also internal factors that could make the region more attractive. One important condition is that FDI should be viewed as a strategic tool of productive development policy (ECLAC, 2024a, 2024c). This perspective is helpful in identifying the best instruments and tools for attracting investment in countries and their territories and the most effective institutional governance mechanisms for productive development and FDI attraction.

The TOPP conceptual framework (technical, operational, political and prospective capabilities) proposed by ECLAC can be a useful analytical approach in identifying the capacities that public institutions require to effective address complex challenges in a changing environment (ECLAC, 2024d). Building on that approach, a non-exhaustive list of guidelines for action is set out below, aimed at helping countries and their territories to improve their policymaking capacities to attract FDI and generate positive productive development outcomes.

1. Technical capabilities

(a) Build the capacity of institutions responsible for attracting and steering FDI

The institutional landscape of investment promotion agencies is highly variable throughout Latin America and the Caribbean.[9] However, there is agreement on the need for solid institutional frameworks that have a wide margin of action and direct decision-making power to effectively attract and sustain FDI (ECLAC, 2024a). In that spirit, the first matter of business is to establish an institution, staffed with qualified personnel and endowed with decision-making autonomy.

[9] See chapters II and III of ECLAC (2024a) for analysis of institutional frameworks for investment promotion in Latin America and the Caribbean at the national and subnational levels, respectively.

(b) Align FDI management policies and productive development policies

FDI management policies include strategies, instruments and tools that are designed and implemented with a view to attracting, sustaining and maximizing the positive economic impact of investments. The design of such policies must be consistent with productive development policies. For example, FDI attraction efforts should focus on sectors prioritized by countries, including at the territorial level, in productive development policies (as detailed further below). Tailoring investments to the productive development objectives of a country or territory increases the probability that transnational corporations' activities will have a positive impact.

(c) Design tools that foster positive FDI impact

It is necessary to design policies that ensure that the economic impact of transnational corporations' activities in the destination country will be positive. The direct and indirect effects of FDI depend on the specific characteristics of the recipient economy, such as whether there is a network of public and private organizations that support science and technology, whether there is interaction and coordination between those organizations and companies and whether there is an education and training system capable of providing skilled labour. One policy option is to create programmes that encourage collaboration between transnational corporations and local providers, including through certification, training and technology transfer plans. Another option is to establish links between research centres, universities and technical training institutions. To achieve these aims, institutions should focus not only on attracting FDI but also on offering services once the investing firm's presence has been established, and they should facilitate interaction and coordination among State entities and public and private organizations.

(d) Evaluate the use of fiscal and financial incentives and regularly monitor their results

Because these incentives require a fiscal sacrifice, countries should bear at least three aspects in mind. First, it is crucial that exemptions be aligned with macroeconomic policies and that they fit within a broader productive development strategy that delineates the specific goals being achieved. Second, countries and territories can require investors wishing to take advantage of these incentives to meet certain conditions as a means of steering investment towards their strategic objectives (Mazzucato and Rodrik, 2023). For example, Costa Rica offers incentives in exchange for fulfilling certain requirements pertaining to skilled job creation and investment size (ECLAC, 2024a). Lastly, it is necessary to monitor how the exemptions evolve, conduct a cost-benefit analysis and evaluate whether, over time, they successfully build a local production system with formal inter-institutional linkages, such as clusters frameworks, in which the competitive advantages of establishing a local presence would be enough to attract investments even if the incentives were removed.

In the region, free zone regimes have been widely deployed with a view to: boosting domestic and international investment, in particular in Costa Rica, the Dominican Republic, Panama and Uruguay; stimulating economic development in specific territories, such as the Manaus Free Zone in Brazil; and driving export growth, as in the case of the Dominican Republic's National Council of Free Export Zone (ECLAC, 2024a).

(e) Identify priority sectors and markets in FDI management strategies

International experience shows that efforts to attract and sustain investments that are focused in certain sectors can be very successful. While the selection of these sectors and investments varies by country and territory, it is recommended that FDI attraction efforts focus on the sectors deemed strategic on account of the initial competitive advantages they present, such as contributions to employment, exports, innovation, productive diversification, infrastructure development, sustainable development or other areas identified on a case-by-case basis.

This prioritization process requires the following: (i) that the country or territory have a productive development policy in place or, absent this, some type of sectoral prioritization strategy as part of a broader public policy framework; (ii) that institutions have information systems in place that facilitate an understanding of the country's or territory's competitive position in the sector in order to determine whether the location is an attractive one for potential investors; and (iii) that there be mechanisms for coordination between investment promotion agencies and productive development institutions on identifying priority sectors and adapting priorities as necessary.

ECLAC (2024c) has identified 14 key sectors that, owing to their growth- and productivity-enhancing characteristics, have the potential to contribute greatly to productive transformation: the pharmaceutical and life sciences industry; the medical device industry; advanced manufacturing; modern services exports enabled by information and communications technology; the care society; labour-intensive services; e-government; the energy transition (renewable energies, green hydrogen and lithium); e-mobility; the circular economy; the bioeconomy (sustainable agriculture, genetic resources and bioindustrialization); agriculture for food security; sustainable water management; and sustainable tourism. In addition, ECLAC has identified the geographical rearrangement of production and value chains worldwide as a key cross-cutting area.

The Brazilian Trade and Investment Promotion Agency (2025) proposes, beyond the identification of priority sectors, preparing a list of 10–15 markets of origin for investors, carrying out a foresight analysis exercise to identify companies with high potential to invest in the country or territory, and developing a unique value proposition outlining the reasons that companies should invest in a given location.

(f) Strengthen the training of human talent for productive development

Transnational corporations often cite the availability of human talent as a consideration in determining where to invest. Institutions responsible for FDI management policies must identify the human talent gaps in strategic priority sectors and pursue solutions in that regard, working hand in hand with the private sector and training institutions.

(g) Strengthen post-investment assistance and monitoring

Monitoring entails a continuous process of evaluation throughout the investment life cycle, not only to resolve unexpected problems but also to ensure retention of the existing investment and create opportunities for future expansion and collaboration (ECLAC, 2024a). Institutions must have the resources and capacities needed to perform this task in order to build trust with investors and encourage them to diversify and expand their investments.

(h) Create spaces for sharing good practices in Latin America and the Caribbean

The countries of the region have had a variety of successful experiences with tackling the shared challenge of attracting and using FDI to drive productive development. Countries and territories have to compete to attract quality investments, but that should not stop them from creating critical spaces for cooperation and shared learning.

2. Operational capabilities

(a) Allocate resources for FDI management policies

The countries of the region face considerable fiscal constraints and major development challenges. Resources are needed to build the capacities of institutions responsible for strategically steering FDI to drive productive development.

(b) Establish information systems to monitor FDI and transnational corporate activities

Balance-of-payments statistics from national accounts do not lend themselves to microeconomic analysis, which is vital for understanding investments' possible impact on countries and territories. Policymakers' access to information is incomplete and dependent on the resources at each institution's disposal. Systems should be implemented to generate and disseminate information, for example using administrative records, to contribute to a better understanding of transnational corporate activities in the countries of the region.

(c) Use tools to make investing easier

It is necessary to adopt measures aimed at streamlining procedures and improving the transparency and predictability of the legal and administrative frameworks that apply to FDI. These measures include simplifying and expediting administrative processes for project approval or implementing one-stop shops for smoother communication between foreign investors and government agencies.

(d) Ensure monitoring and evaluation of FDI management policies

Mechanisms must be in place to monitor the outcomes of policies, tools and programmes and evaluate the performance of institutions responsible for FDI management policies. Information, strategies and adequate resources are required to precisely define evaluation responsibilities and time frames and determine how results will be used.

3. Political capabilities

(a) Establish institutional mechanisms for effective coordination

Close collaboration between the institutions responsible for FDI management policies and those involved in productive development is essential. Cluster initiatives facilitate multi-stakeholder coordination and the uniting of different types of productive development measures and projects around strategic agendas (ECLAC, 2024c), which makes them ideal mechanisms for inclusion in institutional frameworks for FDI management. In addition, these coordination mechanisms can facilitate technology transfer from transnational corporations to local firms and contribute to the training of human talent, both critical factors for maximizing the impact of FDI on destination economies. Lack of coordination and coherence among the different institutions and strategies has been one of the greatest obstacles to attracting quality FDI capable of advancing the region's sustainable development (ECLAC, 2024b). Therefore, governance approaches must be designed to ensure effective coordination to achieve positive outcomes.

(b) Incorporate FDI management in governance frameworks at the highest level

The closer the institutions responsible for policies to attract and sustain investments are to their countries' centres of power, the greater their impact will be. With that in mind, it is essential that FDI attraction policies be supported by governance mechanisms and the highest political levels.

(c) Foster multi-stakeholder participation in designing and adopting FDI attraction policies

Incorporating a productive development perspective into the design of an FDI attraction strategy necessitates the participation of multiple public entities, businesses, the private sector and civil society. Cluster initiatives facilitate this type of coordination.

4. Prospective capabilities

(a) Build desirable future scenarios

Building desirable future scenarios that identify, for each country or territory, the areas in which FDI can best contribute to productive development and alleviate existing bottlenecks in productive sectors can be useful in guiding policies to provide effective solutions. This exercise should include as many stakeholders as possible with links to productive development and investment policies.

(b) Encourage the diversification of FDI by origin

In Latin America and the Caribbean, investors from the United States and the European Union dominate the field. Some countries have had a very active presence globally, but their presence in the region remains marginal. For example, in 2024, FDI project announcements by companies from China, the United Arab Emirates, Taiwan Province of China, the Republic of Korea and Singapore increased globally. The region needs to establish more mechanisms for building future scenarios in which the origins of investment are more diverse. Tools available in this regard include campaigns to expand to other markets, corporations and sectors prioritized in strategies, and seminars —whether held in-person in the target market or virtually— to explore new investment opportunities.

E. Analysis of FDI inflows by country

In 2024, FDI inflows grew in Central America, Mexico and the Caribbean, while results in South American countries were mixed (see map I.1). This section offers country-level analysis of year-on-year change in FDI inflows. It examines trends in FDI components, destination sectors and source countries, according to the availability of 2024 data for each country, and highlights other notable developments not addressed in previous sections of this report. A full presentation of data can be found in annex I.A1.

Map I.1
Latin America and the Caribbean (selected countries and subregions): FDI inflows, 2023 and 2024
(Billions of dollars)

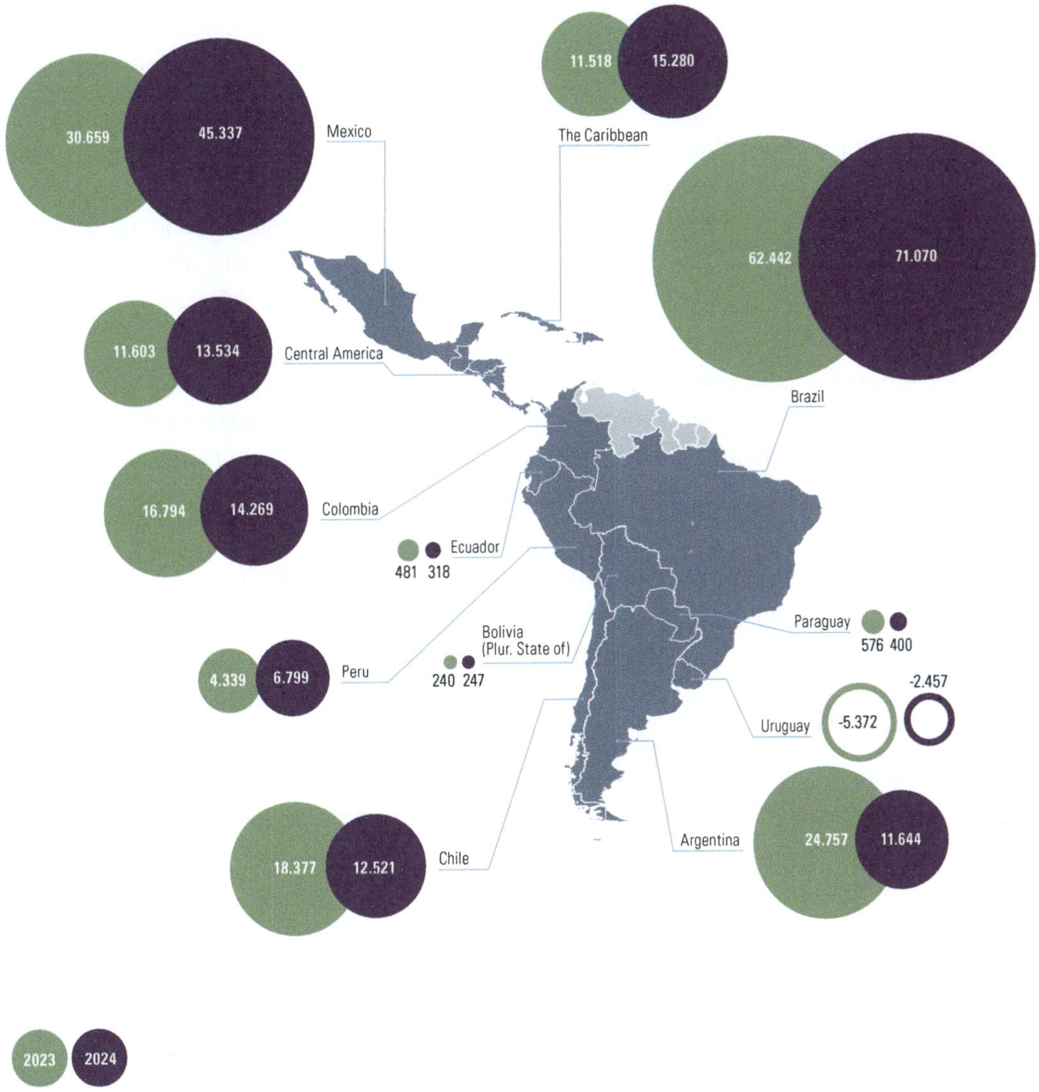

Source: Economic Commission for Latin America and the Caribbean, on the basis of official figures as at 30 June 2025.

1. Brazil

Brazil retained its position as the leading destination of FDI in the region in 2024, attracting US$ 71.070 billion in net inflows, which represents a 14% year-on-year increase[10] but remains approximately 10% below the average for the decade that preceded the COVID-19 pandemic. Growth in 2024 can be attributed to a considerable increase (57%) in reinvested earnings, the largest component of FDI in Brazil that year (47% of total inflows). Equity inflows decreased by 15% to represent 38% of total inflows, while intercompany loans increased by 15% year-on-year.

10 This increase in FDI inflows in Brazil is not evident upon analysis of the information compiled according to MBP5 (IMF, 1993), which indicates that these inflows amounted to US$ 59.187 billion in 2024, 7.6% lower than in 2023. The difference stems from intercompany loans, for which data compiled according to MBP6 (IMF, 2009) show inflows of US$ 19.996 billion in 2024, whereas analysis based on MBP5 indicates negative inflows of US$ 896 million.

By sector,[11] manufacturing attracted the most FDI in Brazil in 2024, with a significant 49% increase relative to 2023, and was the largest sector by total investment, accounting for 57% of the year's net inflows. This growth was largely powered by a substantial increase in investment in the coke, oil derivatives and biofuels subsector, which alone accounted for 42% of all manufacturing inflows, offsetting significant declines in other sectors, including metallurgy (38%), chemical products (42%) and food (39%).

The services sector received the second-largest amount of FDI, accounting for 43% of inflows. Relative to 2023, however, investment in the services sector was down by 24%. Among the subsectors recording the largest declines were financial and auxiliary services (35%), storage and transportation activities (98%) and communications (387%). These decreases were partially offset by significant growth in commerce (35%), electricity and gas (173%) and information services, which recovered from a net negative position in 2023.

The natural resources sector, meanwhile, registered a steep 110% drop in FDI inflows, which entered net negative territory. Declines were recorded in most subsectors, led by oil and gas extraction (which deepened its negative position), mineral extraction (68%) and mining support services (69%).

The composition of FDI inflows in Brazil, by source country, changed considerably in 2024, with the following five countries investing the most: Kingdom of the Netherlands (22% of total investment), United States (21%), Switzerland (7%), United Kingdom (6%) and Chile (5%) In 2023, meanwhile, the top five were the United States (27%), the United Kingdom (12%), Luxembourg (11%), Spain (11%) and Singapore (9%).

For the second consecutive year, Brazil was the top destination for investment announcements by value. Renewable energy has emerged as the foremost sector of interest in the country in recent years for international investors, with a remarkable 193.3% growth in the 2020–2024 period compared to the 2010–2019 period (see figure I.21). In 2024, the sector accounted for US$ 18.1 billion in investment announcements, or 38.3% of the country's total. Within the sector, e-fuels manufacturing predominated, with notable megaprojects by Fotowatio Renewable Ventures, Voltalia and FUELLA at the Pecém Industrial and Port Complex (PV Magazine, 2024; Pecém Industrial and Port Complex, 2024; Habibic, 2024). Other hubs of e-fuel investment in 2024 included the Port of Açu (with project announcements from FUELLA and HIF Global) and the Suape Industrial Port Complex (with a major e-fuel collaboration between Petrobras and European Energy) (FUELLA, 2024; HIF Global, 2024; Petrobras, 2024).

Brazilian assets were the target of 163 mergers and acquisitions in 2024, accounting for half the regional total and 10 of the 20 largest transactions of the year, including three valued at more than US$ 1 billion. Notably, investors from Saudi Arabia and China, both seeking natural resources, bought assets in the country (see table I.5).

By number of transactions, the sectors that led mergers and acquisitions targeting Brazilian assets in 2024 were manufacturing (67 transactions), financial and insurance activities (19), mining and quarrying (16) and electricity, gas and water supply (14).

11 Data by sector do not include reinvested earnings.

Figure I.21
Brazil: FDI project announcements by sector, annual averages for 2010–2019 and 2020–2024
(Billions of dollars)

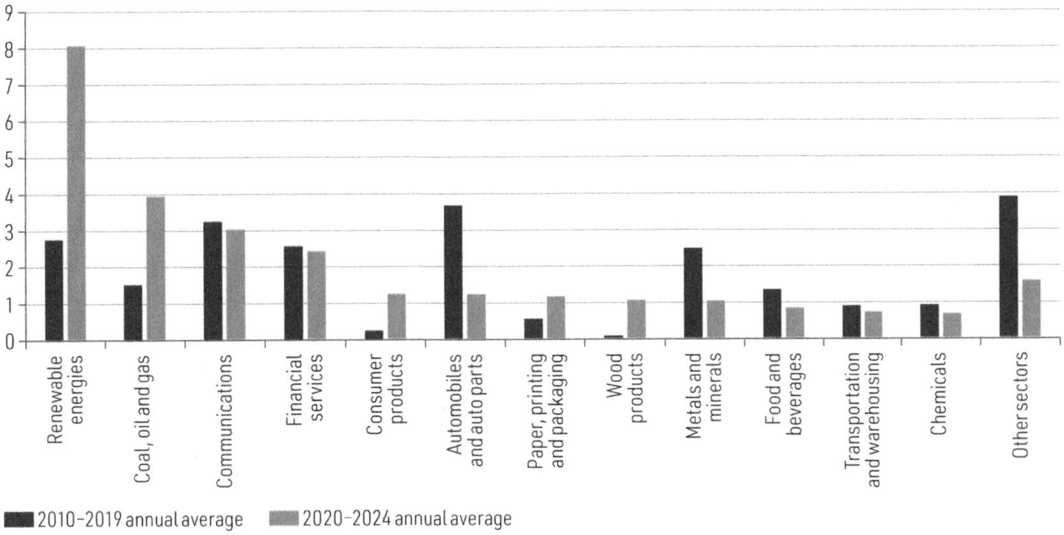

Source: Economic Commission for Latin America and the Caribbean, on the basis of *Financial Times*. fDi Markets. https://www.fdimarkets.com/.

2. Mexico

Mexico received the second-largest amount of FDI in Latin America and the Caribbean in 2024, with net inflows of US$ 45.337 billion, representing a 48% increase over 2023[12] and the highest yearly figure since 2013. By component, reinvested earnings accounted for 63%, followed by intercompany loans (28%) and equity (9%). Intercompany loans reflected the strongest growth relative to 2023, rising from a negative value of US$ 1.212 billion to nearly US$ 13 billion. Reinvested earnings increased moderately, by 8%, while equity fell by 25%.

In terms of sectors,[13] manufacturing was the largest net driver of FDI, with a 10% increase in inflows relative to 2023 and accounting for 53% of the 2024 total. The subsectors exhibiting the most significant year-on-year variation included transportation manufacturing (with increased inflows of 35% and accounting for nearly half of all manufacturing inflows) and drinks and tobacco (which climbed by 56%). Basic metals and machinery, meanwhile, were among the subsectors reporting the largest year-on-year declines.

The services sector was Mexico's second-largest recipient of FDI inflows, accounting for 42% of the total. Relative to 2023, services inflows grew by 9%. By subsector, the largest year-on-year change was in financial and insurance services (down by 18%), which accounted for the largest share of the sector's inflows. These losses were offset by significant growth in the telecommunications subsector, which moved from negative to positive territory, and in the wholesale and retail trade subsectors, which recorded respective increases of 158% and 195%.

The natural resources sector, meanwhile, experienced a larger contraction in FDI inflows, down by 51% relative to 2023. The mining subsector was primarily responsible, with an 83% decrease in inflows. Accordingly, natural resources remained the country's smallest sector by FDI inflows, accounting for 5% of the total.

12 This increase in FDI inflows in Mexico is smaller than that indicated by analysis of data compiled according to MBP5 (IMF, 1993), which point to FDI inflows of US$ 36.872 billion in 2024, 1.1% more than in 2023. The difference is attributable to intercompany loans which, according to MBP6 (IMF, 2009) attracted inflows of US$ 11.978 billion in 2024, compared with US$ 4.994 billion on the basis of MBP5.

13 Mexico presents data on FDI inflows by sector and origin according to MBP5 (IMF, 1993).

Many of the largest source countries increased their investments in Mexico. The United States was the country's biggest source of FDI inflows in 2024, with a 23% jump relative to 2023, followed by Japan and Germany, with increases of 45% and 56%, respectively.

In 2024, Mexico accounted for the second-largest share of FDI project announcements in the region. By value, the coal, oil and gas sector was the top contributor, representing 36.6% of the 2024 total. That figure is almost entirely attributable to a US$ 15 billion plan announced by Mexico Pacific to further develop the Saguaro Energía LNG Facility and Sierra Madre Pipeline (*El Financiero*, 2024a). The size of this investment is a significant outlier for the sector, which in Mexico averaged US$ 1.6 billion in annual announcements between 2010 and 2023 (see figure I.22). Another outlier was the communications sector, which attracted 24 projects for a record US$ 7 billion, or a 255% increase over 2023. The growth was driven in nearly equal measure by project announcements in wired and wireless communications infrastructure (US$ 3.5 billion, with notable announcements from Zayo Group Holdings, Inc. and Tower One Wireless) and data processing, hosting and related activities (US$ 3.4 billion) (Mexico Business News, 2024a; Tower One Wireless, 2024). Lastly, the automobiles and auto parts sector —typically the country's most attractive to international investors— recorded US$ 6.2 billion in project announcements, which represents a 47% year-on-year drop and is below the 2020–2024 annual average.

Figure I.22
Mexico: FDI project announcements, by sector, annual averages for 2010–2019 and 2020–2024
(Billions of dollars)

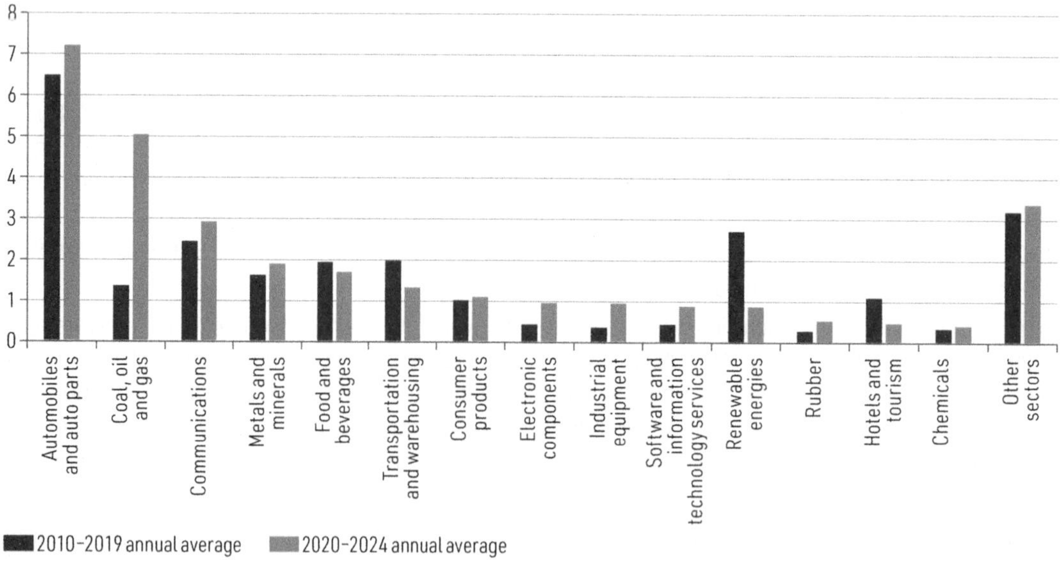

Source: Economic Commission for Latin America and the Caribbean, on the basis of *Financial Times*. fDi Markets. https://www.fdimarkets.com/.

Despite a 25% decline relative to 2023, Mexico was the region's second-largest target for mergers and acquisitions by volume, with 44 transactions. The top sectors were manufacturing (17), mining and quarrying (6) and financial and insurance activities (6). Mexico's largest transaction of 2024, however, was in real estate (see table I.5): Prologis, a United States-based real estate investment trust specialized in logistics facilities, acquired more than 3.9 million m^2 of industrial real estate, hoping to take advantage of growth opportunities in nearshoring and international trade (Prologis, 2024; *El Financiero*, 2024b).

3. Other South American countries

Colombia received US$ 14.269 billion in FDI inflows in 2024. Although this amount constituted a 15% contraction relative to 2023 (and the second consecutive annual decline), the country was the region's third-largest FDI destination. By component, despite a 19% drop, equity inflows retained the top spot, accounting for 52% of Colombia's total, followed by reinvested earnings (36%) and intercompany loans (12%). Reinvested earnings registered an annual increase of 10%, while intercompany accounted for the steepest drop (-43%).

By sector, inflows were concentrated in services (59% of the total). While services inflows increased by 20% compared with 2023, these gains were offset by a 43% decline in the natural resources sector, whose share of total inflows shrank to 27%, and a 33% contraction in the manufacturing sector, whose share dropped to 14%.

The United States was the largest source of FDI inflows to Colombia, representing 39% of the annual total, followed by Spain, which increased its FDI to Colombia by 25% relative to 2023.

In 2024, 158 projects totalling US$ 4.9 billion were announced in Colombia, representing a 43% increase over 2023. Slightly more than half of this amount was attributable to the communications sector, with a record US$ 2.5 billion in announcements driven by a series of investments in data processing, hosting and related services. Taking a longer-term view, Colombia has seen a reduction in project announcement values since the COVID-19 pandemic, with a 2020–2024 average (US$ 3.5 billion) down by 40.5% relative to the 2010–2019 average (US$ 5.8 billion).

In 2024, there were 26 mergers and acquisitions involving Colombian assets. The manufacturing sector accounted for the largest number (10), followed by financial and insurance activities (4). One of these transactions was among the largest in the region (see table I.5): El Salvador's Grupo Calleja displaced French retail company Groupe Casino as the controlling shareholder of the supermarket chain Almacenes Éxito S.A. (America Malls & Retail, 2024).

In Chile, FDI inflows in 2024 totalled US$ 12.521 billion, a 32% decline relative to the high level received in 2023. Nevertheless, Chile remained the fourth-largest recipient of FDI in the region. All components shrank: reinvested earnings (56% of total inflows) remained relatively stable with a year-on-year decrease of just 5%, emerging as the largest component; equity (47% of total inflows) fell by 34%; and intercompany loans were in negative territory with a 122% drop.

In 2024, Chile was the destination of US$ 6.9 billion in project announcements which, despite amounting to a 68.5% decline relative to the record announcements of 2023, is the second-highest annual total since 2019. The renewable energy sector attracted the most investor interest, especially green hydrogen, wind and solar technologies, followed by the metals and minerals sector.

Notably, Chile was the largest source of FDI project announcements in the region in 2024, owing to two megaprojects in Brazil: a US$ 4.6 billion investment by pulp and paper manufacturer CMPC to build a mill in Rio Grande do Sul; and a plan by HIF Global to develop an e-methanol production facility at the Port of Açu in the State of Rio de Janeiro (Fontes, 2024; HIF Global, 2024).

In 2024, 23 mergers and acquisitions targeted Chilean assets (down by 34% year-on-year). The top sectors by number of transactions were manufacturing (6), information and communications (4), electricity, gas and water supply (3) and financial and insurance activities (3).

Argentina recorded US$ 11.644 billion in FDI inflows in 2024. Although this total represented a 53% drop relative to 2023 (when that country registered its largest inflows of the century), it was still 17% higher than the average recorded in the 2010s. In terms of FDI components, reinvested earnings represented the largest share of inflows in 2024 (47%), followed by intercompany loans (29%) and equity (25%). Intercompany loans fell sharply (78%), reflecting an easing of restrictions on import payments that had led companies to accrue debts with their parent companies abroad. Restrictions on profit repatriation that were in place throughout 2024 helped the reinvested earnings component to retain its top position, despite a 24% contraction. Equity inflows were the only component to increase (28%).

Inflows to the natural resources sector, which accounted for 39% of FDI to the country in 2024, climbed by 44%, making it the only sector to record a year-on-year increase. The services sector, meanwhile, remained the largest (accounting for 45% of total inflows), despite a 60% decline relative to 2023. Manufacturing inflows fell by 79% year-on-year, with the sector representing 18% of total inflows.

In terms of origin, the largest investors in Argentina in 2024 were Spain (22% of inflows), Brazil (21%), the United States (14%), France (11%) and Chile (4%).

In 2024, Argentina accounted for the third-largest share of project announcements in the region, attracting a record US$ 34.4 billion in planned projects. Of this total, 87.2% can be attributed to a single megaproject —a collaboration between Shell PLC and YPF to develop LNG capacity in Río Negro province at the Vaca Muerta site— valued at nearly US$ 30 billion. This project, the largest in the region since at least 2005, aims to increase LNG production by 47 million m^3 per day, equivalent to 30% of Argentina's current production (***La Nación***, 2024).

Argentina's minerals sector set a record of its own with US$ 2 billion in announcements, as Arcadium Lithium, Argosy Minerals Limited and Marhen Lithium each announced lithium production projects in the country (S&P Global Commodity Insights, 2024; Mining Technology, 2024; Mining.com, 2024). It is worth noting that Argentina adopted an incentive scheme for large investments (known by its Spanish acronym, RIGI) in mid-2024. RIGI offers fiscal and foreign-exchange incentives for large-scale investments (both foreign and domestic) in strategic sectors, including mining, oil and gas, energy, forestry, infrastructure, metallurgy, technology and tourism.

In terms of mergers and acquisitions, 14 involved Argentine assets in 2024 (down by 52% year-on-year). The manufacturing sector and the mining and quarrying sector accounted for 6 and 5 transactions, respectively, representing more than three quarters of the total.

Peru recorded one of the largest year-on-year increases in FDI inflows, which jumped by 57% to US$ 6.799 billion in 2024. Still, inflows remained approximately 11% below the 2010–2019 average. By component, the largest driver of FDI growth in 2024 was equity, which increased by 43% relative to 2023 and was the only positive inflow. Meanwhile, intercompany loans and reinvested earnings remained net negative (although they closed 71% of the gap), and reinvested earnings went into a steep decline, falling from US$ 29 million to negative US$ 132 million.

In 2024, Peru's project announcements hit a post-pandemic high, with 81 projects valued at US$ 10 billion. While this total represented a 208% year-on-year increase, Peru's average annual announcements have trended down since the crisis, falling from US$ 5.6 billion in 2010–2019 to US$ 3.7 billion in 2020–2024, with particularly large declines in metals and other key sectors. Growth in 2024 was attributable to three megaprojects: the Anillo Vial Periférico consortium (consisting of Spanish firms Ferrovial, Acciona and Sacyr) announced a US$ 3.4 billion concession to construct and operate a new ring road in Lima (Ferrovial, 2024); Phelan Green Energy announced a US$ 2.4 billion investment to develop a green ammonia production facility powered by solar energy in the Arequipa region (Phelan Green Energy, 2024); and authorities approved a US$ 2 billion expansion of the Antamina copper and zinc mine, co-owned by BHP, Glencore, Teck Resources and Mitsubishi Corporation (Antamina, 2024), which represents the metals sector's most significant announcement since 2019.

In addition, Peru was the site of three of the region's highest-valued acquisitions of 2024, in energy, real estate and metal mining (see table I.5). Overall, 24 mergers and acquisitions targeted Peruvian assets in 2024 for a 50% increase over 2023, led by mining and quarrying (7) and manufacturing (6).

In 2024, FDI inflows to Paraguay declined for the second consecutive year, falling by 31% to US$ 400 million. Equity inflows remained stable, increasing by 2% compared with 2023, and accounted for 93% of total inflows. The year-on-year decline was driven by contractions in intercompany loans —already negative in 2023 and down an additional 128%— and in reinvested earnings, which decreased by 32%. Paraguay registered 12 project announcements totalling US$ 551 million, down by 62.4% from the record level announced in 2023. The main sectors were communications (52.4% of the total announced value), hotels and tourism (16.4%) and chemicals (10.9%). While the value of communications projects was roughly half that of the previous year, the sector has gained momentum since 2020, propelled by investment in data centre projects that seek to take advantage of the country's low-cost hydroelectric power.

Net FDI inflows to the Plurinational State of Bolivia rose for the second year in a row, amounting to US$ 247 million, an increase of 3% over 2023. No new investment projects were announced in 2024, marking the first such occurrence since at least 2005.

In 2024, Ecuador received a total of US$ 318 million in FDI, representing a 34% reduction from 2023 and the second consecutive annual decrease. The drop was attributable primarily to a sharp contraction in intercompany loans, which were already negative before falling by an additional 349%. Equity inflows, the largest component of FDI in 2024, also declined by 13% relative to 2023. By contrast, reinvested earnings increased by 16% to their highest level since 2018.

By sector, 38% of FDI inflows to Ecuador were directed towards manufacturing, with total investment expanding more than threefold relative to 2023, to US$ 122 million. Meanwhile, FDI in the services and natural resources sectors contracted sharply, by 66% and 45%, respectively. China was the leading source of inflows to Ecuador, accounting for 35% of the 2024 total. Chinese investment amounted to US$ 111 million, a 50% increase relative to 2023.

Project announcements in Ecuador totalled US$ 822.8 million in 2024, a 40.3% increase year-on-year and the country's highest level since 2018. Among announced projects, the metals sector accounted for an estimated 42.1% of the total value, owing to the approval of the El Domo copper and gold project of Silvercorp Metals Inc. (Silvercorp Metals Inc., 2024). Other notable sectors included communications and transportation and warehousing.

Although only three mergers and acquisitions were reported in Ecuador in 2024, the acquisition of Industrial Pesquera Santa Priscila, the world's largest shrimp farming company, was one of the region's biggest transactions of the year (see table I.5).

Although Uruguay reported negative FDI inflows for the second consecutive year, inflows rose from negative US$ 5.372 billion to negative US$ 2.457 billion. These figures were largely attributable to intercompany loans, despite a narrowing of the shortfall by 30%. Reinvested earnings jumped by 174% relative to 2023, becoming the main positive component, while equity inflows declined by 4%.

Project announcements in Uruguay fell by 93.4% in 2024, to US$ 300.8 million. While 2024 was among the weakest years in recent memory, the country's average annual value of announcements for the current decade (US$ 1.4 billion) remains consistent with the 2010–2019 average. In 2024, transportation and warehousing accounted for 45.9% of investment announcements, followed by financial services (21.6%).

In 2024, the Bolivarian Republic of Venezuela recorded a single project announcement: a plan by Russian automaker Kamaz to build a vehicle assembly plant in the country.

4. Central America

In 2024, FDI inflows to almost every country in Central America increased (see map I.2).

Map I.2
Central America (6 countries): FDI inflows, 2023 and 2024
(Billions of dollars)

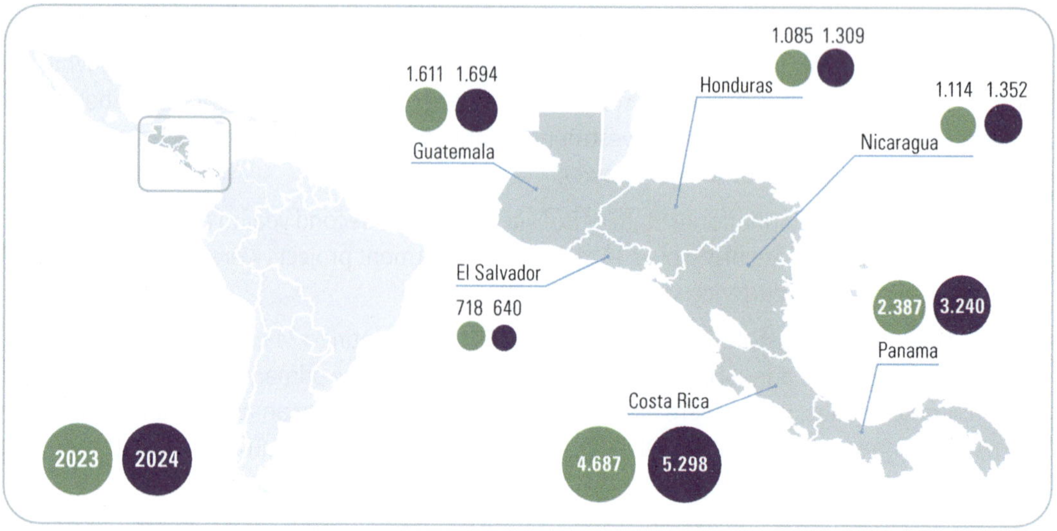

Source: Economic Commission for Latin America and the Caribbean, on the basis of official figures as at 30 June 2025.

Costa Rica was the largest recipient of FDI in Central America in 2024, with inflows totalling US$ 5.298 billion. This is the highest figure ever recorded by the country and represents a 13% increase over 2023, marking the fourth consecutive year of growth in FDI inflows. Reinvested earnings remained the largest component (65% of the total), with no change relative to the previous year. Equity inflows, which accounted for 21% of the country's total, rose sharply by 44%, while intercompany loans —though still the smallest component of inflows at 15%— grew by 61% during this period.

By sector,[14] manufacturing attracted US$ 2.922 billion, a 35% year-on-year increase, and maintained its position as the primary destination for FDI inflows for the seventh consecutive year. The services sector received US$ 1.3 billion in inflows, remaining the second-largest recipient in absolute terms but reflecting a 14% decline from the previous year. The United States was by far the biggest investor, contributing US$ 3.048 billion, a 19% increase over 2023, and accounting for 58% of total inflows to Costa Rica in 2024.

Project announcements in Costa Rica slowed for the second year in a row in 2024. The total announced value was US$ 1.2 billion, representing a 30.2% decrease year-on-year and a 52.8% decline from 2022. Food and beverages was one of the few sectors to attract greater inflows in 2024, propelled by Walmart's US$ 600 million announced investment to expand its operations in the country (Costa Rican Foreign Trade Promoter, 2024). Overall, the sector attracted a record US$ 707.7 million in announced value, representing 59.8% of the national total for 2024. Despite the recent slowdown, average annual investment announcements in Costa Rica have increased substantially during the current decade. Between 2020 and 2024, project announcements averaged US$ 1.8 billion per year, compared with US$ 1.2 billion in 2010–2019. This growth has been driven largely by technology-intensive sectors, which grew by 266.8% during this period, with medical devices emerging as a key area of foreign investor interest.

FDI inflows to Panama totalled US$ 3.240 billion in 2024, a 36% increase over 2023. While this is the highest level recorded in the country since the onset of the COVID-19 pandemic, it remains 22% below the 2010–2019 average. The increase in FDI inflows in 2024 was largely attributable to growth in intercompany loans and reinvested earnings, which rose by 41% and 66%, respectively. In contrast, the equity component plummeted by 886%, to a net negative figure.

14 For Costa Rica, FDI inflow data disaggregated by sector and origin are presented following the approach established in MBP5 (IMF, 2993).

Panama recorded 23 project announcements in 2024, with a total value of US$ 624 million, reflecting a 25.2% decrease from 2023 and a decline for the second consecutive year. The renewable energy sector was the leading recipient in 2024 (68.7% of the country's total announced value) and has seen growing investor interest in the 2020s relative to the previous decade.

In Guatemala, FDI inflows amounted to US$ 1.694 billion in 2024, marking a 5% increase over the previous year and the second consecutive year of growth. By component, reinvested earnings continued to represent almost 100% of total inflows, with a 10% increase in 2024. Equity inflows, while modest in absolute terms, also grew, by 7%. In contrast, intercompany loans remained negative and declined by an additional 97%. By sector, inflows remained relatively stable. The services sector was the principal recipient, accounting for 76% of total inflows and recording 5% growth. Meanwhile, inflows for manufacturing and natural resources weakened.

Panama remained the primary source of FDI in Guatemala, accounting for 32% of total inflows, despite a 6% decrease relative to 2023. Inflows from Mexico, Honduras and the Republic of Korea grew by 63%, 86% and 31%, respectively, as did investments from Luxembourg and the Kingdom of the Netherlands (by 11% and 153%, respectively).

Eleven projects in Guatemala were announced, representing a total value of US$ 737.7 million, the country's highest annual total since 2019 and a 52.2% increase over 2023. The leading sectors for announced projects were oil and gas (38.9%), renewable energy (32.1%) and transportation and warehousing (18.6%).

FDI inflows to Nicaragua totalled US$ 1.352 billion in 2024, representing a 21% increase over 2023 and a record high for the country. By component, reinvested earnings accounted for the largest share (65% of total inflows), followed by equity inflows (24%) and intercompany loans (10%). In 2024, equity inflows registered the strongest growth, of 58%, while reinvested earnings also expanded substantially, by 43%. Intercompany loans, the only component to contract, declined by 51%.

By sector, services captured 52% of total inflows and contributed most to overall growth, with a 32% increase. Though accounting for a smaller share of inflows (just 16%), the natural resources sector also grew substantially, by 95% year-on-year. By contrast, manufacturing inflows fell by 7% relative to 2023.

In 2024, two projects valued at US$ 28.8 million —78.9% lower than the previous year— were announced in Nicaragua. Overall, investment project announcements in that country have slowed in the 2020s, with average annual values falling from US$ 490.4 million (2010–2019) to US$ 136.1 million (2020–2024).

Honduras received US$ 1.309 billion in FDI inflows in 2024, a 21% increase year-on-year and the highest level since 2018. Reinvested earnings remained the largest component, accounting for 74% of total inflows, despite their 15% decline. Intercompany loans, which jumped by 921% relative to 2023, were the strongest contributor to overall growth, representing 29% of total inflows. Equity flows remained negative, though their deficit narrowed by 60%.

The services sector attracted the largest share of inflows, rising to account for 78% of the national total. By contrast, manufacturing inflows declined by 48%, though the sector remained the second largest in 2024, representing 19% of FDI.

The top sources of FDI in Honduras in 2024 were Colombia (30%), Bermuda (16%), Panama (16%), Mexico (15%) and Guatemala (13%).

In 2024, Honduras registered four project announcements valued at US$ 31 million, a significant drop from the record US$ 1.7 billion announced in 2023.

El Salvador recorded FDI inflows of US$ 640 million in 2024, an 11% decline compared with 2023, but the second-highest annual total since 2018. The contraction stemmed from a 37% decrease in inflows to the services sector, which remained dominant with a 62% share of total investment. This reduction was partially offset by growth in the manufacturing sector, where inflows increased by 107% relative to 2023, raising the sector's share to 32% of FDI inflows in 2024.

Spain was the largest source of FDI, accounting for 45% of net inflows, followed by the United States (18%), Panama (16%), Honduras (7%) and Mexico (6%).

In terms of investment announcements, El Salvador attracted 16 projects in 2024 with a record total value of US$ 2.1 billion, far surpassing its 2010–2023 average of US$ 370 million. This surge was largely attributable to the US$ 1.6 billion project announced by Türkiye's YILPORT Holding Inc. in the ports of Acajutla and La Unión, the largest private investment in the country's history (Labrut, 2024). In addition, Mexico's Grupo Bimbo announced a US$ 200 million investment in a new production facility, its largest investment in Central America to date and the largest announcement to date in the country's food and beverages sector (*El Mundo*, 2024).

5. The Caribbean

FDI growth in the Caribbean subregion was driven primarily by investments in Guyana and the Dominican Republic (see map I.3).

Map I.3
The Caribbean: FDI inflows, 2023 and 2024
(Millions of dollars)

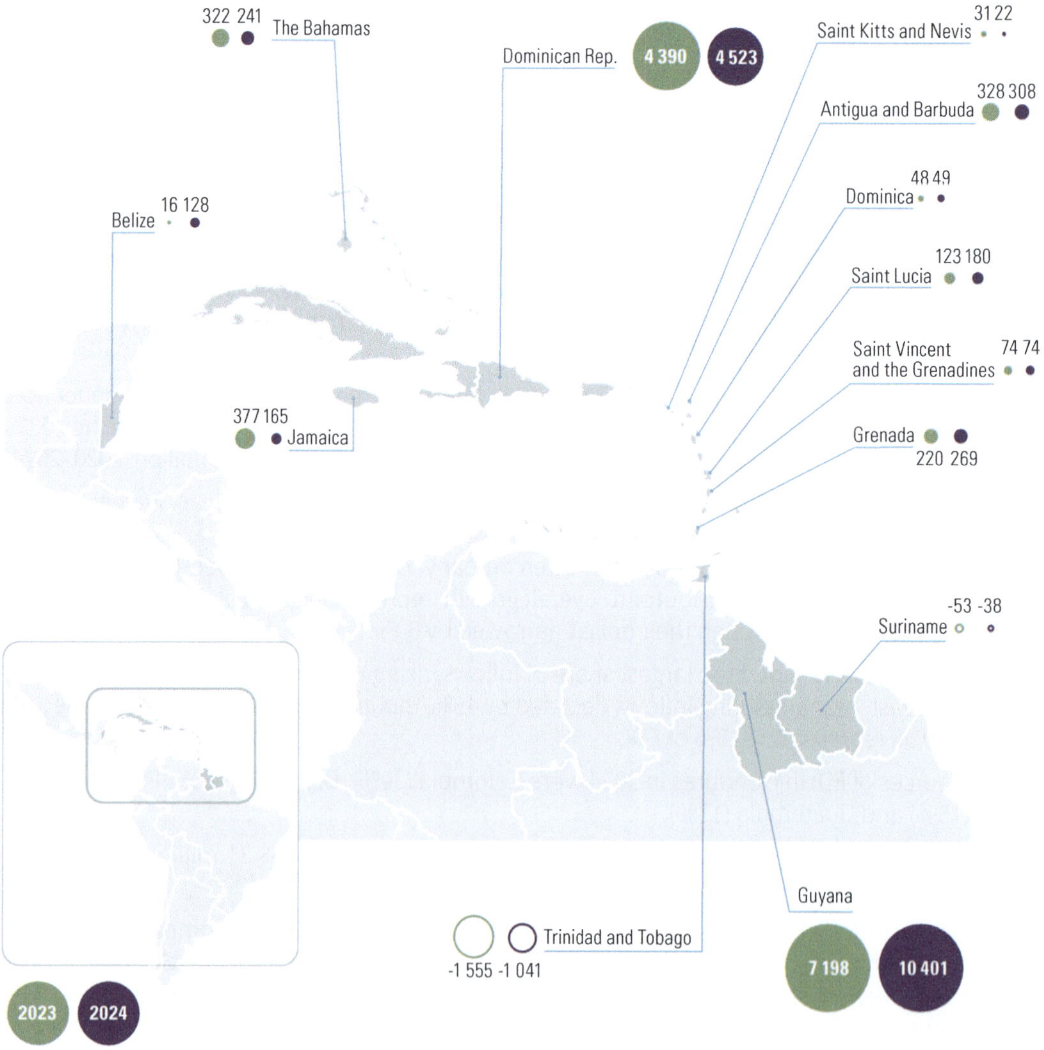

Source: Economic Commission for Latin America and the Caribbean, on the basis of official figures as at 30 June 2024.

Guyana recorded FDI inflows of US$ 10.401 billion in 2024, a 45% increase over 2023 and the second consecutive record year for the country. The natural resources sector —particularly oil and gas extraction— accounted for the vast majority of FDI inflows (98%). As has been the case since 2020, the United States remained the dominant investor, responsible for 97% of the country's total inflows in 2024.

In 2024, Guyana was the fourth-largest destination for FDI projects announced by value, attracting US$ 13 billion, almost entirely attributable to ExxonMobil's investment in the Whiptail development, its sixth project in the offshore Stabroek block (US$ 12.7 billion). The project is estimated to add 250,000 barrels per day to production capacity by late 2027 (ExxonMobil, 2024). In recent years, Guyana has become one of the region's top destinations for investment projects, driven primarily by activity in the oil and gas sector.

In 2024, the Dominican Republic reported FDI inflows of US$ 4.523 billion, a 3% increase over 2023. This marked the fourth consecutive year of growth and a record high annual total for the country. By component, equity inflows accounted for 60% of the year's total FDI, while reinvested earnings represented 37%. While both components registered modest declines compared with 2023, these were offset by a recovery in intercompany loans, which jumped from negative US$ 155 million to US$ 133 million.

FDI growth was driven by the services sector, which expanded by 18% and accounted for 89% of the country's total inflows. In contrast, the manufacturing sector contracted by 36% to represent 10% of the total. Inflows to the natural resources sector, meanwhile, fell by 86%, reducing the sector's share to just 1%. The United States remained the largest source of investment in the Dominican Republic, contributing US$ 1.162 billion. Although this represented 26% of total inflows in 2024, it was a 13% decrease relative to the previous year. Spain followed closely, with investment of a record US$ 1.126 billion, a 68% year-on-year increase.

The Dominican Republic was the destination of 24 projects announced in 2024, representing a total value of US$ 932.8 million, down 49.5% from 2023. Of this amount, an estimated US$ 361 million was allocated to renewable energy, one of the fastest-growing sectors in the country, which has seen average annual project values in the 2020s rise by 385% compared with the 2010s. The hotels and tourism sector attracted US$ 210.8 million in projects, and while it has been surpassed by renewable energy in recent years, investor interest in the sector has also grown significantly since the COVID-19 pandemic. The expansion of these sectors has resulted in average annual project announcements amounting to US$ 1.9 billion in the Dominican Republic in the 2020s, a 14.3% increase over the 2010s.

The Bahamas reported FDI inflows of US$ 241 million in 2024. This 25.2% year-on-year decrease was driven by falling equity inflows (-55.3%), which accounted for 20% of the total, and by a 38.9% contraction in intercompany loans, reducing the component's share to 28%. Reinvested earnings was the only component that increased (by 20.8%), accounting for 52% of total inflows in 2024.

Two projects valued at US$ 35.9 million in total were announced in The Bahamas in 2024. While this marks a significant recovery relative to 2023, when no announcements were reported, activity in the current decade has been weaker overall in comparison to the 2010s. Average annual project values fell from US$ 97.7 million in 2010–2019 to US$ 24.3 million in 2020–2024, a 75.1% decline.

Jamaica recorded inflows of US$ 165 million in 2024, a 56% decline relative to the previous year. The country registered five project announcements with a combined estimated value of US$ 325.2 million, the country's highest since 2019 and a notable rebound following low totals in 2022 and 2023. The hotels and tourism sector accounted for 97.1% of this total. Despite this increase, the pace of project announcements in Jamaica has slowed since the COVID-19 pandemic, averaging US$ 119.6 million annually for the period 2020–2024, compared with US$ 601.5 million in 2010–2019, a decline of 80.1%.

In Belize, FDI inflows recovered in 2024 to US$ 128 million, following a substantial decline in 2023 to US$ 16 million. The country recorded two project announcements in 2024, valued at US$ 5.3 million, representing a 94.3% decrease from the peak in 2023.

Suriname reported net negative FDI inflows of US$ 38 million, compared with negative US$ 53 million in 2023. Intercompany loans remained negative, although the net balance improved from negative US$ 131 million to negative US$ 32 million. The equity component was the only positive figure, at US$ 2 million, although this represented a 93% decline relative to 2023. Reinvested earnings fell by 115% to negative US$ 7 million.

In Trinidad and Tobago, net FDI flows were negative US$ 1.041 billion in 2024. Although this figure represented a 33% closure of the deficit relative to 2023, it marked the fourth consecutive year of negative net inflows for the country. As in 2023, all components reflected a net negative position. Intercompany loans closed their deficit by 96%, ending the year at negative US$ 15 million. Reinvested earnings also improved, with the deficit narrowing by 55% to US$ 514 million. However, the deficit for equity widened, from US$ 60 million in 2023 to US$ 512 million in 2024.

All sectors registered net negative inflows in 2024. The services sector recorded a net decline, falling by 133% from a net positive position into net negative territory. Meanwhile, net manufacturing inflows remained negative but registered a relative increase, closing the deficit by 31%. Likewise, the deficit in natural resources decreased by 71%, the largest net improvement in 2024.

The primary sources of investment in the country were the United States, the Kingdom of the Netherlands and Canada, although these inflows were offset by significant negative flows to Barbados and the United Kingdom.

Trinidad and Tobago recorded five project announcements in 2024 valued at US$ 147.5 million, a 189% year-on-year increase. The transportation and warehousing sector accounted for 93.2% of this total. Despite this uptick, the average annual announcement value in 2020–2024 stood at US$ 107 million, down 62.6% from the period 2010–2019.

In Cuba, three projects worth a total US$ 53.4 million were announced in 2024, an 11.3% decrease from 2023. Project announcements have fallen sharply since 2020, averaging US$ 41.5 million annually in 2020–2024, compared with US$ 966 million in the 2010s, a 95.7% decline.

No project announcements were reported in Haiti in 2024, marking the sixth consecutive year without announcements, amid the country's ongoing crises.

The member countries of the Organisation of Eastern Caribbean States (OECS) —Antigua and Barbuda, Dominica, Grenada, Saint Kitts and Nevis, Saint Lucia and Saint Vincent and the Grenadines— collectively received FDI inflows amounting to US$ 901 million, a 9% increase over 2023 and the highest annual total recorded since 2007. By component, equity represented the largest share of this total, with net inflows of US$ 781 million, or 87%. Reinvested earnings amounted to 9% of inflows, while intercompany loans accounted for 4%.

Within this group, Antigua and Barbuda reported US$ 308 million in inflows. While this was the largest volume of FDI, it represented a modest decrease of 6% relative to 2023. Grenada was the second-largest recipient, with inflows totalling US$ 269 million, an increase of 22% from the previous year. Saint Lucia recorded the highest relative growth in percentage terms, with inflows rising by 46% to US$ 180 million. Inflows to Saint Vincent and the Grenadines remained unchanged at US$ 74 million, while Dominica recorded a modest increase to US$ 49 million. Saint Kitts and Nevis registered the steepest decline, with inflows falling by 29% to US$ 22 million.

Across this group of countries, the only project announced in 2024 was the opening of new offices in Antigua and Anguilla by the Italian company Acquera Yachting (Yacht Harbour, 2024). Although the annual value of project announcements in OECS countries has always varied widely from year to year, it has dropped markedly since the onset of the COVID-19 pandemic. During the period 2010–2019, OECS countries collectively averaged US$ 435.6 million in project announcements annually, driven by investments in real estate and hotels and tourism. From 2020 to 2024, however, the annual average value of announced projects plummeted to just US$ 19.1 million, a 95.6% decline compared with the previous decade.

Bibliography

America Malls & Retail. (2024, 22 January). *Calleja Group acquires 86.51% of Éxito stores*. https://america-retail.com/malls/colombia-malls/grupo-calleja-adquiere-el-8651-de-almacenes-exito-transformando-su-estructura-accionaria/

Antamina. (2024, 15 February). *Gobierno peruano aprueba Modificación del Estudio de Impacto Ambiental (MEIA) de Antamina*. https://www.antamina.com/noticias/gobierno-peruano-aprueba-modificacion-estudio-de-impacto-ambiental-meia-antamina/

Bonvillian, W. B. (2024). Industrial policies for the twenty-first century: lessons from the United States. *Project Documents* (LC/TS.2024/13). Economic Commission for Latin America and the Caribbean.

Brazilian Trade and Investment Promotion Agency. (2025). *Guia de Atração de Investimentos Estrangeiros: Estruturando Agências de Promoção de Investimentos em Estados e Municípios*.

CNOOC Limited. (2024, 17 October). *CNOOC Limited subsidiary signed 4 concession contracts for exploration blocks offshore Brazil*. https://www.cnoocltd.com/english/presscenter/pressreleases/202410/t20241023_98671.html

Costa Rican Foreign Trade Promoter. (2024, 21 May). *Walmart Centroamérica anuncia fuerte compromiso de inversión en Costa Rica*. https://www.procomer.com/noticia/walmart-centroamerica-anuncia-fuerte-compromiso-de-inversion-en-costa-rica/#:~:text=Se%20proyecta%20que%20para%202028,tiendas%20y%20centros%20de%20distribución

De Camino, C., Pérez Caldentey, E. and Vera, C. (2023). Non-financial corporations as financial intermediaries and their macroeconomic implications: an empirical analysis for Latin America. In A. Gevorkyan (Ed.), *Foreign Exchange Constraint and Developing Economies*. Edward Elgar.

Dussel Peters, E. (2025). *Monitor de la OFDI china en América Latina y el Caribe 2025*. Red Académica de América Latina y el Caribe sobre China.

Economic Commission for Latin America and the Caribbean. (2021). *Foreign Direct Investment in Latin America and the Caribbean*, 2021 (LC/PUB.2021/8-P).

Economic Commission for Latin America and the Caribbean. (2024a). *Foreign Direct Investment in Latin America and the Caribbean*, 2024 (LC/PUB.2024/8-P).

Economic Commission for Latin America and the Caribbean. (2024b). *Preliminary Overview of the Economies of Latin America and the Caribbean, 2024* (LC/PUB.2024/27-P).

Economic Commission for Latin America and the Caribbean. (2024c). *Panorama of Productive Development Policies in Latin America and the Caribbean, 2024* (LC/PUB.2024/15-P/Rev.1).

Economic Commission for Latin America and the Caribbean. (2024d). *Development Traps in Latin America and the Caribbean: Vital Transformations and How to Manage Them. Summary* (LC/SES.40/4).

Economic Commission for Latin America and the Caribbean. (2025). *Relations between Latin America and the Caribbean and China: areas of opportunity for more productive, inclusive and sustainable development* (LC/TS.2025/16).

El Financiero. (2024a, 7 June). *Mexico Pacific, empresa de gas natural, invertirá otros 15 mil mdd en el sexenio de Sheinbaum*. https://www.elfinanciero.com.mx/economia/2024/06/07/mexico-pacific-empresa-de-gas-natural-invertira-otros-15-mil-mdd-en-el-sexenio-de-sheinbaum/

El Financiero. (2024b, 5 August). *Prologis anuncia la conclusión de la compra de Terrafina*. https://www.elfinanciero.com.mx/empresas/2024/08/05/prologis-anuncia-la-conclusion-de-la-compra-de-terrafina/

El Mundo. (2024, 18 April). *Bimbo invertirá $200 millones en una planta de producción en El Salvador*. https://diario.elmundo.sv/economia/bimbo-invertira-200-millones-en-una-planta-de-produccion-en-el-salvador

ExxonMobil. (2024, 12 April). *ExxonMobil Guyana moves forward with sixth offshore development*. https://corporate.exxonmobil.com/news/news-releases/2024/0412_guyana-offshore-development-whiptail

Ferrovial. (2024, 5 April). *Ferrovial, Acciona and Sacyr to develop Lima's Peripheral Ring Road for USD 3.4 billion*. https://newsroom.ferrovial.com/en/press-releases/develop-limas-peripheral-ring-road/

Financial Times. (2023, 28 November). *The cheque book COP: UAE's $200bn bid for climate influence*. https://www.ft.com/content/36a2f00d-eb7a-4057-bc31-6be6c4f01d16

Fontes, S. (2024, 4 December). *CMPC moves forward with $4.6bn pulp mill project in Brazil*. Valor International. https://valorinternational.globo.com/business/news/2024/12/04/cmpc-moves-forward-with-46bn-pulp-mill-project-in-brazil.ghtml

Forbes. (2024, 15 April). *Mallplaza confirma la adquisición de Open Plaza en Perú por 848 millones de dólares*. https://forbes.pe/negocios/2024-04-15/mallplaza-lanzara-opa-para-adquirir-open-plaza-de-propiedad-de-falabella-en-peru

FUELLA. (2024, 6 September). *Prumo and Fuella announce first Area Reservation Contract for Hydrogen Hub at Port of Açu*. https://fuella.no/it-is-a-great-pleasure-to-announce-our-first-project-in-brazil-and-the-signing-of-a-land-reservation-agreement-and-an-mou-with-prumo-and-porto-do-acu-a-subsidiary-of-prumo-for-a-green-ammonia-plant/

Habibic, A. (2024, 6 November). *Fuella reveals second green ammonia project in Brazil*. Offshore Energy. https://www.offshore-energy.biz/fuella-reveals-second-green-ammonia-project-in-brazil/

HIF Global. (2024, 24 September). *HIF Global announces e-Fuels project in Brazil*. https://www.hifglobal.com/media/news-description/2024/09/24/hif-global-announces-e-fuels-project-in-brazil

International Monetary Fund. (1993). *Balance of Payments Manual: Fifth Edition*.

International Monetary Fund. (2009). Balance of Payments and International Investment Position Manual: Sixth Edition *(BPM6)*.

Katz, J. and Stumpo, G. (2001). Sectoral regimes, productivity and international competitiveness. *CEPAL Review* (75) (LC/G.2150-P). Economic Commission for Latin America and the Caribbean.

La Nación. (2024, 19 December). *YPF firmó con Shell un convenio para desarrollar el gas licuado en la Argentina*. https://www.lanacion.com.ar/economia/ypf-firmo-con-shell-un-convenio-para-desarrollar-el-gas-licuado-en-la-argentina-nid19122024/

Labrut, M. (2024, 15 August). *Yilport investing $1.6 billion in two El Salvador ports*. Seatrade Maritime News. https://www.seatrade-maritime.com/ports-logistics/yilport-investing-1-6-billion-in-two-el-salvador-ports

Mazzucato, M. and Rodrik, D. (2023). Industrial policy with conditionalities: a taxonomy and sample cases. *Working Paper* (2023/07). Institute for Innovation and Public Purpose.

Mexico Business News. (2024a, 6 February). *Zayo, Fermaca Ally to expand North American connectivity*. https://mexicobusiness.news/infrastructure/news/zayo-fermaca-ally-expand-north-american-connectivity

Mexico Business News. (2024b, 10 July). *ENGIE signs agreement to promote biomethane projects*. https://mexicobusiness.news/energy/news/engie-signs-agreement-promote-biomethane-projects

Microsoft. (2024, 26 September). *Microsoft announces 14.7 billion Reais investment over three years in Cloud and AI infrastructure and provide AI training at scale to upskill 5 million people in Brazil*. https://news.microsoft.com/pt-br/microsoft-announces-14-7-billion-reais-investment-over-three-years-in-cloud-and-ai-infrastructure-and-provide-ai-training-at-scale-to-upskill-5-million-people-in-brazil/

Mining Technology. (2024, 24 April). *Argosy obtains approval to expand Rincon Lithium Project*. https://www.mining-technology.com/news/argosy-obtains-rincon-lithium/

Mining.com. (2024, 21 April). *Emirati company to invest $550 million in Argentinian lithium project*. https://www.mining.com/emirati-company-to-invest-550-million-in-argentinian-lithium-project/

Ohmium International. (2024, 18 April). *H2 Green Mining and Ohmium Sign Agreement to Boost Green Hydrogen in Chile*. https://www.ohmium.com/news/h2-green-mining-and-ohmium-sign-agreement-to-boost-green-hydrogen-in-chile

Organisation for Economic Co-operation and Development. (2025, 30 April). *FDI in Figures: April 2025*. https://www.oecd.org/en/publications/fdi-in-figures-april-2025_d5a76fd0-en.html

Pecém Industrial and Port Complex. (2024, 9 April). *Governo do Ceará assina sexto pré-contrato para produção de hidrogênio verde no Pecém*. https://www.complexodopecem.com.br/governo-do-ceara-assina-sexto-pre-contrato-para-producao-de-hidrogenio-verde-no-pecem/

Petrobras. (2024, 27 November). *Petrobras signs Heads of Agreement with European Energy*. https://agencia.petrobras.com.br/en/w/negocio/petrobras-assina-acordo-de-principios-com-a-european-energy

Phelan Green Energy. (2024, 5 July). *Phelan Green Energy, US$2.4 Billion Investment in Peru*. https://ammoniaenergy.org/wp-content/uploads/2024/07/Press-Release-Peru-05-July-2024.pdf

Prologis. (2024, 6 August). *FIBRA Prologis secures majority owner position of Terrafina; makes significant commitment to Mexican industrial market*. https://www.prologis.com/about/news-press-releases/fibra-prologis-secures-majority-owner-position-terrafina-makes

PV Magazine. (2024, 17 June). *FRV planea invertir en Brasil cerca de 5 mil millones de dólares en 2 GW de capacidad de hidrógeno verde*. https://www.pv-magazine-latam.com/2024/06/17/frv-planea-invertir-en-brasil-cerca-de-5-mil-millones-de-dolares-en-2-gw-de-capacidad-de-hidrogeno-verde/

Reuters. (2024, 11 September). *Amazon's AWS to invest $1.8 billion in Brazil through 2034*. https://www.reuters.com/technology/amazons-aws-unit-invest-18-bln-brazil-through-2034-2024-09-11/

S&P Global Commodity Insights. (2024, 20 September). *Arcadium looks beyond EVs in plan to double lithium output by 2028*. https://cilive.com/commodities/metals-mining/news-and-insight/092324-arcadium-looks-beyond-evs

Salazar-Xirinachs, J. M. (2025, 23 April). *Latin America should take the long view on Tariffs*. Project Syndicate. https://www.project-syndicate.org/commentary/latin-america-caribbean-response-to-us-tariffs-should-focus-on-structural-change-by-jose-manuel-salazar-xirinachs-2025-04

Silvercorp Metals Inc. (2024, 6 August). *El Domo – Curipamba project fully permitted to start construction*. https://silvercorpmetals.com/el-domo-curipamba-project-fully-permitted-to-start-construction/

TotalEnergies. (2024, 27 May). *Brazil: final investment decision for Atapu-2 and Sépia-2 oil developments*. https://totalenergies.com/news/press-releases/brazil-final-investment-decision-atapu-2-and-sepia-2-oil-developments

Tower One Wireless. (2024, 7 February). *Tower One Wireless announces seven towers completed - Additional non-cancellable rent of $ 1,511,525*. https://toweronewireless.com/tower-one-wireless-announces-seven-towers-completed-additional-non-cancellable-rent-of-1511525/

United Arab Emirates. (2023). *We the UAE 2031: Towards New Peaks*. https://wetheuae.ae/en

United Nations Conference on Trade and Development. (2025). *World Investment Report 2025: International Investment in the Digital Economy* (UNCTAD/WIR/2025).

Yacht Harbour. (2024, 20 November). *Acquera Yachting Expands to Caribbean with New Offices in Antigua and Anguilla*. https://www.yachtharbour.com/news/acquera-yachting-expands-to-caribbean-with-new-offices-in-antigua-and-anguilla-7629

YPF. (2024, 19 December). *YPF and Shell sign a Project Development Agreement (PDA) for the first phase of the Argentina LNG Project*. https://novedades.ypf.com/r/documents.html?p=ypf-y-shell-firman-acuerdo-argentina-lng.pdf

Annex I.A1

Table I.A1.1
Latin America and the Caribbean (32 countries): FDI inflows, by country, 2004–2024[a]
(Millions of dollars)

	2004	2005	2006	2007	2008	2009	2010	2011	2012	2013	2014	2015	2016	2017	2018	2019	2020	2021	2022	2023	2024
Antigua and Barbuda	95	238	361	341	161	85	101	68	138	101	46	114	97	151	205	128	77	290	313	328	308
Argentina	4 125	5 265	5 537	6 473	9 726	4 017	11 333	10 840	15 324	9 822	5 065	11 759	3 260	11 517	11 717	6 649	4 884	6 658	15 206	24 757	11 644
Bahamas (The)	804	1 054	1 492	1 623	1 512	646	1 097	1 409	1 034	1 590	3 551	713	1 260	901	947	611	435	383	531	322	241
Barbados	228	390	342	476	615	255	446	456	527	118	592	418	269	206	242	215	262	237	-	-	-
Belize	111	127	109	143	170	109	97	95	189	95	153	65	44	24	118	94	76	125	141	16	128
Bolivia (Plurinational State of)	85	-287.8	281	366	513	423	643	859	1 060	1 750	657	555	335	712	302	-217.0	-1.1	584	6	240	247
Brazil	18 161	15 460	19 418	44 579	50 716	31 481	82 390	102 427	92 568	75 211	87 714	64 738	74 295	68 885	78 184	69 174	38 270	46 441	74 606	62 442	71 070
Chile	4 969	5 991	4 755	10 545	18 812	12 750	14 849	26 369	31 802	21 121	25 528	17 766	11 363	5 237	7 943	13 579	11 447	15 177	18 772	18 377	12 521
Colombia	3 116	10 235	6 751	8 886	10 564	8 035	6 430	14 647	15 040	16 210	16 169	11 621	13 858	13 701	11 299	13 989	7 459	9 561	17 182	16 794	14 269
Costa Rica	794	861	1 469	1 896	2 078	1 615	1 907	2 733	2 696	3 205	3 242	2 956	2 620	2 925	3 015	2 719	2 103	3 593	3 673	4 687	5 298
Dominica	27	32	29	48	57	58	43	35	59	25	12	7	42	23	78	63	22	28	17	48	49
Dominican Republic	909	1 123	1 085	1 667	2 870	2 165	2 024	2 277	3 142	1 991	2 209	2 205	2 407	3 571	2 535	3 021	2 560	3 197	4 099	4 390	4 523
Ecuador	837	493	271	194	1 057	309	166	646	567	727	772	1 323	767	632	1 391	980	1 119	650	882	481	318
El Salvador	363	511	241	1 551	903	369	-113.2	123	467	179	306	397	347	889	826	636	24	386	172	718	640
Grenada	66	73	96	172	141	104	64	45	34	114	84	154	109	153	186	204	136	152	163	220	269
Guatemala	296	508	592	745	738	522	658	1 219	1 270	1 479	1 442	1 231	1 174	1 130	981	976	935	3 462	1 442	1 611	1 694
Guyana	30	77	102	152	178	164	198	247	294	214	255	122	58	212	1 232	1 712	2 074	4 468	4 393	7 198	10 401
Haiti	6	26	161	75	30	55	186	114	174	159	94	106	105	375	105	75	25	51	39	-	-
Honduras	547	600	669	928	1 006	509	969	1 014	1 059	1 069	1 704	1 317	1 147	941	1 380	947	224	800	759	1 085	1 309
Jamaica	602	682	882	866	1 437	541	228	218	413	545	582	925	928	889	775	665	265	320	319	377	165
Mexico	25 143	25 162	22 129	31 020	29 761	19 652	30 525	23 895	18 232	50 930	28 438	36 251	38 900	33 132	37 859	29 947	31 538	35 460	39 136	30 659	45 337
Nicaragua	250	241	287	382	627	434	490	936	776	965	1 077	967	989	1 035	838	503	747	1 047	1 287	1 114	1 352

	2004	2005	2006	2007	2008	2009	2010	2011	2012	2013	2014	2015	2016	2017	2018	2019	2020	2021	2022	2023	2024
Panama	1 012	1 027	2 498	1 777	2 402	1 259	2 363	3 132	2 980	3 943	4 459	5 058	5 585	3 977	5 487	4 451	-2 477	1 353	2 467	2 387	3 240
Paraguay	70	42	161	443	398	168	731	626	822	396	975	709	799	607	246	430	326	358	745	576	400
Peru	1 599	2 579	3 467	5 491	6 924	6 431	8 455	7 682	14 182	9 571	4 263	7 337	6 805	7 413	5 873	4 775	663	7 142	11 201	4 339	6 799
Saint Kitts and Nevis	63	104	115	141	184	136	119	112	110	139	157	128	121	48	40	62	6	19	53	31	22
Saint Lucia	81	82	238	277	166	152	127	100	78	95	65	152	162	90	46	76	48	91	59	123	180
Saint Vincent and the Grenadines	66	41	110	121	159	111	97	86	115	160	124	124	71	165	40	69	65	168	65	74	74
Suriname	-37.3	28	-63.4	-246.7	-231.4	-93.4	-247.7	70	174	188	164	267	300	96	131	84	1	-132.7	-9.3	-53.1	-37.6
Trinidad and Tobago	998	940	883	830	2 801	709	549	41	-1 904.3	-1 130.0	661	177	-23.6	-470.9	-700.2	184	1 056	-935	-914	-1 555	-1 041
Uruguay	332	847	1 493	1 329	2 106	1 529	2 289	2 504	6 394	987	4 085	2 673	-515.7	2 687	1 727	1 467	973	5 165	8 810	-5 372.5	-2 457.2
Venezuela (Bolivarian Republic of)	1 483	2 589	-508.0	3 288	2 627	-983.0	1 574	5 740	5 973	2 680	-1 028.0	769	1 068	-68.0	886	…	…	…	…	…	…
Total	**67 231**	**77 141**	**75 352**	**126 580**	**151 206**	**93 716**	**170 787**	**210 766**	**215 787**	**204 647**	**193 619**	**173 100**	**168 746**	**161 788**	**175 930**	**158 271**	**105 342**	**146 300**	**205 618**	**176 414**	**188 962**

Source: Economic Commission for Latin America and the Caribbean, on the basis of official figures up to 30 June 2025.

[a] Except in the cases of the Bolivarian Republic of Venezuela and Peru, data are compiled using the methodology of International Monetary Fund. (2009). *Balance of Payments and International Investment Position Manual: Sixth Edition (BPM6)*. The methodology of the fifth edition (1993) is used in part of the series for the following countries: Antigua and Barbuda, Argentina (2003-2005); Dominica, Ecuador, Plurinational State of Bolivia (2003-2015); Dominican Republic (2003-2009); Grenada, Guatemala (2003-2007); Guyana (2003-2016); Honduras (2003-2012); Nicaragua (2003-2005); Panama (2003-2014); Paraguay (2003-2007); Saint Kitts and Nevis, Saint Lucia (2003-2013); Suriname (2003-2016); Trinidad and Tobago (2003-2010); Uruguay (2003-2011).

Table I.A1.2
Latin America and the Caribbean (19 countries): FDI inflows, by destination sector, 2008–2024[a]
(Millions of dollars)

	2008	2009	2010	2011	2012	2013	2014	2015	2016	2017	2018	2019	2020	2021	2022	2023	2024
Argentina[b]																	
Natural resources	1 537	946	2 741	1 056	6 586	5 084	-828.6	2 141	352	2 177	4 966	3 377	1 993	1 322	2 399	2 854	4 105
Manufacturing	5 477	264	3 991	4 096	3 963	3 841	5 850	6 420	-1 577.5	5 216	4 741	2 430	744	2 572	6 741	9 271	1 933
Services	5 126	2 556	4 140	5 830	6 295	4 511	6 454	6 704	1 620	3 843	5 287	4 697	2 308	4 132	6 445	11 852	4 754
Belize																	
Natural resources	37	7	13	31	101	22	10	12	28	10	21	-	-	-	-	-	-
Manufacturing	-	-	-	-	-	-	-	-	-	-	-	-	-	-	-	-	-
Services	117	93	79	59	82	64	113	40	10	7	86	79	67	119	-	-	-
Other	16	9	5	5	6	9	30	13	6	7	11	15	9	9	-	-	-
Bolivia (Plurinational State of)[c]																	
Natural resources	859	420	531	622	1 166	1 550	1 558	916	372	638	448	221	2	495	508	316	211
Manufacturing	154	74	276	240	119	317	390	23	137	260	147	148	39	380	201	77	164
Services	290	193	128	171	220	162	173	227	592	312	309	206	124	177	281	254	226
Brazil[d]																	
Natural resources	11 210	4 288	20 278	8 901	10 140	17 180	9 391	5 924	10 140	5 030	10 644	11 448	5 283	-244.0	8 861	5 003	-496.9
Manufacturing	9 763	9 952	25 852	33 551	37 580	39 323	42 484	34 349	37 025	21 383	33 494	24 905	15 019	7 647	16 030	14 630	21 744
Services	9 091	5 667	7 233	28 574	27 494	23 873	34 585	31 952	22 631	32 317	17 630	12 002	12 352	21 905	28 900	21 483	16 320
Other	-	-	223	207	162	123	82	144	157	106	85	67	157	244	258	207	344
Chile																	
Natural resources	4 599	6 062	6 053	12 673	13 184	6 152	6 591	8 966	1 017	993	-1 570.5	1 666	2 722	6 095	6 851	10 238	-
Manufacturing	1 570	28	1 572	-54.1	1 107	1 465	3 630	526	303	-275.9	-223.9	328	-225.8	207	648	757	-
Services	8 725	7 092	7 805	12 918	14 288	10 758	14 318	7 759	7 175	636	8 822	8 438	5 576	9 491	7 398	7 202	-
Other	256	674	589	-1 387.2	3 224	2 747	989	515	2 868	3 884	915	3 147	3 376	-615.0	3 339	3 542	-

	2008	2009	2010	2011	2012	2013	2014	2015	2016	2017	2018	2019	2020	2021	2022	2023	2024
Colombia																	
Natural resources	5 176	5 670	4 976	7 236	7 972	8 513	7 091	3 264	2 501	4 339	3 931	4 482	1 089	1 431	4 380	6 836	3 906
Manufacturing	1 696	1 260	210	1 108	1 925	2 138	2 826	2 638	1 844	2 368	1 310	1 499	894	1 719	1 508	2 967	1 985
Services	3 693	1 105	1 244	6 303	5 143	5 560	6 252	5 718	9 513	6 994	6 058	8 008	5 476	6 411	11 294	6 991	8 379
Costa Rica																	
Natural resources	71	78	-3.2	-18.7	20	2	13	403	110	34	93	5	-60.1	-61.1	-4.5	92	105
Manufacturing	431	373	980	887	399	329	614	622	953	1 269	1 352	1 668	1 163	2 425	2 137	2 166	2 922
Services	1 696	875	530	1 548	1 847	2 392	2 271	1 726	1 138	1 481	1 038	1 119	650	887	1 032	1 512	1 300
Other	122	118	176	45	-7.8	19	27	1	3	-6.1	5	20	10	-20.5	-0.6	19	-4.6
Dominican Republic																	
Natural resources	357	758	240	1 060	1 169	93	-38.5	6	486	410	185	225	-6.5	536	371	279	39
Manufacturing	574	280	566	355	1 257	404	607	368	413	1 365	540	356	441	307	609	689	441
Services	1 938	1 128	1 218	862	716	1 494	1 640	1 831	1 508	1 796	1 811	2 440	2 125	2 354	3 118	3 422	4 043
Ecuador																	
Natural resources	265	58	189	382	243	274	725	629	512	196	880	524	545	118	-116.0	216	118
Manufacturing	198	118	120	122	136	139	108	264	38	144	105	110	37	194	83	36	122
Services	595	133	-143.1	142	189	314	-56.8	441	217	293	406	345	536	338	915	229	78
El Salvador																	
Natural resources	31	9	1	-0.6	-	-	-	-	-	-	-	-	-	-	-	-	-
Manufacturing	28	92	-65.3	149	-47.3	289	82	291	268	458	586	51	-201.0	-45.4	41	97	201
Services	479	243	-224.8	66	488	-149.3	246	80	80	374	159	553	252	392	93	631	398
Other (maquila)	365	21	59	4	29	35	-22.5	28	-1.4	58	81	33	-28.3	38	44	-13.6	38
Guatemala																	
Natural resources	209	110	147	391	461	440	51	23	59	-49.6	-98.2	64	19	18	91	-12.4	57
Manufacturing	76	23	199	187	132	190	197	238	242	277	274	227	240	184	173	271	267
Services	447	383	290	711	644	789	1 159	963	881	804	713	660	589	3 224	1 141	1 228	1 292
Other	6	6	23	-69.2	33	60	37	8	-6.6	99	92	26	86	36	37	124	79

	2008	2009	2010	2011	2012	2013	2014	2015	2016	2017	2018	2019	2020	2021	2022	2023	2024
Guyana																	
Natural resources	87	65	94	108	122	173	113	59	41	161	1 138	1 480	2 015	4 415	4 345	7 122	10 196
Manufacturing	12	8	16	30	44	10	31	13	4	2	6	30	26	44	40	28	94
Services	62	77	70	92	113	17	44	17	1	41	12	4	0	1	2	34	36
Other	17	14	18	17	14	14	67	33	12	8	76	199	32	9	7	14	75
Honduras																	
Natural resources	4	10	84	62	41	70	72	64	-94.0	-67.0	57	9	6	62	-119.2	13	34
Manufacturing	267	98	341	392	426	325	667	385	430	635	-37.4	-110.3	70	119	108	360	187
Services	736	402	545	560	591	665	678	755	803	607	942	600	343	557	932	703	773
Jamaica																	
Natural resources	152	54	31	57	107	87	56	82	118	235	483	342	95	35	29	1	-
Manufacturing	-	-	-	-	-	-	-	-	-	-	-	-	-	-	-	-	-
Services	453	292	155	93	100	155	139	369	371	213	106	121	63	163	188	321	-
Other	832	195	42	68	206	303	387	474	439	441	186	203	108	122	102	55	-
Mexico																	
Natural resources	4 905	1 352	1 497	1 341	3 246	5 911	3 113	1 994	1 458	1 998	1 947	2 176	1 904	5 016	2 064	3 827	1 876
Manufacturing	8 907	8 108	14 125	12 175	10 540	32 171	18 807	18 620	18 258	16 903	16 291	16 616	11 625	14 575	14 040	18 148	19 885
Services	15 694	8 388	11 567	12 113	7 980	10 272	8 411	15 327	11 458	15 134	15 862	15 821	14 692	13 950	20 220	14 507	15 852
Nicaragua																	
Natural resources	57	47	77	191	123	272	109	32	71	33	128	207	159	212	323	113	220
Manufacturing	122	70	108	226	302	234	246	280	292	301	131	-25.8	215	25	445	452	419
Services	447	318	323	550	347	350	378	501	596	650	573	312	348	802	561	539	711
Other	-	-	-	-	22	125	151	137	30	52	6	10	24	8	-42.5	10	10
Panama																	
Natural resources	-59.0	-33.9	77	94	1 164	468	27	1 679	730	2 043	820	1 450	195	17	-375.0	198	...
Manufacturing	161	104	-113.8	298	520	142	250	-7.6	221	316	27	133	-65.5	255	193	247	...
Services	2 106	1 190	2 760	2 761	1 526	2 957	4 182	2 885	3 795	1 923	3 197	2 808	1 271	1 859	2 495	1 751	...

	2008	2009	2010	2011	2012	2013	2014	2015	2016	2017	2018	2019	2020	2021	2022	2023	2024
Paraguay																	
Natural resources	19	22	21	43	71	121	94	-87.6	162	64	-44.0	15	-29.9	63	-5.5	-33.6	-
Manufacturing	98	11	370	271	172	-17.4	5	132	152	185	181	314	33	79	445	-14.1	-
Services	235	69	257	391	574	425	589	532	382	92	63	29	320	126	364	372	-
Uruguay																	
Natural resources	604	253	329	383	435	342	43	42	182	-88.9	-43.0	-61.1	55	65	129	-11.2	-
Manufacturing	261	242	131	190	568	507	677	163	-759.1	-90.9	200	481	506	1 407	1 465	677	-
Services	1 068	1 027	1 037	1 482	1 007	3 369	1 431	855	-1 218.4	-447.0	-82.6	1 646	306	1 552	1 673	1 552	-
Other	238	71	820	572	64	36	42	47	42	1	-55.1	21	-9.9	-5.3	83	30	-
Total																	
Natural resources	30 120	20 174	37 376	34 612	46 351	46 754	28 190	26 149	18 243	18 156	23 986	27 627	15 984	19 596	29 732	37 051	20 367
Manufacturing	29 794	21 103	48 677	54 223	59 144	81 804	77 473	65 323	58 244	50 716	59 123	49 161	30 562	32 095	44 908	50 859	50 364
Services	52 997	31 229	39 013	75 225	69 645	67 977	83 007	78 681	61 562	67 068	62 990	59 888	47 398	68 438	87 052	74 582	54 162
Other	1 851	1 108	1 955	-537.7	3 753	3 471	1 789	1 401	3 548	4 650	1 401	3 740	3 764	-173.7	3 826	3 986	541

Source: Economic Commission for Latin America and the Caribbean, on the basis of official figures up to 30 June 2025.

[a] Except in the cases of Costa Rica, Honduras, Mexico, Panama, Paraguay and Uruguay, data are compiled using the methodology of International Monetary Fund. (2009). *Balance of Payments and International Investment Position Manual: Sixth Edition (BPM6)*. The methodology of the fifth edition (1993) is used in part of the series for Ecuador (2008–2015).

[b] According to data from the Central Bank of the Argentine Republic.

[c] Gross FDI flows, excluding divestments.

[d] Data do not include reinvested earnings.

Table I.A1.3
Latin America and the Caribbean (17 countries): FDI inflows, by country of origin, 2008–2024[a]
(Millions of dollars)

	2008	2009	2010	2011	2012	2013	2014	2015	2016	2017	2018	2019	2020	2021	2022	2023	2024
Argentina[b]																	
Spain	812	1 248	1 166	217	2 835	2 354	-2 323	3 310	1 275	1 584	2 102	1 399	740	1 575	2 253	3 077	2 306
Brazil	1 626	-380	1 663	1 756	621	367	584	1 077	-527	-1 661	1 634	649	466	313	1 585	3 960	2 285
United States	2 395	1 276	1 060	2 167	2 221	2 310	4 200	3 372	-1 110	1 813	2 717	1 596	754	949	2 585	4 531	1 486
France	162	112	332	251	448	490	950	546	-53	166	582	355	380	307	576	694	1 145
Chile	862	245	1 080	1 085	1 255	590	838	929	120	860	778	540	357	78	-295	326	434
Australia	58	67	229	11	50	52	7	74	54	47	42	201	56	56	90	176	419
China	30	17	75	47	332	110	126	81	49	161	234	638	160	190	525	1 728	415
Canada	684	-274	154	383	1 723	916	329	379	-400	519	1 161	652	155	477	-23	408	407
Bolivia (Plurinational State of)[c]																	
Spain	25	145	271	235	364	676	537	369	164	167	208	274	64	159	157	76	168
Sweden	339	22	169	280	178	347	15	79	-13	413	212	40	-154	286	140	13	101
Chile	23	27	5	4	-11	1	20	6	-7	6	20	12	10	22	28	18	68
Canada	51	16	4	23	19	14	-32	30	4	17	-10	-3	4	21	10	-5	51
Peru	26	40	82	12	56	102	442	-5	247	13	145	37	121	254	218	57	33
Brazil[d]																	
Netherlands (Kingdom of the)	3 136	3 803	2 762	18 693	15 365	23 614	24 650	23 907	23 885	8 327	18 416	6 742	5 504	-1 555	10 222	778	8 251
United States	2 207	1 277	7 180	4 531	20 926	10 715	11 530	10 159	8 614	14 820	10 311	7 698	10 399	11 963	13 838	11 139	8 118
Switzerland	663	-66	8 346	1 644	5 957	3 790	4 687	-459	1 787	-2 252	2 237	-40	312	-3 220	-586	959	2 664
United Kingdom	582	990	1 451	3 302	2 606	1 745	1 904	1 855	-1 735	1 299	602	2 899	-1 178	133	2 515	4 839	2 210
Chile	-8	971	1 459	1 686	2 210	3 316	1 385	726	418	1 395	859	3 675	596	936	3 148	954	2 003
Singapore	91	91	59	314	1 114	290	376	251	88	398	818	1 523	2 105	943	1 039	3 886	1 926
Spain	2 594	3 016	632	9 965	2 450	2 180	6 356	5 311	2 482	753	2 979	2 231	1 543	-632	3 264	4 414	1 910
Canada	946	1 227	547	1 619	1 832	1 855	2 131	2 679	1 440	-559	1 460	1 361	298	1 342	1 494	1 370	1 400

	2008	2009	2010	2011	2012	2013	2014	2015	2016	2017	2018	2019	2020	2021	2022	2023	2024
Chile																	
Canada	...	423	515	3 244	2 227	2 430	3 129	-1 226	326	1 104	2 661	1 348	2 085	2 374	3 716	4 842	...
Japan	...	297	1 452	803	1 016	897	391	-31	-156	681	-166	806	98	825	948	3 741	...
Spain	...	2 325	-585	2 347	1 136	1 787	7 398	1 523	1 301	861	1 306	-66	1 017	-3 045	1 709	2 648	...
United States	...	1 042	1 087	5 141	8 501	2 058	3 538	1 471	1 660	-3 588	52	1 758	1 555	-2 045	838	2 379	...
Italy	...	316	392	268	25	-138	58	69	2 495	17	1 043	2 094	89	9 047	2 571	1 798	...
Colombia																	
United States	2 874	2 343	1 593	2 154	2 476	2 838	2 240	2 123	2 099	2 172	2 410	2 475	1 843	1 733	5 096	5 449	5 552
Spain	1 040	830	113	1 164	628	884	2 214	1 324	1 463	2 612	1 677	2 536	1 709	1 418	2 766	2 240	2 793
Anguilla	1 224	920	337	482	598	856	-163	-191	-237	35	295	500	11	313	1 305	2 361	1 580
Panama	1 141	789	1 368	3 508	2 395	2 040	2 436	1 650	1 433	1 429	1 215	968	598	618	2 241	-158	1 191
Switzerland	140	166	180	994	698	2 096	2 804	958	731	741	877	1 154	583	1 057	1 050	1 161	590
United Kingdom	1 505	1 400	949	1 408	1 357	1 400	1 088	718	879	1 260	1 248	994	285	402	833	1 360	573
Costa Rica																	
United States	1 352	1 008	1 107	1 499	907	449	796	1 263	764	1 611	1 631	1 962	1 163	2 547	2 481	2 550	3 048
Belgium	...	...	...	...	12	28	29	27	-4	17	7	41	70	-9	15	436	248
Mexico	16	5	40	172	225	160	234	114	115	136	85	94	15	10	-22	-59	167
Colombia	49	6	98	138	104	57	170	135	84	195	69	104	37	206	89	105	149
Brazil	-8	-5	-6	6	80	17	44	-55	2	13	51	6	33	-14	1	80	78
Spain	119	68	28	247	301	211	270	95	119	111	21	44	49	60	20	58	70
Dominican Republic																	
United States	360	455	1 055	499	252	374	321	405	356	732	709	937	730	1 410	1 553	1 329	1 162
Spain	181	151	203	137	128	33	7	32	281	206	288	355	194	213	372	668	1 126
Brazil	54	85	24	-2	1 042	52	428	-425	148	999	71	24	96	-194	110	-120	229
Mexico	1 055	273	433	73	-32	6	244	-19	118	-45	-80	609	337	392	482	349	210
Canada	383	773	696	1 126	851	143	158	91	480	473	329	259	80	380	372	287	207

	2008	2009	2010	2011	2012	2013	2014	2015	2016	2017	2018	2019	2020	2021	2022	2023	2024
Ecuador																	
China	47	56	45	82	86	94	81	114	62	98	61	28	60	76	62	74	111
Switzerland	34	24	6	8	18	9	28	19	19	-0	17	9	39	82	30	5	62
United States	-29	-607	-535	12	94	43	14	188	88	35	60	74	87	83	36	63	57
Chile	5	19	8	15	16	24	18	77	14	44	37	20	32	39	20	77	46
Sweden	...	-2	-1	-1	3	-3	...	29	1	...	3	6	1	1	17	1	37
Peru	32	14	13	7	13	12	7	173	5	8	12	2	-3	3	5	-2	26
El Salvador																	
Spain	...	...	-41	-0	17	170	149	143	31	47	54	233	353	98	-331	40	285
United States	129	74	-99	23	3	31	116	248	49	24	354	215	-24	146	81	118	113
Panama	321	80	206	27	-514	236	12	120	226	367	172	270	320	500	-111	256	100
Guatemala																	
Panama	9	5	9	15	28	9	27	53	19	-24	52	24	178	209	413	578	542
Mexico	75	44	79	97	98	231	181	111	202	203	102	108	-13	167	174	134	218
United States	224	132	280	151	232	207	372	359	299	263	292	236	96	121	308	182	194
Luxembourg	36	19	1	10	18	-5	73	70	63	22	23	31	41	2248	136	115	128
Honduras	3	31	-35	16	23	61	31	62	31	14	34	35	26	41	52	62	116
Netherlands (Kingdom of the)	6	2	35	7	5	7	2	49	...	-32	5	69	43	114	5	45	115
Republic of Korea	4	20	52	45	35	104	63	38	48	86	40	26	15	-22	28	47	62
Honduras																	
Colombia	...	...	...	20	22	31	128	97	99	31	106	105	156	169	171	224	298
Bermuda	...	23	11	12	15	16	5	42	11	-24	33	33	25	75	89	37	162
Panama	16	1	14	16	22	63	152	232	273	156	188	89	56	132	239	167	161
Mexico	30	168	124	154	192	266	140	138	161	219	116	140	-25	-39	13	76	147
Guatemala	44	14	61	44	52	37	88	60	158	56	40	121	72	133	43	64	124
Belgium	...	...	...	...	...	...	...	...	78	1	127	8	-35	-64	78	279	120

	2008	2009	2010	2011	2012	2013	2014	2015	2016	2017	2018	2019	2020	2021	2022	2023	2024
Mexico																	
United States	11 081	7 408	10 413	13 413	9 179	15 717	10 430	17 219	10 534	15 554	11 379	12 342	9 763	13 474	19 532	13 625	16 748
Japan	823	746	1 151	846	2 004	1 642	2 494	2 128	1 973	2 405	2 258	1 759	1 332	1 445	2 209	2 963	4 287
Germany	766	435	975	814	1 461	2 374	2 175	1 371	3 127	2 774	3 163	3 938	1 560	2 277	-48	2 419	3 774
Canada	4 575	1 983	1 924	1 315	1 618	5 360	2 868	1 357	2 577	3 855	4 423	2 219	4 026	2 403	3 795	3 594	3 499
Netherlands (Kingdom of the)	189	275	5 499	295	414	1 145	238	1 164	338	-22	851	1 036	698	165	82	1 073	1 976
Belgium	815	855	177	381	-142	13 323	1 269	826	942	1 027	68	1 281	273	1 695	50	753	1 533
Republic of Korea	786	181	360	487	481	471	595	969	1 112	245	737	192	571	729	685	498	1 311
Nicaragua																	
Panama	4	1	1	34	137	94	116	128	182	143	164	181	97	121	179	230	336
United States	126	88	88	159	54	324	78	224	162	261	79	100	180	331	384	242	283
Spain	59	25	33	116	57	96	94	57	70	50	-20	7	33	40	22	-7	96
Costa Rica	5	10	2	39	38	22	-0	-9	40	36	68	19	31	-7	136	87	82
Mexico	164	48	90	115	134	136	248	140	154	159	143	103	84	131	198	136	67
Panama																	
United States	224	-19	1 120	652	28	715	2 154	711	1 059	-25	896	687	969	216	594	434	...
Netherlands (Kingdom of the)	420	...	126	-114	244	-2	109	398	-152	13	474	183	124	-3	-29	255	...
Switzerland	122	301	444	216	152	232	244	161	232	546	1	-8	-103	410	304	246	...
Colombia	60	135	82	486	9	29	1 162	659	913	346	864	778	371	516	773	171	...
United Kingdom	6	68	114	486	-701	78	101	193	313	-159	276	190	319	-15	4	158	...
Singapore	...	...	...	17	2	1	38	77	20	-4	117	-57	74	25	14	152	...
Brazil	59	33	-2	20	...	...	37	154	64	-50	-163	77	-229	28	149	148	...
Paraguay																	
Brazil	58	7	85	60	173	151	160	107	-7	104	59	104	74	143	225	181	...
Uruguay	-14	18	23	27	40	53	141	-105	69	41	28	15	2	9	11	87	...
Spain	66	...	98	166	70	99	7	37	90	112	10	20	-57	-232	22	69	...
Argentina	38	14	17	30	84	48	-7	73	64	16	-24	-19	15	60	-53	59	...
Ireland	5	...	5	13	9	6	10	4	6	8	6	18	23	17	26	53	...

	2008	2009	2010	2011	2012	2013	2014	2015	2016	2017	2018	2019	2020	2021	2022	2023	2024
Trinidad and Tobago																	
United States	403	469	363	-12	-16	-520	-153	13	26	...	-15	74	1 008	-403	893	-1 752	304
Netherlands (Kingdom of the)	...	...	...	...	...	...	...	...	7	1	-3	3	2	-33	-29	30	34
Uruguay																	
Netherlands (Kingdom of the)	14	110	-2	172	-104	119	-979	27	-228	-149	-955	119	1 996	-1 780	465	2 617	...
Brazil	183	110	108	170	331	515	-252	534	-884	167	-1 201	468	-1 591	4 227	945	1 767	...
China	...	...	...	...	48	27	-33	-10	-113	-7	-35	-19	215	908	306	439	...
Cameroon	3	...	14	18	-125	110	149	203	-79	-43	80	284	204	-152	-50	267	...
Luxembourg	4	12	10	-4	-726	102	-140	67	281	-82	-53	-2 012	1 095	879	-691	266	...
Peru	1	...	...	...	-13	-24	-119	-100	45	-19	-15	-110	11	-407	-19	188	...

Source: Economic Commission for Latin America and the Caribbean, on the basis of official figures up to 30 June 2025.

[a] Except in the cases of Costa Rica, Honduras, Mexico, Panama, Paraguay and Uruguay, data are compiled using the methodology of International Monetary Fund. (2009). *Balance of Payments and International Investment Position Manual: Sixth Edition (BPM6)*. The methodology of the fifth edition (1993) is used in part of the series for Ecuador (2008–2015).

[b] According to data from the Central Bank of the Argentine Republic.

[c] Gross FDI flows, excluding divestments.

[d] Data do not include reinvested earnings.

Table I.A1.4
Latin America and the Caribbean (28 countries): FDI inflows, by component, 2008-2024[a]
(Millions of dollars)

	2008	2009	2010	2011	2012	2013	2014	2015	2016	2017	2018	2019	2020	2021	2022	2023	2024
Antigua and Barbuda																	
Equity	149	79	96	61	110	65	67	94	94	156	209	128	93	290	301	299	297
Intercompany loans	...	1	1	2	6	29	-25	-6	-4	7	3	9	15	-9	-15	18	-2
Reinvested earnings	12	5	5	5	22	7	5	26	8	-11	-8	-9	-31	9	27	12	12
Argentina																	
Equity	4 552	2 133	2 504	4 508	4 861	2 784	-112	1 319	3 716	1 958	3 259	2 231	1 373	746	628	2 251	2 886
Intercompany loans	4 777	-1 010	3 507	2 600	3 120	-783	-945	2 382	-4 732	2 422	1 424	167	839	974	8 800	15 327	3 326
Reinvested earnings	396	2 894	5 322	3 732	7 343	7 821	6 121	8 058	4 276	7 137	7 034	4 251	2 672	4 938	5 777	7 179	5 433
Bahamas (The)																	
Equity	1 032	753	960	971	575	868	617	408	511	351	573	373	181	61	286	107	48
Intercompany loans	481	-107	137	438	458	723	2 934	304	749	550	374	238	299	279	104	112	68
Reinvested earnings	...	...	...	...	...	...	...	...	...	...	...	...	-45	43	141	103	125
Barbados																	
Equity	340	140	393	227	230	135	307	398	82	295	321	311	310	215	...	...	...
Intercompany loans	231	103	41	324	113	-110	-76	-190	-260	-192	-165	-154	-100	-27	...	...	...
Reinvested earnings	45	13	13	-95	184	92	361	210	447	102	85	58	53	49	...	...	...
Belize																	
Equity	141	80	80	103	193	101	145	57	29	2	94	57	68	28	118	...	...
Intercompany loans	8	6	2	1	...	...	...	...	...	...	...	...	...	...	...	...	...
Reinvested earnings	21	23	15	-8	-4	-6	7	7	15	22	24	37	8	13	16	...	...
Bolivia (Plurinational State of)																	
Equity	45	...	1	5	19	17	313	20	406	152	70	126	36	70	52	38	38
Intercompany loans	850	177	141	130	282	331	889	741	568	417	438	345	350	444	258	326	281
Reinvested earnings	407	509	793	899	1 204	1 682	919	405	127	640	397	103	-221	538	680	282	281

	2008	2009	2010	2011	2012	2013	2014	2015	2016	2017	2018	2019	2020	2021	2022	2023	2024
Brazil																	
Equity	30 064	19 906	40 117	54 782	52 836	42 152	47 501	49 520	44 512	53 950	41 013	42 878	28 118	29 998	36 584	31 725	26 915
Intercompany loans	20 652	11 575	13 470	16 451	22 541	38 346	39 040	22 851	25 440	4 886	20 840	5 543	4 693	-445	17 465	9 598	10 976
Reinvested earnings	...	...	28 803	31 194	17 192	-5 288	1 174	-7 632	4 342	10 049	16 330	20 753	5 459	16 887	20 557	21 119	33 159
Chile																	
Equity	7 775	1 905	4 662	10 911	8 532	4 778	10 506	6 494	6 148	2 075	2 476	6 361	5 245	11 605	10 344	9 023	5 927
Intercompany loans	3 086	1 144	3 856	3 233	11 067	8 714	9 619	9 785	2 552	-943	-795	1 846	936	-979	485	1 975	-433
Reinvested earnings	7 951	9 701	6 332	12 225	12 203	7 629	5 404	1 488	2 663	4 105	6 262	5 372	5 267	4 551	7 943	7 379	7 028
Colombia																	
Equity	7 861	4 903	3 733	8 282	9 091	9 755	9 181	7 423	6 399	8 053	4 558	7 285	3 386	3 269	7 860	9 163	7 407
Intercompany loans	47	731	-635	1 872	1 239	2 368	2 493	2 006	4 672	1 794	1 604	2 411	2 527	2 485	2 955	2 923	1 669
Reinvested earnings	2 657	2 400	3 332	4 493	4 710	4 087	4 495	2 191	2 787	3 854	5 137	4 293	1 546	3 807	6 367	4 709	5 193
Costa Rica																	
Equity	1 594	1 050	818	959	852	1 704	1 352	1 180	414	685	769	507	461	900	652	761	1 094
Intercompany loans	39	-174	150	711	1 136	714	912	665	1 153	573	794	574	511	693	425	486	781
Reinvested earnings	446	471	497	509	708	788	978	1 110	1 054	1 667	1 452	1 638	1 130	2 000	2 596	3 441	3 423
Dominica																	
Equity	39	39	28	25	45	16	6	8	36	26	60	52	39	32	26	53	...
Intercompany loans	9	13	13	7	9	4	2	-7	...	15	...	-2	...	-3	-2	-2	...
Reinvested earnings	9	6	3	2	4	5	4	6	6	-19	18	13	-17	-1	-6	-4	...
Dominican Republic																	
Equity	2 199	704	667	804	1 256	233	955	995	1 126	2 403	1 513	1 583	1 688	1 629	2 401	2 837	2 722
Intercompany loans	278	1 096	554	468	904	471	-166	18	66	-162	-141	225	-330	-82	309	-155	133
Reinvested earnings	394	365	803	1 005	982	1 286	1 420	1 192	1 214	1 331	1 164	1 213	1 201	1 650	1 389	1 708	1 663
Ecuador																	
Equity	229	278	265	252	227	424	848	985	679	521	470	431	837	579	1 171	356	310
Intercompany loans	530	-225	-312	66	40	-7	-390	51	-112	-49	689	379	125	-70	-434	-41	-185
Reinvested earnings	298	256	213	328	301	310	314	287	200	161	232	170	157	142	145	166	193

	2008	2009	2010	2011	2012	2013	2014	2015	2016	2017	2018	2019	2020	2021	2022	2023	2024
Grenada																	
Equity	128	97	56	39	29	109	58	122	85	122	123	149	130	121	133	187	233
Intercompany loans	1	2	3	1	...	...	14	-2	20	-6	24	5	-12	-6	-9	-8	-8
Reinvested earnings	12	5	5	5	5	5	12	34	4	38	40	49	19	37	40	40	44
Guatemala																	
Equity	177	-33	168	405	448	288	439	772	157	112	212	31	53	2 209	74	156	167
Intercompany loans	153	175	-136	149	318	382	269	-255	392	250	-57	46	40	34	159	-82	-162
Reinvested earnings	408	381	626	666	505	809	734	714	625	768	825	899	841	1 219	1 210	1 537	1 689
Honduras																	
Equity	568	84	29	284	310	174	247	137	201	474	120	27	-18	-178	-9	-86	-35
Intercompany loans	-40	65	378	56	52	250	540	342	-34	79	614	231	-73	-60	-33	37	378
Reinvested earnings	479	360	562	674	697	645	917	838	981	388	647	689	314	1 038	802	1 135	966
Mexico																	
Equity	13 062	11 009	15 637	9 699	4 316	22 041	5 763	13 450	10 992	11 958	11 326	13 570	6 756	15 396	18 180	5 232	3 909
Intercompany loans	7 370	3 278	9 583	3 439	3 251	10 392	4 639	10 845	17 225	9 193	13 220	-1 802	8 647	7 151	4 754	-1 212	12 717
Reinvested earnings	9 329	5 365	5 306	10 756	10 664	18 497	18 037	11 955	10 683	11 981	13 313	18 179	16 135	12 913	16 202	26 639	28 710
Nicaragua																	
Equity	...	...	...	...	567	360	686	595	446	630	496	247	226	205	312	208	329
Intercompany loans	...	...	...	...	29	321	235	145	209	55	40	109	44	301	32	288	140
Reinvested earnings	...	...	...	...	180	265	157	227	335	351	302	147	477	541	943	617	883
Panama																	
Equity	918	898	948	759	1 561	1 614	687	77	923	-24	31	-25	-668	119	101	42	-327
Intercompany loans	136	105	540	1 224	682	550	343	1 599	2 258	2 211	3 557	2 756	-1 108	-375	1 280	1 292	1 820
Reinvested earnings	1 348	257	874	1 150	737	1 779	3 429	3 382	2 404	1 790	1 900	1 720	-700	1 608	1 085	1 053	1 747
Paraguay																	
Equity	181	205	134	633	358	466	685	431	389	431	219	304	323	252	203	363	370
Intercompany loans	-3	-98	292	111	232	-287	22	271	297	205	-251	305	263	-189	305	-72	-165
Reinvested earnings	220	62	305	-118	232	216	268	6	113	-29	278	-180	-259	295	237	286	195

	2008	2009	2010	2011	2012	2013	2014	2015	2016	2017	2018	2019	2020	2021	2022	2023	2024
Peru																	
Equity	2 981	1 828	2 445	896	7 337	4 258	3 589	2 876	3 325	5 297	4 921	392	96	6 726	8 276	4 973	7 126
Intercompany loans	656	-782	693	2 117	1 459	2 300	2 460	401	906	173	-811	1 419	88	500	1 080	-663	-195
Reinvested earnings	3 287	5 385	5 317	4 670	5 387	3 013	-1 786	4 060	2 574	1944	1 763	2 965	480	-84	1 845	29	-132
Saint Kitts and Nevis																	
Equity	178	132	116	107	106	137	161	132	113	34	39	78	14	14	19	29	19
Intercompany loans	3	1	1	1	2	…	-7	-7	…	8	-5	2	-5	8	28	-2	-2
Reinvested earnings	2	2	2	4	1	1	2	3	9	6	6	-18	-3	-3	5	4	4
Saint Lucia																	
Equity	135	135	109	80	54	76	25	83	136	68	64	40	44	60	59	112	111
Intercompany loans	21	13	13	15	16	10	2	11	11	15	-31	17	10	17	-42	-15	41
Reinvested earnings	11	3	4	5	8	9	38	58	14	7	12	18	-7	14	42	26	28
Saint Vincent and the Grenadines																	
Equity	142	100	91	79	112	157	99	123	99	167	62	77	71	155	56	77	68
Intercompany loans	8	8	2	2	2	2	15	4	-15	11	-10	2	3	8	5	8	10
Reinvested earnings	9	2	4	4	1	1	10	-3	-14	-13	-12	-11	-8	6	5	-11	-4
Suriname																	
Equity	…	…	…	…	…	…	…	…	…	10	-3	5	…	-1	1	28	2
Intercompany loans	-231	-93	-248	-51	113	71	-21	186	254	55	89	96	-32	31	55	-131	-32
Reinvested earnings	…	…	0	121	11	69	27	1 291	1 519	31	44	-17	33	-163	-65	50	-7
Trinidad and Tobago																	
Equity	2 322	426	309	517	-251	-1 899	518	-223	-268	-367	-790	137	12	-82	-134	…	..
Intercompany loans	-16	-12	-11	-476	-1 653	769	143	400	245	-104	90	47	387	105	-582	…	..
Reinvested earnings	495	296	251	…	…	…	…	…	…	…	…	…	658	-957	-198	…	..
Uruguay																	
Equity	1 012	990	1 617	1 412	1 242	2 057	1 708	1 422	1 019	646	277	636	1 006	733	970	539	516
Intercompany loans	540	82	8	263	2 676	-1 704	1 569	2 501	-924	854	332	1 449	187	1 124	4 221	-6 468	-4 500
Reinvested earnings	554	457	664	828	2 476	634	809	-1 250	-610	1 187	1 117	-619	-220	3 307	3 620	557	1 527

	2008	2009	2010	2011	2012	2013	2014	2015	2016	2017	2018	2019	2020	2021	2022	2023	2024
Venezuela (Bolivarian Republic of)																	
Equity	302	-3 348	-1 319	-495	-307	-79	67	123	21	20	20	...	...	...	...	...	...
Intercompany loans	-11	367	1 457	2 752	3 292	1 784	-1 605	1 051	622	-1 440	-697	...	...	...	...	...	...
Reinvested earnings	2 336	1 993	1 436	3 483	2 988	975	510	-405	425	1 352	1 563	...	...	...	...	...	...
Total																	
Equity	78 124	44 492	74 663	96 304	94 707	92 792	86 419	89 020	81 790	90 205	72 501	77 993	49 878	75 152	88 663	68 473	60 132
Intercompany loans	39 573	16 439	33 500	35 907	51 387	65 641	62 904	56 095	51 556	20 876	41 168	16 266	18 304	11 909	41 602	23 538	26 674
Reinvested earnings	31 124	31 213	61 487	76 538	68 741	45 350	44 365	28 258	36 201	48 839	59 927	61 714	34 938	54 397	71 406	78 055	92 167

Source: Economic Commission for Latin America and the Caribbean, on the basis of official figures up to 30 June 2025.

[a] Except in the cases of the Bolivarian Republic of Venezuela and Peru, data are compiled using the methodology of International Monetary Fund. (2009). *Balance of Payments and International Investment Position Manual: Sixth Edition (BPM6)*. The methodology of the fifth edition (1993) is used in part of the series for the following countries: Antigua and Barbuda, Dominica, Grenada, Plurinational State of Bolivia, Saint Kitts and Nevis, Saint Lucia (2003–2013); Argentina (2003–2005); Dominican Republic (2003–2009); Ecuador (2003–2015); Guatemala (2003–2007); Guyana (2003–2016); Honduras (2003–2012); Mexico, Nicaragua (2003–2005); Panama (2003–2014); Paraguay (2003–2007); Suriname (2003–2016); Trinidad and Tobago (2003–2010); Uruguay (2003–2011).

Table I.A1.5
Latin America and the Caribbean (23 countries): FDI stock, by country, 2015–2024
(Billions of dollars and percentages)

A. Value *(Billions of dollars)*

	2015	2016	2017	2018	2019	2020	2021	2022	2023	2024
Argentina	79.773	74.868	80.700	72.589	70.458	85.269	99.995	116.685	135.561	178.663
Belize	2.051	2.095	2.119	2.237	2.331	2.409	2.538	2.679	2.636	2.764
Bolivia (Plurinational State of)	11.598	11.565	12.241	11.835	11.7[illegible]0	10.276	10.586	9.839	9.377	9.566
Brazil	568.226	703.328	767.757	737.894	873.979	765.401	901.421	1 056	1 283	1 091
Chile	222.984	236.752	257.748	254.160	257.709	260.715	253.725	269.368	283.757	285.790
Colombia	149.073	164.428	179.334	188.833	204.916	212.299	219.677	234.230	253.672	267.476
Costa Rica	34.278	37.309	40.788	44.524	47.753	50.129	53.721	57.492	62.180	67.457
Dominican Republic	31.284	33.794	37.371	40.183	43.013	45.473	48.823	52.873	57.624	62.099
Ecuador	15.894	16.676	17.308	18.699	19.679	20.798	21.448	22.330	22.811	23.128
El Salvador	9.995	10.178	10.351	10.877	11.591	11.972	12.921	12.980	13.746	14.638
Guatemala	12.228	13.850	15.099	15.587	16.670	17.574	21.367	22.409	24.153	26.417
Haiti	1.265	1.370	1.745	1.850	1.925	1.940	1.992	2.031	...	...
Honduras	13.564	14.900	15.461	16.503	17.029	17.421	17.952	18.660	19.537	20.017
Jamaica	14.171	15.099	15.988	16.762	17.428	17.693	18.013	18.332	18.709	...
Mexico	478.453	486.671	544..480	570.381	616.321	592.508	641.298	712..753	845.412	774.675
Nicaragua	7.208	7.935	8.620	9.056	9.240	9.986	11.206	12.500	13.730	14.787
Panama	39.629	44.839	55.110	59.869	65.937	62.914	62.118	64.668	66..994	70.887
Paraguay	6.739	7.677	8.696	8.591	8.523	8.391	8.863	9.231	9.829	10.229
Peru	91.203	98.008	105.421	111.294	116.069	116.733	123.875	135.076	139.415	146.215
Suriname	1.477	1.894	2.034	2.173	2.266	2.275	2.144	2.138	2.067	2.029
Trinidad and Tobago	10.049	9.545	9.083	8.452	8.455	10.496	11.105	...	...	...
Uruguay	47.419	46.563	50.404	51.257	51.619	50.582	54.140	63.493	58.328	54.954
Venezuela (Bolivarian Republic of)	28.142	23.569	22.175	22.918	...	...	...	...	...	...
Total	**1 877**	**2 063**	**2 260**	**2 277**	**2 475**	**2 373**	**2 599**	**2 906**	**3 330**	**3 131**

B. Share of GDP *(Percentages)*

	2015	2016	2017	2018	2019	2020	2021	2022	2023	2024
Argentina	12	13	13	13	16	22	21	19	21	28
Belize	94	94	94	98	98	118	105	94	86	82
Bolivia (Plurinational State of)	35	34	33	29	29	28	26	22	21	20
Brazil	31	39	37	38	47	52	54	54	58	50
Chile	92	95	93	86	93	102	80	89	85	87
Colombia	51	58	58	56	63	78	69	68	69	64
Costa Rica	61	63	67	71	74	80	83	83	72	71
Dominican Republic	44	45	47	47	48	58	51	47	48	50
Ecuador	16	17	17	17	18	22	20	19	19	19
El Salvador	43	42	41	42	43	48	44	41	41	41
Guatemala	20	21	21	21	22	23	25	23	23	23
Haiti	9	10	11	12	14	12	10	11	...	...
Honduras	65	69	67	69	68	75	64	59	57	54
Jamaica	100	107	108	106	110	128	123	107	96	...
Mexico	39	44	46	45	47	52	49	49	47	42
Nicaragua	57	60	63	70	73	78	79	80	77	75
Panama	71	75	85	89	94	110	92	85	80	82
Paraguay	19	21	22	21	22	24	22	22	23	23
Peru	48	51	50	50	51	58	55	55	52	51
Suriname	29	57	57	54	53	55	64	56	60	46
Trinidad and Tobago	37	40	38	35	36	50	46	36	32	33
Uruguay	81	81	78	78	83	94	89	90	75	68
Venezuela (Bolivarian Republic of)	19	12	14	17	...	...	...	...	...	...
Total	**52**	**58**	**57**	**60**	**69**	**80**	**75**	**74**	**78**	**72**

Source: Economic Commission for Latin America and the Caribbean, on the basis of official figures up to 30 June 2025.

Table I.A1.6
Latin America and the Caribbean (27 countries): FDI outflows, by country, 2004–2024
(Millions of dollars)

	2004	2005	2006	2007	2008	2009	2010	2011	2012	2013	2014	2015	2016	2017	2018	2019	2020	2021	2022	2023	2024
Antigua and Barbuda	15	17	2	2	2	4	5	3	4	6	6	14	38	12	-1	-11	2	-10	9	18	18
Argentina	676	1 311	2 439	1 504	1 391	712	965	1 488	1 055	890	1 921	875	1 787	1 156	1 726	1 523	1 177	1 544	2 090	3 023	2 757
Bahamas	169	143	333	459	410	217	150	524	158	277	2 679	170	359	151	117	148	60	85	214	...	...
Barbados	54	157	44	82	73	27	345	556	39	40	-229	52	-194	-28	9	28	8	28	...	...	...
Belize	0	1	1	1	3	0	1	1	1	1	3	0	2	0	1	2	4	2	1	2	3
Bolivia (Plurinational State of)	3	3	3	4	5	-4	-29	0	77	-255	-33	-2	89	80	-84	48	-111	91	-81	257	233
Brazil	9 822	2 910	28 798	17 061	26 115	-4 552	26 763	16 067	2 083	15 644	20 607	3 134	14 693	21 341	2 025	22 820	-3 467	16 239	33 355	25 148	24 319
Chile	1 951	1 997	2 027	4 361	8 463	5 806	8 561	16 892	19 935	9 323	10 080	15 851	7 876	2 535	1 847	10 345	6 398	14 573	14 055	8 765	3 592
Colombia	192	4 796	1 268	1 279	3 085	3 505	5 483	8 420	-606	7 652	3 899	4 218	4 517	3 690	5 126	3 153	1 733	3 181	3 384	1 269	4 576
Costa Rica	206	150	219	430	197	274	318	405	894	804	424	414	493	273	581	24	459	447	613	987	337
Dominica	1	13	3	7	0	1	1	0	0	2	-2	-12	1	-1	0	0	-0	2	-1	0	0
El Salvador	-3	113	-26	95	79	3	112	-96	-36	66	200	98	132	-385	-413	61	384	427	-117	-45	288
Grenada	1	3	6	16	6	1	3	3	3	1	7	19	17	4	18	24	-19	-9	10	-2	3
Guatemala	0	0	0	0	17	31	50	80	44	30	55	183	209	196	201	180	149	476	722	615	691
Honduras	-6	1	1	2	-1	4	-1	2	208	77	390	365	247	-94	485	419	-105	288	21	228	689
Jamaica	52	101	85	115	76	61	58	75	90	75	59	34	270	34	13	446	7	56	60	-4	1
Mexico	4 559	5 835	6 676	8 332	688	11 663	17 895	11 573	18 775	18 032	5 594	10 978	7 870	3 045	12 245	6 084	5 033	-150	17 343	755	13 301
Panama	0	0	0	0	0	0	0	176	-274	331	329	1 091	933	-338	570	725	-2 535	-9	188	1 001	865
Paraguay	0	0	0	0	46	67	202	40	-145	458	734	388	420	377	-177	212	91	168	-59	252	65
Peru	0	0	0	-66	-736	-411	-436	-343	2 308	237	337	-663	1 526	1 422	-790	-500	1 880	1 969	-587	1 476	1 174
Saint Kitts and Nevis	7	11	4	6	6	5	3	2	2	2	5	-5	-3	6	29	12	3	-15	2	-1	2
Saint Lucia	5	4	4	6	5	6	5	4	4	3	-32	23	12	-6	-9	45	-6	-18	-18	-30	-9
Saint Vincent and the Grenadines	0	1	1	2	0	1	0	0	0	0	5	8	-9	21	7	5	2	-0	-1	-0	-0
Suriname	0	0	0	0	0	0	0	0	0	0	0	0	0	-2	12	92	1	-9	-13	10	-11
Trinidad and Tobago	25	341	370	0	700	0	0	67	189	63	-18	128	-25	-12	65	114	98	769	1 354	531	215
Uruguay	-18	-36	1	-89	11	-16	60	7	4 154	-2 058	1 838	1 898	1 308	4 724	2 456	104	-120	2 620	5 932	-8 211	-75
Venezuela (Bolivarian Republic of)	619	1 167	1 524	-495	1 311	2 630	2 492	-370	4 294	752	1 024	-399	-1 041	-2 234	-661	...	...	...	...	...	...
Total	**18 333**	**19 037**	**43 782**	**33 114**	**41 952**	**20 034**	**63 006**	**55 576**	**53 256**	**52 453**	**50 382**	**38 864**	**41 527**	**35 965**	**25 396**	**46 104**	**11 125**	**42 744**	**78 477**	**36 045**	**53 033**

Source: Economic Commission for Latin America and the Caribbean, on the basis of official figures up to 30 June 2025.

CHAPTER

II

Foreign direct investment in mining and the potential of critical minerals in Latin America and the Caribbean

Introduction

Humanity is facing an unprecedented environmental crisis, which is triggering extreme weather and climate events around the world and causing significant loss and damage to both nature and people. In this context, the energy transition —which includes the electrification of various production and consumption processes, such as e-mobility— is urgently needed to mitigate the adverse effects of climate change and promote sustainable development.

Clean energy technologies, such as solar panels, wind turbines and electric batteries, are more mineral-intensive than conventional fossil fuel-based technologies. These minerals, referred to as critical energy transition minerals, include lithium, copper, graphite, cobalt, nickel and rare earth elements. According to the International Energy Agency (IEA, 2021), electric vehicles require 6 times more of these minerals than gasoline-powered vehicles, while solar photovoltaic and offshore wind power plants require 6 and 13 times more minerals, respectively, than a natural gas plant of equivalent capacity. This suggests a sharp increase in demand for these minerals over the medium and long term, along with a significant mobilization of investment flows aimed at expanding their production.

There is no single definition or universal list of critical minerals. In various countries, especially developed countries, the designation of a mineral as "critical" depends on its importance to industrial systems, new technologies, national defence or the energy transition, and on associated supply risks. Several institutions have defined critical minerals for the energy transition on the basis of their role as key inputs for creating renewable energy and e-mobility technologies (IEA, 2024b; Secretary-General's Panel on Critical Energy Transition Minerals, 2024; United Nations, 2025b), particularly for the production of wind turbines, solar panels, electric vehicles and rechargeable batteries.

In Latin America and the Caribbean, several mineral-rich countries have opted to refer to these as strategic minerals, emphasizing their importance not only for the energy transition and regional and global geopolitics, but also for national productive and social development (Chilean Copper Commission [COCHILCO], 2024a; Government of Chile, 2023). In this chapter, critical or strategic minerals are defined as those essential to the energy transition and to fostering productive, inclusive and sustainable development in the region's countries with high geological potential. According to this definition, the main critical minerals found in Latin America and the Caribbean are aluminium (bauxite and alumina), cobalt, copper, graphite, lithium, nickel and rare earth elements.

Global geopolitical competition is currently centred on critical minerals, owing not only to the projected increase in demand for such minerals, but also to the risk of insufficient supply of some of them, especially for countries leading the development of new technologies. This strategic interest is already evident in global foreign direct investment (FDI) announcements: in the past decade (2015–2024), 52% of all FDI announcements in the mining and metals sector have been related to critical minerals. However, announced investments are estimated to meet only 70% and 50% of demand for copper and lithium, respectively, in 2035 (IEA, 2024a).

Against this backdrop, Latin America and the Caribbean has emerged as a region of increasing interest, given its high levels of reserves and production of some critical minerals, especially lithium and copper, making it an attractive destination for FDI in the sector.

The relative scarcity of these minerals, combined with geopolitical competition, creates both new opportunities and substantial challenges for Latin America and the Caribbean. Historically, the region has not fully leveraged its natural resource endowment, specifically in terms of building stronger productive linkages (both upstream and downstream) in sectors that produce more differentiated and complex goods and services, are more knowledge-intensive and offer higher-skilled, better-paying jobs.

Given its natural competitive advantages, the region could capitalize on its strategic position to strengthen the alignment of policies for FDI attraction and for productive development in the sector. Beyond mining and processing of strategic minerals, countries could attract FDI to support economic diversification through productive linkages along the value chains of critical minerals and energy transition technologies. To encourage the emergence of new productive activities in these value chains and build up domestic production and technological capabilities, it is essential that countries in the region reinforce these policies, an approach that the Economic Commission for Latin America and the Caribbean (ECLAC) has emphasized in recent years (ECLAC, 2024a; 2024b). Regional cooperation and coordination should also be enhanced, through coordinated initiatives aimed not only at greater productive integration, but also at avoiding harmful competitive practices reflecting a race to the bottom, which is an ever-present risk in policies to attract FDI.

The global energy transition will have a decisive impact on the volume and type of minerals that countries in the region will be able to produce and export. Rising global demand for critical minerals will require more exploration and extraction projects. This, in turn, means that the mining industry will need to scale up its investments and adopt more socially responsible and environmentally sustainable practices.

This chapter examines FDI trends in the mining sector in Latin America and the Caribbean and assesses the sector's potential in terms of its contribution to productive, inclusive and sustainable development in mineral-rich countries. Section A compares the regional context of critical minerals with the global landscape, analysing the region's share of reserves, production and exports of these minerals over the past two decades. Section B reviews trends in FDI flows in mining in selected countries of the region and offers an in-depth analysis of FDI announcements in the minerals and metals sectors in both the region and the world. Section C explores investment attraction and productive development policies in mining, examining regional and national initiatives aimed at leveraging the opportunities presented by the sector. The final section summarizes the main conclusions.

A. Critical minerals in Latin America and the Caribbean and the world

This section analyses the region's position in the international market for critical minerals, focusing on its reserves, production and exports. It also examines key trends stemming from competition among regions and countries for the supply of these minerals.

1. Status of critical mineral reserves and production

Critical minerals for the energy transition are geographically concentrated in a limited number of regions, including Latin America and the Caribbean (see figure II.1). For example, Chile holds 31.3% of the world's lithium reserves, followed by Argentina with 13.3% and Brazil with 1.3%.[1] A similar pattern is observed for copper, with Chile accounting for 19.4% of global reserves, Peru for 10.2% and

1 The Plurinational State of Bolivia has the world's largest lithium reserves, but these remain uncertified.

Mexico for 5.4%. Brazil also possesses 26.5% of the world's graphite reserves, while Mexico accounts for 1.1%. Brazil is the second-largest holder of global reserves of rare earth elements, with a 23% share. Brazil and Jamaica are the fourth- and fifth-largest holders of global reserves of bauxite and alumina, which are key inputs for aluminium production, with shares of 9% and 7%, respectively. Brazil ranks third globally in nickel reserves, with a 12.2% share, while Cuba ranks fourth in cobalt reserves, with 4.7% of the world total.

Figure II.1
Selected regions and countries: share of global reserves of seven critical minerals, 2024
(Percentages)

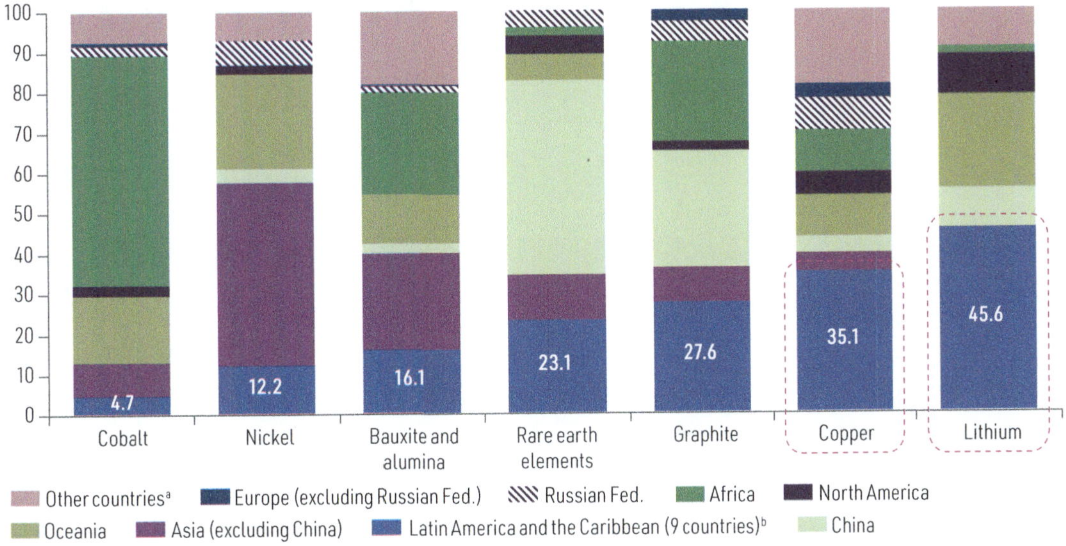

Source: Economic Commission for Latin America and the Caribbean, on the basis of UnitedStates. Geological Survey. (2025). *Mineral Commodity Summaries*.

[a] Other countries in the selected regions with critical mineral reserves that have not been identified in the source.

[b] Argentina, Brazil, Chile, Colombia, Cuba, Jamaica, Mexico, Peru and the Plurinational State of Bolivia.

Ownership of a significant share of global mineral reserves does not necessarily translate into a high share of production, owing to economic, technical and institutional factors that determine a country's capacity to convert reserves into effective production. Mining is a capital- and technology-intensive industry that faces considerable uncertainty given the volatility of international mineral prices and the lengthy investment and recovery periods involved. The exploitation of mining resources requires significant investments at various stages throughout the life cycle of each project (from exploration to mine closure), including expenditures on infrastructure, equipment and machinery, and specialized services. Not all countries with reserves possess the multiple financial, technical and infrastructure capacities necessary to undertake these investments.

Within the region, there are countries with a strong mining tradition where the sector accounts for a considerable share of the economy, such as Chile, Colombia, Guyana, Jamaica, Peru, the Plurinational State of Bolivia and Suriname, alongside countries with less of a mining tradition or where the sector represents a smaller share. Table II.1 lists the countries that play a prominent role in the production of selected minerals.

Table II.1
Latin America and the Caribbean (18 countries): main minerals produced, by country, latest year for which information is available

Type	Mineral	Argentina	Bolivia (Plurinational State of)	Brazil	Chile	Colombia	Cuba	Dominican Republic	Ecuador	El Salvador	Guatemala	Guyana	Honduras	Jamaica	Mexico	Nicaragua	Panama	Peru	Trinidad and Tobago
Metals	Aluminium	X		X															
	Bauxite			X				X				X		X					
	Cobalt						X												
	Copper			X	X										X		X	X	
	Tin		X	X															
	Ferroalloys			X				X							X				
	Iron			X	X		X		X	X					X			X	X
	Magnesium			X															
	Manganese			X											X				
	Molybdenum				X										X			X	
	Niobium			X															
	Nickel			X		X	X	X			X								
	Silver	X	X	X	X	X		X					X		X	X		X	
	Lead	X	X	X			X						X		X			X	
	Gold	X	X	X	X	X		X	X			X			X			X	
	Rhenium				X														
	Selenium																	X	
	Titanium			X															
	Zinc	X	X	X	X		X						X		X			X	
Industrial minerals	Barite		X																
	Boron	X	X		X													X	
	Celestine														X				
	Graphite														X				
	Lithium	X		X	X														
Fuels	Coal					X												X	

Source: Economic Commission for Latin America and the Caribbean, on the basis of United States Geological Survey. (various years). *Mineral Commodity Summaries*.

The region is the world's leading producer of mined copper, accounting for 38% of global production. Chile is the top global copper producer, with a 23.7% share, followed by Peru with 10.2%. The region is also the second-largest global producer of lithium, with a 33% share. Chile again stands out as the second-largest global lithium producer, with 20.8%, while Argentina ranks fourth with 7.6% and

Brazil fifth with 4.2%. The region's production of bauxite and alumina represents 11.2% of the global total, and although it accounts for a smaller share of global production of graphite, nickel, cobalt and rare earth elements, identified reserves point to significant potential (see figure II.2).

Figure II.2
Selected regions and countries: share of global production of seven critical minerals, 2024
(Percentages)

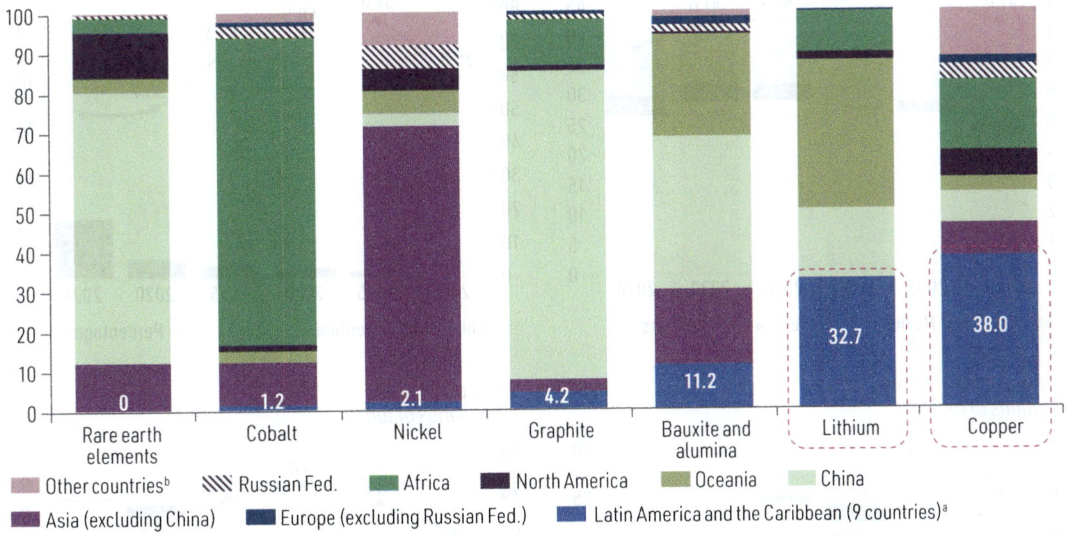

Source: Economic Commission for Latin America and the Caribbean, on the basis of United States Geological Survey. (2025). *Mineral Commodity Summaries*.
[a] Argentina, Brazil, Chile, Colombia, Cuba, Jamaica, Mexico, Peru and the Plurinational State of Bolivia.
[b] Other countries in the selected regions with critical mineral reserves that have not been identified in the source.

The growth in global demand for critical minerals is driven by decarbonization (net-zero emissions) agreements and the deployment of technologies enabling the transition to low-carbon energy (Kelley et al., 2021; IEA, 2024a). Globally, China leads in the development and production of these technologies (e.g. solar panels, rechargeable batteries and wind turbines), and in the processing and refining of the critical minerals they require, making it the world's largest consumer of these minerals. Given the insufficient domestic reserves and production of such minerals (except for graphite and rare earth elements), China depends heavily on mining outside its territory (IEA, 2024a).

The growth in global demand for critical minerals has prompted increased exploration and attraction of these minerals around the world. In Latin America and the Caribbean, this stronger demand has not translated into a larger share of global production. Although production of copper, lithium, bauxite, alumina and graphite increased between 2000 and 2024, the region lost global market share to other regions. For nickel, cobalt and rare earth elements, both production levels and global shares declined (see figure II.3), confirming the challenge facing the region in converting reserves into effective production, even in the cases of lithium and copper, for which conditions are relatively more favourable.

Figure II.3
Latin America and the Caribbean (12 countries): critical mineral production and global market share, 2000, 2005, 2015, 2020 and 2024
(Millions of tons or thousands of tons and percentages)

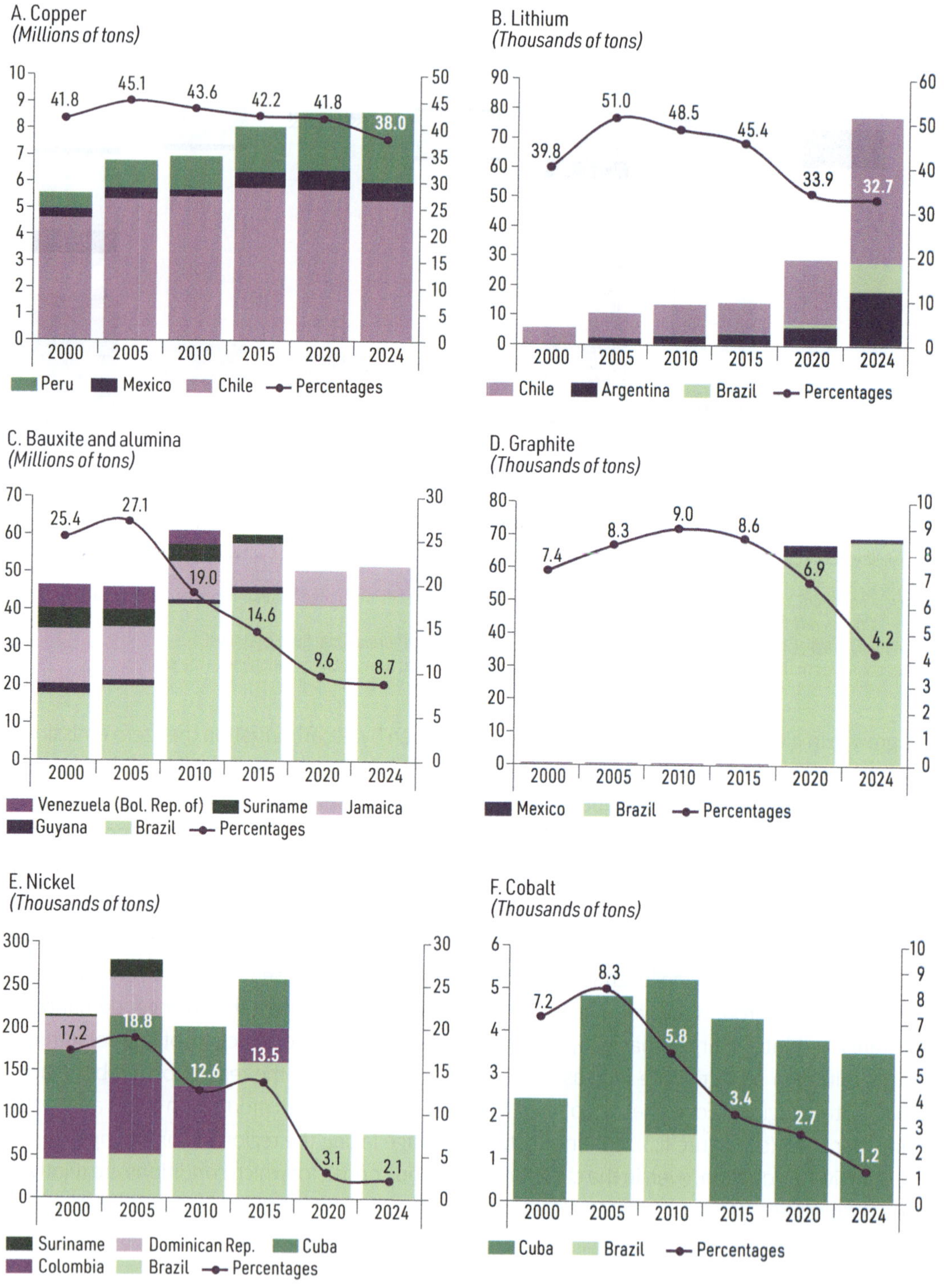

G. Rare earth elements
(Thousands of tons)

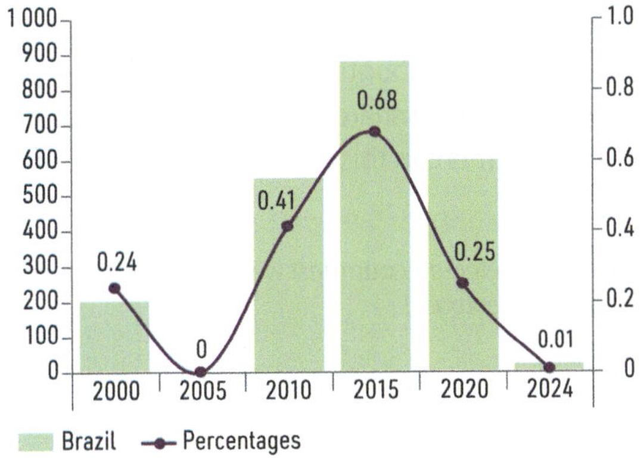

Source: Economic Commission for Latin America and the Caribbean, on the basis of United States Geological Survey. (various years). *Mineral Commodity Summaries*.

Global production of lithium increased 39-fold between 1994 and 2024, to approximately 235,000 tons in 2024. Despite holding the world's largest reserves and having maintained a global market share above 40% since the early 2000s —with peaks surpassing 50% in some years— the region's share in this market declined after 2016, to 33% in 2024. Australia and China have managed to strengthen their position and gain market share during this period (see figure II.4).

Figure II.4
Latin America and the Caribbean and selected countries: world lithium production, 1994–2024
(Thousands of metric tons and percentages)

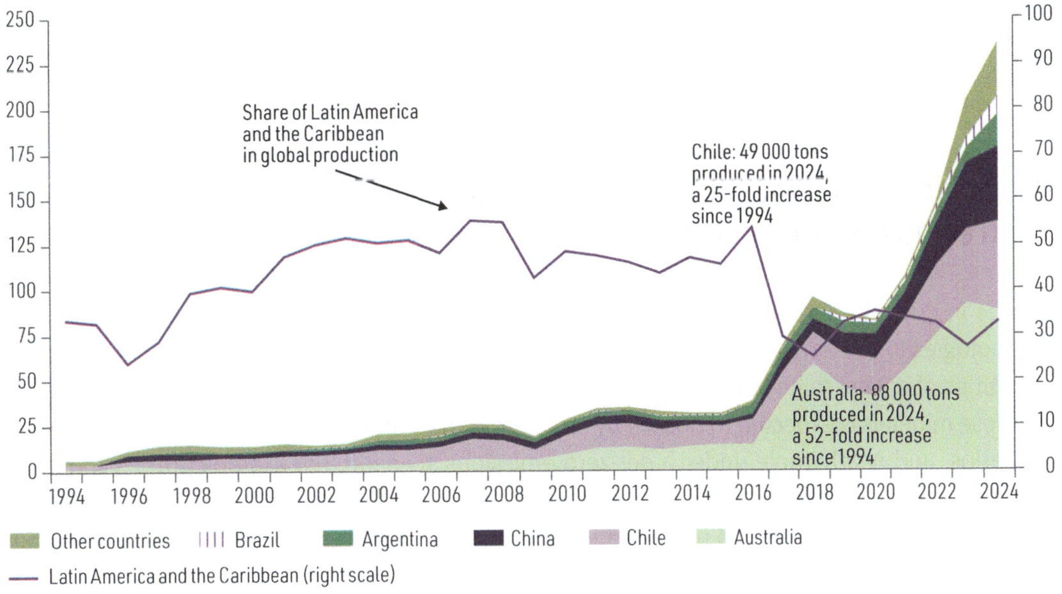

Source: Economic Commission for Latin America and the Caribbean, on the basis of United States Geological Survey. (various years). *Mineral Commodity Summaries*.
Note: "Other countries" may include lithium-producing countries not specifically identified in the source.

Global production of copper, which has a much more mature market, jumped by 71% in the period 2000–2024, from 13.2 million tons to 22.6 million tons. While the region's share of global production remained stable above 40% until 2021, and even exceeded 45% in certain years, it has since declined, to 38% in 2024. Other copper-producing countries outside the region, particularly the Democratic Republic of the Congo, have gained market share in recent years (see figure II.5), reflecting significant international competition for investment in this sector, as in the case of lithium.

Figure II.5
Latin America and the Caribbean and selected countries: world copper production, 1994–2024
(Millions of tons of mined copper and percentages)

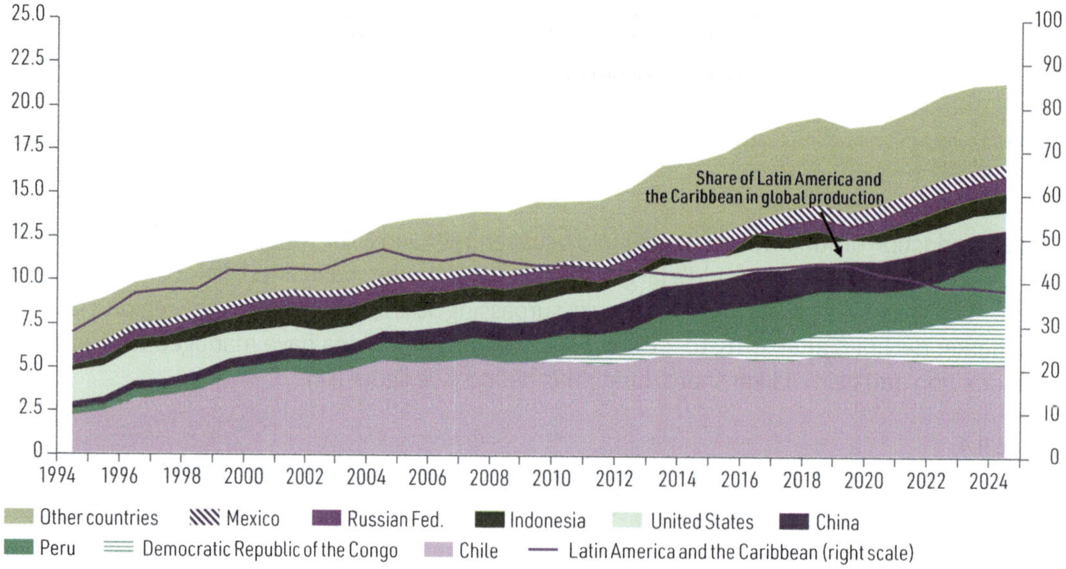

Source: Economic Commission for Latin America and the Caribbean, on the basis of United States Geological Survey. (various years). *Mineral Commodity Summaries*.
Note: "Other countries" may include copper-producing countries not specifically identified in the source.

2. Critical mineral supply, demand and prices: trends and projections

Trends in critical mineral demand, supply and prices are determined by the development of technologies for the energy transition. As previously noted, these technologies require increasing quantities of critical mineral-based materials and compounds. According to IEA (2024a), demand for these minerals is expected to double by 2030 under the stated policies and announced pledges scenarios, and nearly triple under a net-zero emissions scenario. For example, under the latter, global demand would more than triple by 2050 for copper (see figure II.6), grow 17-fold for lithium, increase 6-fold for graphite and nickel, and rise 5-fold for cobalt and rare earth elements. Meeting this growing demand will require raising current levels of critical mineral production, which implies greater investment in all phases (exploration, extraction, processing and refining), as well as expanding mining into unexploited territories.

Figure II.6
Projected growth in demand for selected critical minerals up to 2050, by scenario
(Multiples of estimated 2023 demand)

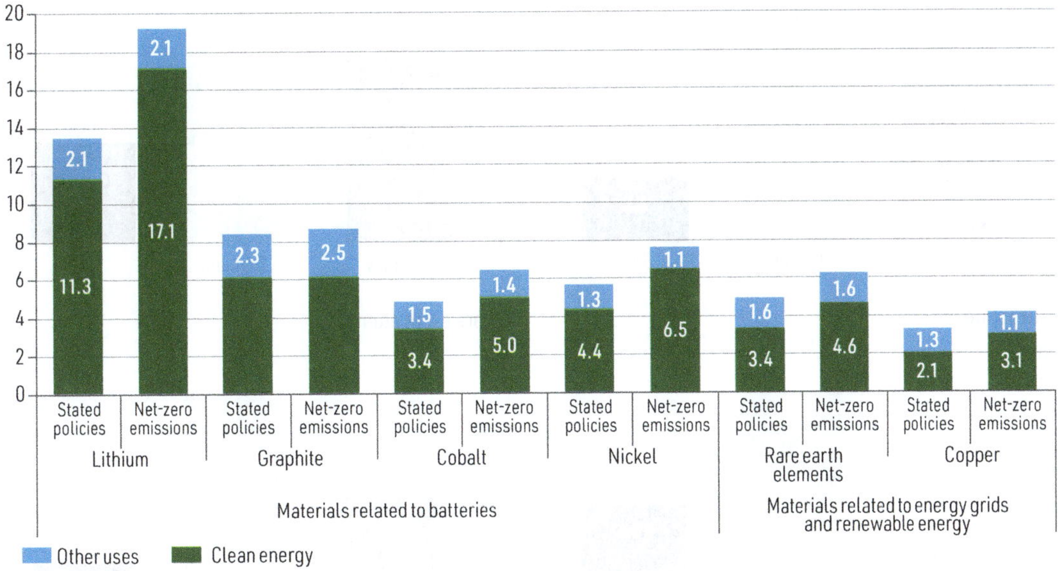

Source: Economic Commission for Latin America and the Caribbean, on the basis of International Energy Agency (2024), *Global Critical Minerals Outlook 2024*.
Note: Critical mineral demand increases by a certain factor (multiples of demand = 2050 demand/2023 demand) depending on the requirements of current transition technologies and deployment projections.

There is a significant gap between projections for global critical mineral demand and supply, which poses a threat to both the transition to a low-carbon economy and to the potential development of high-tech and innovation-intensive sectors that rely on a stable supply of these inputs. According to IEA (2024a), on the basis of ongoing or announced mining projects, copper and lithium production would meet only 77% and 54% of demand by 2040, respectively. The situation is similar for nickel, cobalt, graphite and rare earth elements, with supply expected to cover only 76%, 65%, 42% and 62% of demand, respectively (see figure II.7). These gaps between demand and supply —which may widen owing to disruptions in supply chains from extreme weather events or geopolitical tensions— represent both a risk to the speed of the energy transition and a major opportunity for the region.

Figure II.7
Gaps between supply and demand for selected critical minerals, projections for 2040
(Millions of tons and percentages)

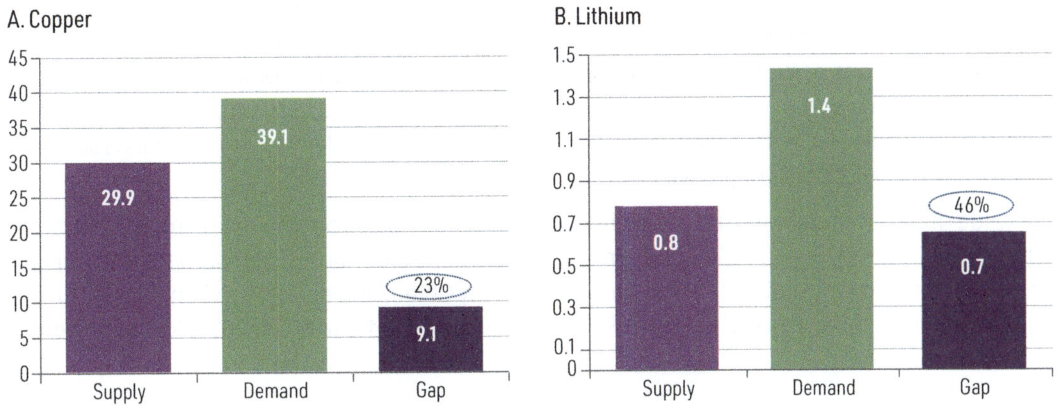

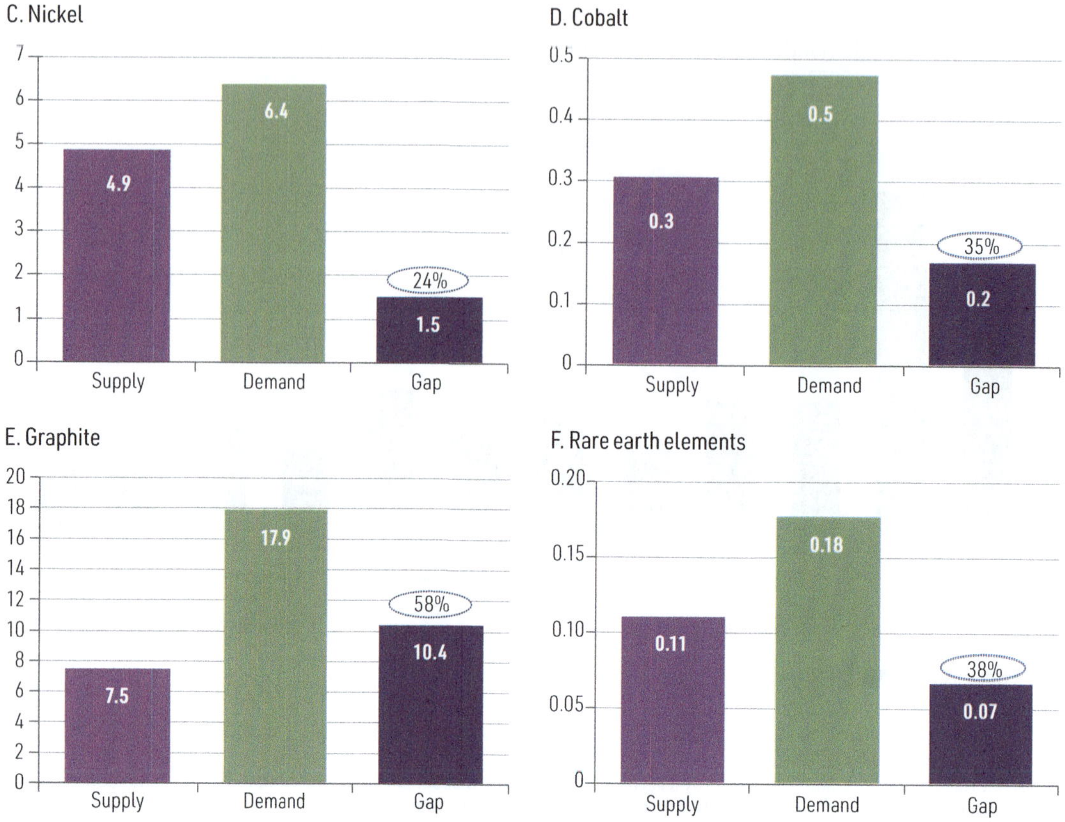

Source: Economic Commission for Latin America and the Caribbean, on the basis of International Energy Agency (2024), *Global Critical Minerals Outlook 2024*.

Note: Total demand is projected under the net-zero emissions scenario. Supply projections derive from the base-case scenario. The supply gap is the difference between projected demand and available supply for selected critical minerals. The circle indicates the percentage of global demand with uncertain coverage. Supply figures for copper, cobalt, nickel and rare earth elements refer to refined products, while those for lithium and graphite include both mineral and refined (chemical or battery-grade) products.

3. Trends in critical mineral exports for the region

So far this century, the production of strategic minerals in Latin America and the Caribbean has reflected sustained growth, driven primarily by copper and, to a lesser extent, by lithium, bauxite and alumina, and graphite. However, this growth has not been sufficient for the region to maintain its share in global mineral production. Trade has recorded a similar trend, albeit with some nuances. The region has maintained a prominent role since its mineral production is primarily export-oriented. Although production in other regions —such as Asia and, to a lesser extent, Europe— grew more than in Latin America and the Caribbean, their share in the international market did not increase because a significant portion of their output is consumed domestically for industrial purposes. As such, Latin America and the Caribbean faces the structural challenge of maintaining its position in mineral trade, while also reassessing whether its role as a global supplier of raw materials is sufficient to achieve its development objectives.

The value of total mineral exports (not limited to critical minerals) from the region rose significantly between 2004 and 2023, from US$ 61 billion to US$ 208 billion (see figure II.8). This pace of expansion was in line with growing global demand, driven chiefly by China, and enabled a slight increase in the region's share of global exports, from 10.3% in 2004–2008 to 11.4% in 2019–2023. Regional exports of critical minerals expanded markedly over the same period, from US$ 29 billion to US$ 102 billion, accounting for approximately 50% of the region's total mineral exports. The region's share in global critical mineral exports also rose, from 17.7% to 18.8%.

Figure II.8
Latin America and the Caribbean (33 countries): value of mineral and critical mineral exports and global market share, 2004–2023
(Billions of dollars and percentages)

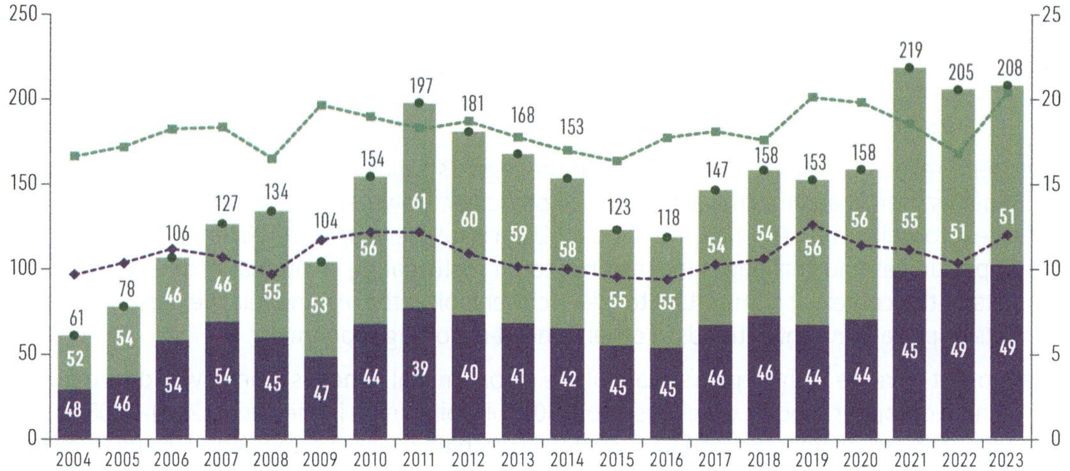

Source: Economic Commission for Latin America and the Caribbean, on the basis of United Nations, UN Comtrade Database. https://comtrade.un.org/.
Note: "All minerals" includes all mineral groups. "Critical minerals" includes the following: aluminium (including alumina and bauxite), cobalt, copper, graphite, lithium, nickel and rare earth elements.

This reflects stable, though limited, growth compared to other regions that have also maintained or strengthened their positions, such as Asia (excluding China), China, Oceania and Africa (see table II.2). Latin America and the Caribbean benefited the least as a region from the relative decline in the market shares of North America and Europe (excluding the Russian Federation), both in the case of overall mineral exports and in critical mineral exports. As will be discussed in section B, this export performance —consistent with the expansion of global demand but less dynamic than that of other developing regions— reflects broader FDI trends.

Table II.2
Selected regions and countries: market share and change in share of mineral and critical mineral exports, 2004–2023
(Percentages and changes in percentage points)

A. All minerals								
Period	Latin America and the Caribbean	Africa	North America	Asia (excluding China)	China	Europe (excluding Russian Federation)	Russian Federation	Oceania
2004-2008	10.3	4.5	11.3	19.8	5.7	38.6	4.7	3.9
2019-2023	11.4	5.6	10.5	24.2	7.3	30.8	4.5	6.5
Δ	**1.10**	**1.10**	**-0.81**	**4.47**	**1.66**	**-7.82**	**-0.18**	**2.65**

B. Critical minerals								
Period	Latin America and the Caribbean	Africa	North America	Asia (excluding China)	China	Europe (excluding Russian Federation)	Russian Federation	Oceania
2004-2008	17.7	4.5	13.0	14.9	4.0	33.8	5.8	6.2
2019-2023	18.8	6.5	9.9	20.2	7.2	28.2	3.8	5.3
Δ	**1.07**	**2.08**	**-3.09**	**5.28**	**3.22**	**-5.66**	**-1.96**	**-0.92**

Source: Economic Commission for Latin America and the Caribbean, on the basis of United Nations. UN Comtrade Database. https://comtrade.un.org/.

Note: "All minerals" includes all mineral groups; "Critical minerals" includes the following: aluminium (including alumina and bauxite), cobalt, copper, graphite, lithium, nickel and rare earth elements.

This trend reflects a notable improvement in the region's capacity to meet rising global demand for minerals overall, and for critical minerals in particular. However, it also raises questions about the extent to which Latin America and the Caribbean is fully leveraging its potential and highlights the opportunities and challenges the region faces in participating in international critical mineral markets. In this context, it is important to take a closer look at the region's relative position in these markets, especially in light of trends in other mineral-exporting economies.

The modest increase in the region's share of the global critical minerals market was driven mainly by its share of copper exports, which rose from 30% of global trade in the period 2004–2008 to 32% in 2019–2023, and of lithium exports, which nearly doubled over the same period, rising from 12% to 24%. China's share of global lithium exports tripled —from 10% to 30%— and Australia's grew 15-fold —from 2% to 30%— consolidating both as the leading exporters of this mineral. By contrast, the region's share of exports of other critical minerals, such as nickel, aluminium, cobalt and rare earth elements, declined, in line with production trends (see figure II.9). This indicates that, within the critical minerals category, the region's specialization has been concentrated in copper and, to a lesser but growing extent, lithium.

Figure II.9

Latin America and the Caribbean (33 countries): market share based on the value of global exports of seven critical minerals, 2004–2023

(Percentages)

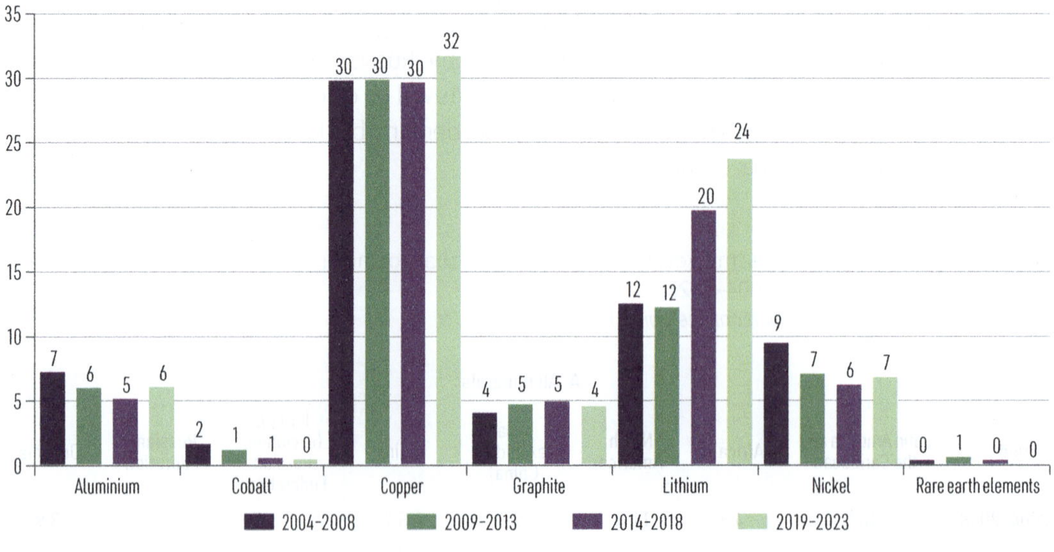

Source: Economic Commission for Latin America and the Caribbean, on the basis of United Nations. UN Comtrade Database https://comtrade.un.org/.

Note: "Critical minerals" includes the following: aluminium (including alumina and bauxite), cobalt, copper, graphite, lithium, nickel and rare earth elements.

Chile remains the leading exporter of copper in the region and has maintained its global market share. Peru, meanwhile, has nearly doubled its share of global copper exports, becoming the main contributor to the region's growth in this market in the 2019–2023 period. As for lithium, Chile has consolidated its position as the regional leader, accounting for 90% of lithium exports from Latin America and the Caribbean over the last five years and more than doubling its global share between 2004 and 2023 (from 8% to 20%). Half of Chile's copper and lithium exports are destined for China. While Argentina's lithium exports have also increased, they account for only about 3% of the global total. Brazil's position in the markets for aluminium, graphite and nickel has strengthened and the country has emerged as the region's leading exporter of these minerals. In contrast, other countries' shares have shown little variation or have declined, particularly in the cobalt and rare earth markets. In both cases, the reduction in Cuba's and Brazil's shares explains the contraction of the region's overall share in these markets (see figure II.10).

Figure II.10
Latin America and the Caribbean (33 countries): market share based on the value of global exports of seven critical minerals, by country, 2004–2023
(Percentages)

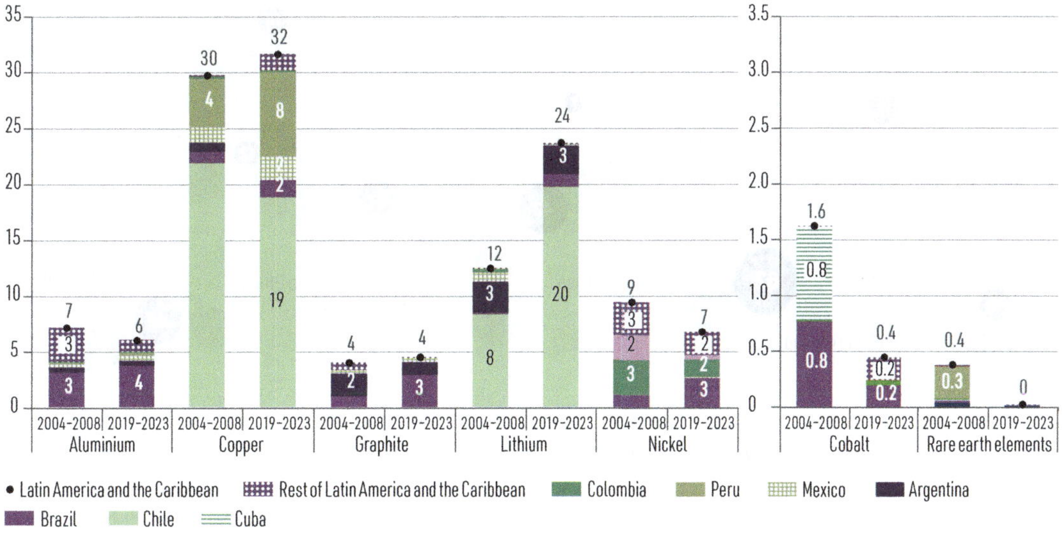

Source: Economic Commission for Latin America and the Caribbean, on the basis of United Nations, UN Comtrade Database. https://comtrade.un.org/.
Note: "Critical minerals" includes the following: aluminium (including alumina and bauxite), cobalt, copper, graphite, lithium, nickel and rare earth elements.

Over the past two decades, the region has maintained its position in the international copper market, owing to the expansion and consolidation of new players such as Brazil, Mexico, Panama and Peru[2] and despite increasing competition from other countries, including the Democratic Republic of the Congo and Zambia, thanks largely to China's growing presence in metal value chains. In addition to being one of the leading producers of mined copper globally and the top producer of smelted and refined copper, China is also the world's largest importer of this metal in its various processing stages.

The increased production and export of critical minerals from Latin America and the Caribbean has not been accompanied by greater diversification of the export basket, as raw materials continue to

[2] Between 2019 and 2022, the Minera Panamá S.A. project, a subsidiary of Canada's First Quantum Minerals, accounted for approximately 1.5% of annual global copper production. Amid widespread public protests over the project's environmental impact, the Supreme Court of Justice of Panama revoked the company's operating permit in 2023, declaring the concession contract unconstitutional. Since then, the project has remained suspended.

represent a substantial share of the region's exports. For instance, between 2019 and 2023, 62% of the region's critical mineral exports consisted of unprocessed products or those having undergone only basic refining, the highest share among the main exporters of these minerals. By contrast, North America, Europe and China export critical minerals with higher levels of value added and economic complexity, including semi-processed products, which account for over 80% of such exports (see map II.1). Consequently, the main importers of the region's critical minerals are industrialized countries, with China in the lead, followed by the United States, Japan, the Republic of Korea and some European countries.

Map II.1
Selected countries, regions and groupings: composition of critical mineral export values, by level of processing, 2019–2023
(Percentages)

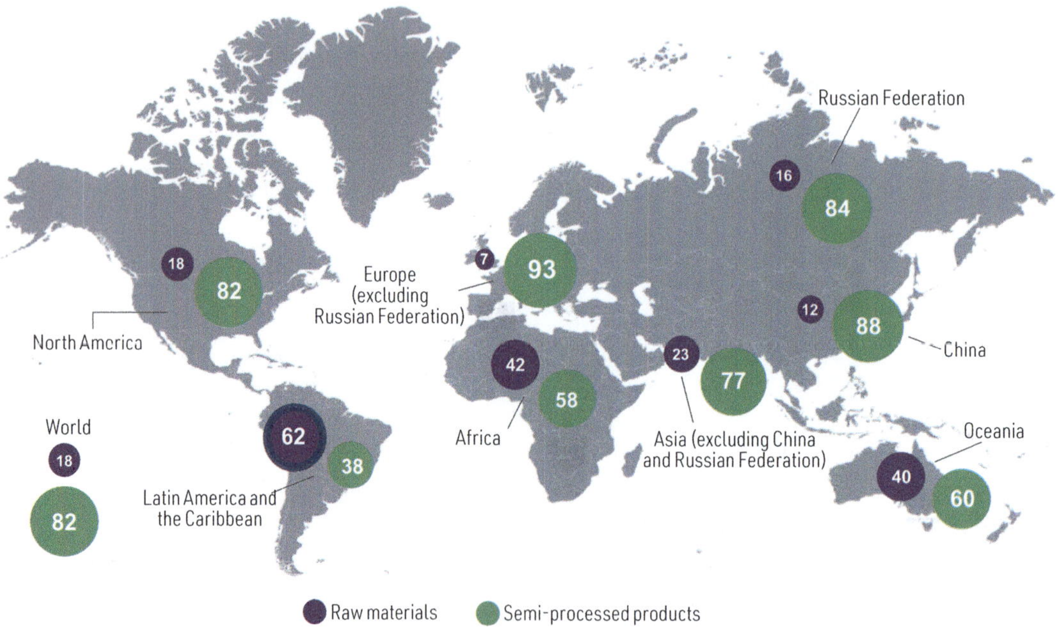

Source: Economic Commission for Latin America and the Caribbean, on the basis of United Nations. UN Comtrade Database. https://comtrade.un.org/.
Note: "Critical minerals" includes the following: aluminium (including alumina and bauxite), cobalt, copper, graphite, lithium, nickel and rare earth elements.

These results suggest that, although Latin America and the Caribbean has consolidated its global position as a producer and exporter of certain critical minerals in recent years (despite some losses in market share), it continues to face the challenge of adding value to its raw materials and diversifying its export basket.

B. Mining investment trends in the region

Mining investment in Latin America and the Caribbean has been driven by both domestic and foreign capital, with their respective shares fluctuating over time. The share of foreign capital has been growing since the 1990s. Nevertheless, domestic investment has maintained a prominent role in many countries through key State actors, such as the National Copper Corporation of Chile

(CODELCO),[3] and private enterprises such as Vale in Brazil[4] and Grupo México in Mexico and Peru.[5] The share of domestic and foreign capital varies across countries. For example, when comparing investment projects planned for the coming years in Chile and Peru, more than 64% of investment in Chile is of domestic origin, whereas in Peru this proportion is just 7% (COCHILCO, 2024b; Ministry of Energy and Mines of Peru, 2024).

FDI has played a fundamental role in the development of mining in several countries of the region. It comes from countries with a strong extractive tradition, such as Australia, Canada, Japan, Switzerland, the United Kingdom, the United States and, more recently, China, and is mainly concentrated in countries with consolidated mining sectors, such as Brazil, Chile, Mexico and Peru, and in emerging ones such as Argentina, Colombia, Ecuador, Guyana, Panama and Suriname. In recent years, these investment flows have increasingly targeted critical minerals such as copper, lithium and nickel, which dominate the region's export supply, alongside gold, silver and iron.

The main transnational companies leading mining investment include the following:

- BHP (Australia and the United Kingdom), operating in Chile since the mid-1980s with the Escondida copper project and in Peru since the early 2000s through the Antamina polymetallic project.
- Rio Tinto (Australia and the United Kingdom), present in Brazil since the mid-1980s with the Alumar alumina project, in Chile with the Escondida copper project and in Argentina since the mid-2000s with the Río Colorado potash project and since 2021 with the Rincón lithium project.
- Glencore (Switzerland), which acquired Xstrata in 2013, operating in Peru since the mid-2000s with the Las Bambas copper project and in Chile since 2010 with the Punitaqui copper project.
- Anglo American (United Kingdom), operating in Brazil since the 1970s with the Morro Velho gold project and in Chile since the late 1990s with the Los Bronces copper project.
- Freeport-McMoRan (United States), present in Peru since the mid-1970s with the Cerro Verde copper project and in Chile since the mid-1990s with the El Abra copper project.
- First Quantum Minerals (Canada), operating in Panama since 2013 with the Cobre Panamá project.
- Mitsui & Co. (Chile) Ltd. (Japan), operating in Chile since the early 1970s with investments in copper projects and in Brazil since the early 1960s with investments in iron projects.
- Zijin Mining Group (China), present in Argentina since 2016 with the Salar Tres Quebradas lithium project and with gold projects in Colombia, Guyana, Peru and Suriname since 2020.

These are mostly publicly listed private companies traded on major global stock exchanges, with primarily institutional shareholders. As will be shown below, their increasing interest in the critical minerals of Latin America and the Caribbean —particularly copper and lithium— reflects the strategic importance of the region in global supply chains associated with the energy transition.

---

3 CODELCO is a State-owned enterprise that produces copper and by-products such as molybdenum, silver and gold, and will produce lithium as part of the National Lithium Strategy. Established in 1976, its operations are exclusively located in Chile. The company has significant experience in partnerships and joint ventures with other mining companies, including Freeport-McMoRan (since 1994, in El Abra), KINROSS (since 2003, in Sociedad Contractual Minera Purén), Anglo American, Mitsui & Co. (Chile) Ltd. and Mitsubishi (since 2012, in Anglo American Sur), Rio Tinto (since 2023, in Nuevo Cobre), Teck-Sumitomo (since 2024, in Quebrada Blanca), and SQM (since 2024, in Salar de Atacama).

4 Vale is a publicly traded private company based in Brazil, listed on the São Paulo (B3), New York (NYSE) and Madrid (BME-Latibex) stock exchanges. It produces iron, nickel, copper and by-products such as cobalt, platinum group metals, silver and gold. In addition, it owns and operates logistics, transportation and energy assets. Founded in 1942 as a State-owned enterprise (Companhia Vale do Rio Doce), it was privatized in 1997. Vale is currently the world's second-largest producer of iron and sixth-largest producer of nickel, with operations in Brazil, Canada, Indonesia, Japan, Oman and the United Kingdom. Since 2010, its business strategy has focused on the iron market and energy transition metals, leading to the divestment of its aluminium, fertilizer, manganese and coal assets.

5 Grupo México is a publicly traded private company based in Mexico and listed on the Mexican Stock Exchange (BMV). It produces copper and by-products such as molybdenum, silver, gold, selenium and zinc. The company also owns and operates assets in logistics and transportation, energy, engineering, construction and real estate. With origins dating back to 1890, Grupo México is the fourth-largest copper producer in the world and maintains operations in Argentina, Chile, Ecuador, Mexico, Peru, Spain and the United States.

This section begins by examining trends in FDI in mining in Latin America and the Caribbean over the past two decades, on the basis of official sources from 11 countries in the region. It then draws on data on announced investments in minerals and metals from the *Financial Times* database,[6] to expand the geographical scope and identify investment specifically related to critical minerals. The second and third parts of this section use the same source to analyse the characteristics of FDI in mining globally and in the region, with a focus on critical minerals, and provide information on cross-border mergers and acquisitions of related assets.

1. FDI trends in the region's mining sector

So far this century, FDI inflows in the mining sector of Latin America and the Caribbean have largely followed the trend in international mineral prices, in line with global patterns (United Nations, 2025a). Global mining investment has been shaped by growing demand, primarily from China, with fluctuations associated with various global crises, including the 2008–2009 financial crisis, the coronavirus disease (COVID-19) pandemic in 2020, and the energy crisis triggered by the conflict between the Russian Federation and Ukraine since 2022. Government strategies in energy, production, technology and even defence have also had an impact on the sector, by increasing demand for critical minerals required for the development and deployment of technologies associated with the energy transition. In this regard, the sector is highly vulnerable to global geopolitical tensions, which have intensified over the past decade and are reflected in the proliferation of restrictive or discriminatory trade measures. These measures also affect (and will continue to affect) international investment flows in mining (see figure II.11).

Figure II.11
Latin America and the Caribbean (11 countries): mining sector FDI inflows, 2005–2023
(Billions of dollars and index 2016 = 100)

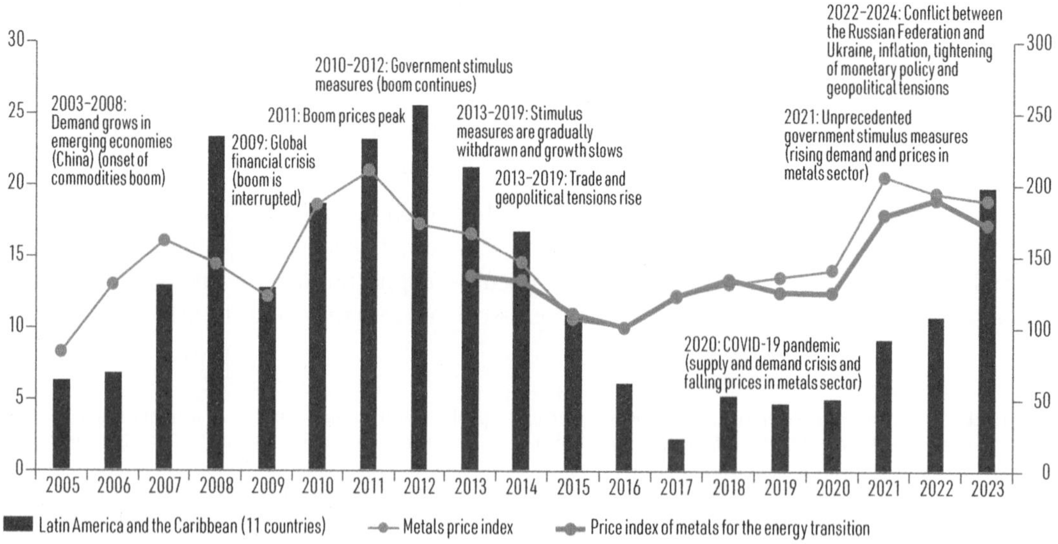

Source: Prepared by the authors on the basis of official sources and International Monetary Fund.
Note: The countries included are Brazil, Chile, Colombia, Costa Rica, the Dominican Republic, Ecuador, Guatemala, Honduras, Mexico, Nicaragua and the Plurinational State of Bolivia. Mining sector FDI refers to inflows (net of disinvestment); in the case of Costa Rica, Ecuador, Guatemala and Honduras, the mining and hydrocarbon sectors are included.

[6] *Financial Times*. fDi Markets. https://www.fdimarkets.com/.

Apart from the obvious prerequisite of having sufficient mineral resources, a country's ability to attract mining investments is affected by many factors in addition to those mentioned above (see box II.1).

Box II.1

Determinants of investment in mining

Investing in the mining sector is different from investing in other sectors, owing to a combination of characteristics inherent to extractive activity, such as: high capital intensity, with high sunk costs; low labour intensity, but requiring specialized training; protracted timelines for investment and cost recovery; finite useful life of projects; non-renewable resources; and considerable environmental and social impacts, including significant environmental liabilities for future generations. These characteristics come with risks, which are intensified by factors including geological uncertainty, mineral price volatility, environmental and social concerns, political and social instability and legal uncertainty.

In theory, according to Vivoda (2017), investments should flow to the countries with the largest and highest-quality reserves. In practice, however, investment decisions are influenced by other factors —besides geological wealth—, which collectively form the "investment climate" (Jara, 2017).

Conventionally, the investment climate refers to the overall conditions affecting investors' willingness and ability to invest in a given country or sector, including economic, political, social and legal factors that may affect their perception of risk and opportunity. In the mining sector, the factors that define the investment climate include adequate infrastructure, availability of human resources, social and political stability, strong institutions and sector-specific regulations (Jara, 2017).

In a review of the literature, Vivoda (2017) highlighted a cross-cutting study of nine Asia-Pacific countries (Economic and Social Commission for Asia and the Pacific, 1992), which provides a list of criteria that can influence mining investment decisions, as set out below.

- Geological conditions: general mineral abundance; target minerals; strategic or critical minerals; historical production, availability of geoscientific information; ability to apply geological assessment techniques.
- Political conditions: system and government regime stability; form of government; domestic security; consistency and constancy of mineral policies.
- Market conditions: geographical location; presence of domestic markets; availability of infrastructure services; export policies; trade agreements with other countries.
- Regulatory conditions: mineral legislation; stability of exploration or mining terms; mineral ownership; land ownership (access and use); security of tenure; quality of mineral title system; right to transfer ownership; size of exploration blocks or duration of exploration rights; procedural efficacy and clarity.
- Fiscal conditions: method and level of taxation; ability to predetermine tax liability; availability of tax incentives; stability of fiscal system; tax treaties with countries of origin.
- Monetary and financial conditions: foreign-exchange regulations and external accounts; ability to repatriate profits; ability to raise external financing.
- Environmental and social conditions: legal environmental protection requirements; ability to predetermine environmental obligations; socioenvironmental conflicts; relative sensitivity of the environment in areas with mining potential.
- Operational conditions: equity ownership held by the company; company control over management; access to infrastructure services and affordability; climate conditions; availability of experienced workforce; availability of technical support and maintenance services; labour market conditions; technological requirements; control of administrative processes.

- Profit considerations: profitability; competitive cost position.
- Other criteria: prior company experience in the country; company employee experience; specialized company experience.

Naturally, conceptions of the investment climate vary —especially in the mining sector— according to the level of consideration given to other dimensions of the comprehensive development agenda. For example, what an investor might consider a necessary condition of an acceptable investment climate might be considered unacceptable from an environmental, social, tax or regulatory standpoint, or from the point of view of the authorities tasked with implementing productive development policies, who might have an interest in requiring foreign investor firms to agree to local sourcing or technology transfer terms. Depending on their interpretation, these requirements could be deemed detrimental according to certain criteria mentioned above, including equity ownership held by the company, the company's control over management, technological requirements or competitive positioning.

The investment climate is thus an idea that should be thoroughly deliberated, especially when it comes to mining sector development, to synthesize and balance the different objectives and dimensions of a comprehensive development agenda. Such an approach would not only consider the economic and profit interests of investors but also effectively incorporate the environmental, social and productive development concerns of host countries.

Source: Vivoda, V. (2017). Determinants of foreign direct investment in the mining industry. In T. O'Callaghan y G. Graetz (Eds.), *Mining in the Asia-Pacific* (pp. 25-45). Springer. https://doi.org/10.1007/978-3-319-61395-6_2; Jara, J. J. (2017). Determinants of country competitiveness in attracting mining investments: An empirical analysis. *Resources Policy, 52*, 65-71. https://doi.org/10.1016/j.resourpol.2017.01.016; Economic and Social Commission for Asia and the Pacific. (1992). *Mineral investment conditions in selected countries of the Asia-Pacific region*. https://hdl.handle.net/20.500.12870/3900.

As seen in figure II.12, which shows FDI inflows to the region's mining sector and global investment in the sector by the top mining companies specializing in non-ferrous metals (i.e. excluding iron, gold, coal and other minerals), FDI inflows to the region's mining sector have rebounded in recent years, totalling US$ 19.8 billion in 2023, but are still below the peak recorded in 2012. Indeed, the US$ 9.9 billion annual average in the period 2019–2023 was 20% lower than the 2005–2009 average and 53% lower than the 2010–2014 average. Meanwhile, capital expenditure by the major global mining companies specializing in non-ferrous metals reached new heights in 2022.[7]

The partial "decoupling" of the sector's regional FDI and global investment trends could be an indication that, despite its recovery in mining FDI in the past five years, Latin America and the Caribbean is falling behind other regions in terms of its capacity to attract capital. There is, however, reason for optimism. According to S&P Global Market Intelligence data on mining exploration budgets for non-ferrous metals (excluding iron, aluminium and coal), between 2005 and 2023, Latin America and the Caribbean and North America were the most attractive destinations, with North America in the lead from 2005 to 2011 and from 2020 onward, and Latin America and the Caribbean leading in the intervening period (2012–2019). It should be noted that this indicator includes gold exploration, which attracts the largest exploration budgets; if gold and diamonds are excluded from the data, the largest budgets in recent years have gone to Latin America and the Caribbean, largely for copper exploration (S&P Global Market Intelligence, 2024).

7 Expenditure rose to US$ 46 billion in 2022 and US$ 50 billion in 2023, compared with the previous record of US$ 45 billion in 2012. These figures offer a useful point of comparison in considering the required annual capital expenditure from 2024 to 2040 to meet projected demand for cobalt, copper, lithium, nickel and rare earth elements under the announced pledges scenario (US$ 34.9 billion) and the net zero emissions by 2040 scenario (US$ 46.6 billion) (IEA, 2024a).

Figure II.12
Latin America and the Caribbean (11 countries) and world: capital expenditure on non-ferrous metal mining, non-ferrous metal exploration budgets and mining sector FDI inflows, 2005–2023
(Index 2012 = 100)

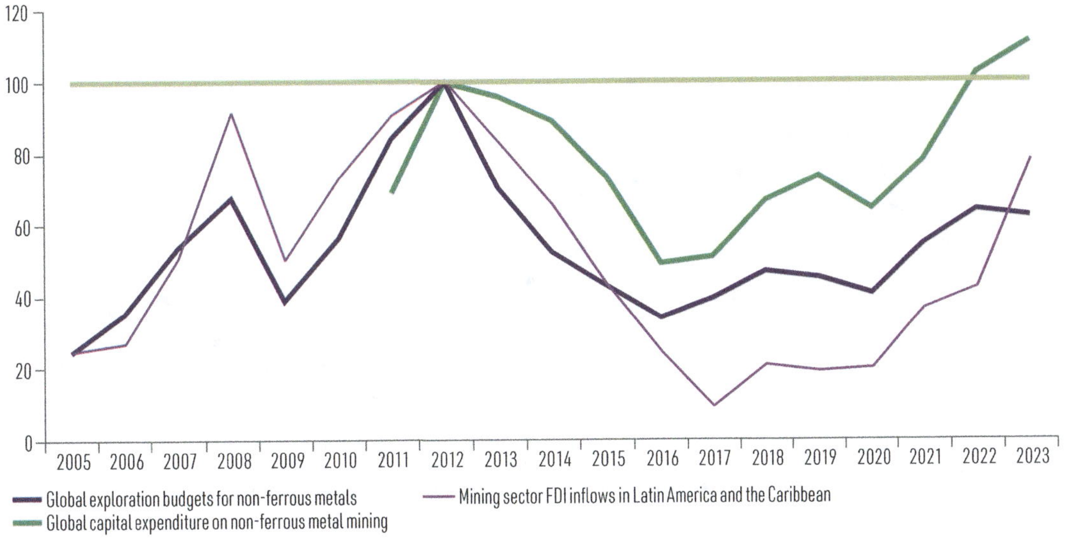

Source: Prepared by the authors on the basis of official sources; International Energy Agency. (2024b). *Energy Technology Perspectives 2024*. https://www.iea.org/reports/energy-technology-perspectives-2024; S&P Global Market Intelligence. (2024). *World Exploration Trends 2024. PDAC Special Edition*.

Note: The countries included are Brazil, Chile, Colombia, Costa Rica, the Dominican Republic, Ecuador, Guatemala, Honduras, Mexico, Nicaragua and the Plurinational State of Bolivia. Mining sector FDI refers to inflows (net of disinvestment); in the case of Costa Rica, Ecuador, Guatemala and Honduras, the mining and hydrocarbon sectors are included. Capital expenditure on non-ferrous metal mining includes copper, cobalt, lithium, nickel and by-products (and excludes coal, iron, gold and other energy products). Exploration budgets for non-ferrous metals include gold, copper, lithium, nickel, cobalt, uranium, silver, zinc-lead, diamonds, and lanthanides and rare earth elements (for a complete list of minerals, see S&P Global Market Intelligence, 2024).

Only 11 countries of the region have official mining FDI figures. This sample includes several countries that have a mining tradition, such as Brazil, Chile, Colombia, Ecuador, Mexico and the Plurinational State of Bolivia, but does not include Peru (a country with a polymetallic mining tradition and a significant foreign capital presence in the sector), Guyana, Jamaica or Suriname. According to the official figures, between 2005 and 2023, the mining sector accounted for an average 11% of total FDI in the 11 countries, with the lowest share recorded in 2017 (1.8%) and the highest recorded in 2008 (24.5%). These net mining inflows amounted to 0.3% of GDP, with a low of 0.1% and a high of 0.7% in the same period (see figure II.13).

In terms of absolute value, mining sector FDI is concentrated in four countries: Chile, Brazil, Mexico and Colombia (again, according to the information available). Chile is the most notable, accounting for more than 50% of FDI inflows to the 11 countries included in the sample for the past five years (see figure II.14).

Figure II.13
Latin America and the Caribbean (11 countries): mining sector FDI in index values, as a share of total FDI and as a share of GDP, 2005–2023
(Percentages and index 2012 = 1)

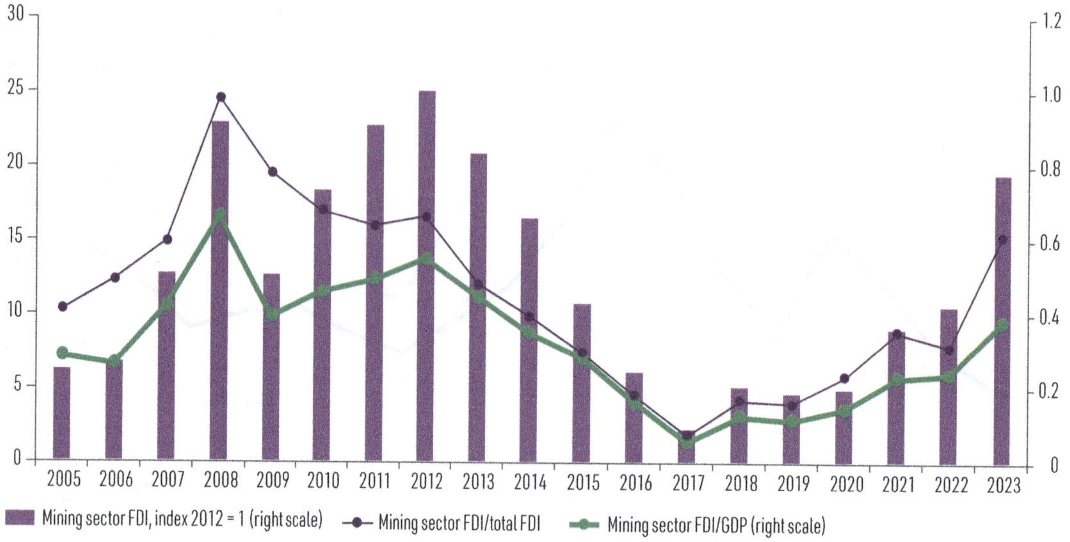

Source: Prepared by the authors on the basis of official sources; and CEPALSTAT.
Note: The countries included are Brazil, Chile, Colombia, Costa Rica, the Dominican Republic, Ecuador, Guatemala, Honduras, Mexico, Nicaragua and the Plurinational State of Bolivia. Mining sector FDI refers to inflows (net of disinvestment); in the case of Costa Rica, Ecuador, Guatemala and Honduras, the mining and hydrocarbon sectors are included.

Figure II.14
Latin America and the Caribbean (11 countries): share of mining sector FDI, 2005–2023
(Percentages)

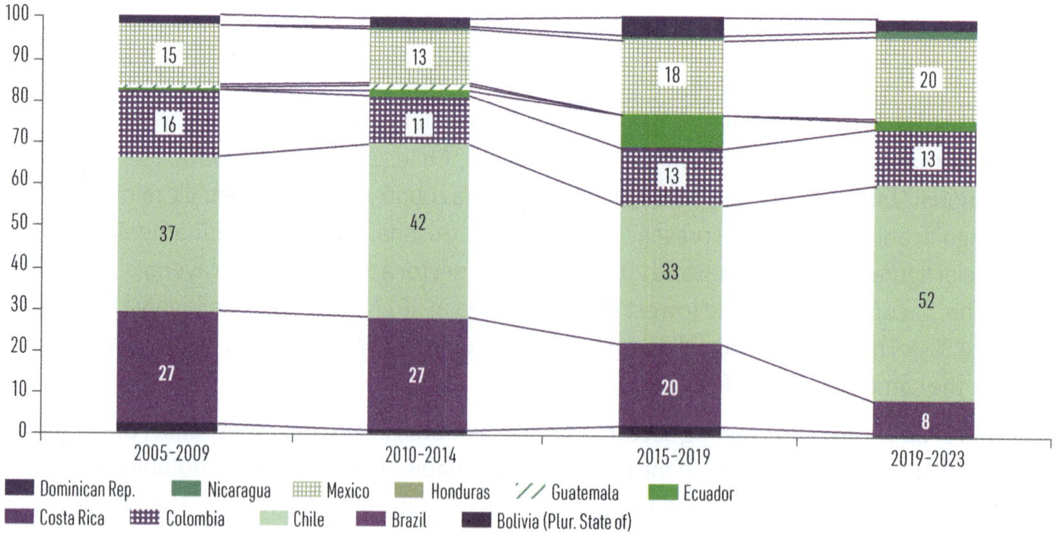

Source: Prepared by the authors on the basis of official sources.
Note: Mining sector FDI refers to inflows (net of disinvestment); in the case of Costa Rica, Ecuador, Guatemala and Honduras, the mining and hydrocarbon sectors are included.

Apart from absolute values, the trends and relative impact of FDI inflows to the mining sector vary significantly by country. For example, in countries such as Chile, Colombia, the Dominican Republic and the Plurinational State of Bolivia, these inflows have in some years exceeded 35% of total FDI. Here again, Chile where the sector accounted for an average 31.3% of total FDI in the period of analysis, is noteworthy (see table II.3). This variation among countries is also borne out in GDP terms.

Table II.3
Latin America and the Caribbean (11 countries): average, minimum, maximum and coefficient of variation in mining sector shares of total FDI and GDP, 2005–2023
(Percentages)

	Mining sector FDI/total FDI, 2005-2023				Mining sector FDI/GDP, 2005-2023			
	Average	Minimum	Maximum	Coefficient of variation	Average	Minimum	Maximum	Coefficient of variation
Bolivia (Plurinational State of)	17.0	-45.9 (2020)	58.4 (2006)	123.0	0.9	-0.2 (2020)	3.0 (2006)	101.6
Brazil	6.4	-4.1 (2021)	36.5 (2008)	131.9	0.1	-0.1 (2021)	0.6 (2008)	111.7
Chile	31.3	-21 (2018)	51.7 (2011)	57.8	2.3	-0.6 (2018)	5.0 (2011)	64.6
Colombia	14.4	-1.3(2016)	37.5 (2009)	65.7	0.6	-0.1 (2016)	1.5 (2005)	67.2
Costa Rica	0.2	-0.5 (2008)	2.5 (2016)	312.1	0.0	0.0 (2008)	0.1 (2016)	356.8
Ecuador	32.2	-52.9 (2007)	107.3 (2010)	122.3	0.3	-0.3 (2006)	0.8 (2018)	102.9
Dominican Republic	12.6	-1.7 (2014)	46.5 (2011)	104.0	0.5	-0.1 (2014)	1.9 (2012)	114.6
Guatemala	10.7	-11.4 (2018)	34.1 (2012)	125.7	0.2	-0.2 (2018)	0.9 (2012)	135.0
Honduras	1.4	-11.1 (2022)	6.4 (2010)	285.7	0.1	-0.3 (2022)	0.4 (2010)	203.2
Mexico	6.2	1.0 (2005)	16.1 (2008)	62.9	0.2	0.0 (2005)	0.4 (2013)	68.1
Nicaragua	9.9	0.0 (2005)	26.2 (2019)	81.4	0.7	0.0 (2005)	1.9 (2013)	82.9
Latin America and the Caribbean	**11.1**	**1.8 (2017)**	**24.5 (2008)**	**52.9**	**0.3**	**0.1 (2017)**	**0.7 (2008)**	**50.3**

Source: Prepared by the authors on the basis of official sources.
Note: Mining sector FDI refers to inflows (net of disinvestment); in the case of Costa Rica, Ecuador, Guatemala and Honduras, the mining and hydrocarbon sectors are included.

To sum up, FDI inflows to the mining sector are significant in the countries of Latin America and the Caribbean that have a mining tradition, accounting for a considerable share of total inflows, but have trended down over the past 20 years. Despite a recovery starting in 2017, values have yet to regain the record levels reached during the global commodities price boom, indicating that the region has become a less attractive destination for FDI compared with other regions.

Nevertheless, Latin America and the Caribbean still attracts the largest copper exploration budgets of any region, a promising fact in view of other trends and with regard to its future market position. These observations are supported by the analysis of FDI project announcements provided in the next section, which shows that FDI inflows have primarily been funnelled into mining development in copper, gold and silver, iron and, more recently, lithium. Still, the Latin American and Caribbean share of FDI has decreased as other regions, including Asia (excluding China) and North America, have increased their shares.

Although the information considered in the analysis is based on official sources and a robust and internationally accepted methodology (using balance-of-payments and international investment position statistics for the countries included), only a small number of countries in the region have such information available, and what information is available is not disaggregated by mineral, limiting the possibility of a more consistent analysis of FDI in critical minerals. Project announcement information is less statistically robust than information based on official statistics. It is less accurate because project announcements do not equate to the effective implementation of projects, and sums announced do not always correspond to sums invested, nor do they necessarily take into account reinvested earnings of foreign firms already present in the region which, from a macroeconomic standpoint, constitute a highly consequential source of financing for FDI. However, using project announcement information does enable the inclusion of more countries in the sample, comparisons with other regions and, most importantly, greater clarity in the analysis of the mining sector and its subsectors, and of the critical minerals subgroup. The systematic nature and coverage of the analysis make it a useful and informative exercise, given that mining is one of the largest recipients of FDI from developed economies (Casella and Formenti, 2022).

2. Mining investment project announcements in the region

An analysis of investment project announcements provides a more detailed picture of FDI trends in the region's mining sector, as projects can be categorized according to location, country of origin, sector and activity, using available information from 2005 onward.[8]

For expository purposes, the analysis will be divided in two periods: 2005–2014, a decade characterized by the boom in global commodities prices, including for minerals; and 2015–2024, a decade characterized by falling global prices and a succession of systemic shocks, including the COVID-19 pandemic and the conflict between the Russian Federation and Ukraine. According to the analysis of *Financial Times*[9] data on project announcements in the minerals and metals sectors, the value of global FDI announcements in the mining sector surpassed US$ 1.166 trillion in the two decades analysed, for an annual average of US$ 58.323 billion. This amount was distributed across 8,686 announcements. Asia was the destination of 36% of the total, followed by Latin America and the Caribbean (21%), Africa (17%), Europe (12%), North America (10%) and Oceania (4%). Unlike with other economic activities, in which FDI tends to be concentrated in countries with higher per capita GDP, mining sector FDI announcements were concentrated in developing countries (79%). This is consistent with the taxonomy proposed by Dunning (1993, 1998) and the identification of natural resource availability —in this case, mineral reserves— as the deciding factor in this type of investment.[10]

FDI announcements in mining by region show that Asia was a major destination over the period and that its share of the global total increased after the COVID-19 pandemic. In Latin America and the Caribbean, the trend has been less consistent: the region's share fluctuated between 7% and 38% in the period 2005–2024 (see figure II.15). In the medium-to-long term, that share has contracted, from 24% in 2005–2014 to 19% in 2015–2024, reflecting the region's diminished role relative to other parts of the world. By region, the top destination countries were India and Indonesia, in Asia; Australia, in Oceania; Guinea and the Democratic Republic of the Congo, in Africa; and Chile, Brazil and Peru, in Latin America and the Caribbean.

8 Owing to the non-equivalence of methodologies employed, a quantitative comparison cannot be made between the data used in this section and those analysed in the previous section.

9 *Financial Times*. fDi Markets. https://www.fdimarkets.com/.

10 According to Dunning, the selection of a given country as an investment destination depends on four main factors: the availability of resources, market size, production costs and the presence of strategic assets.

Figure II.15
Selected regions and countries: FDI project announcements in mining, 2005–2024
(Billions of dollars and percentages)

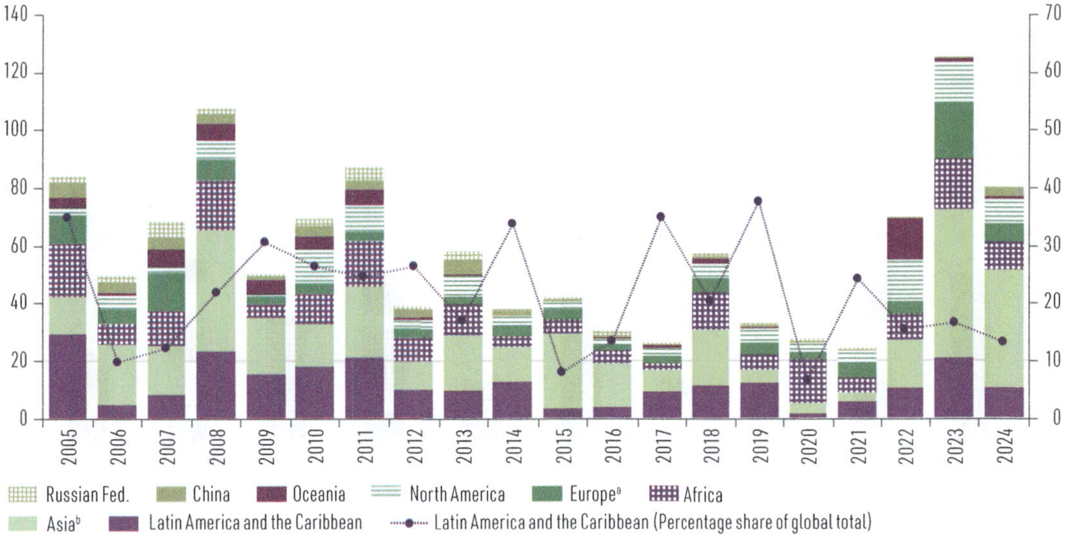

Source: Economic Commission for Latin America and the Caribbean, on the basis of *Financial Times*. fDi Markets. https://www.fdimarkets.com/.
Note: FDI project announcements in mining correspond to the minerals and metals sectors as defined in the source.
[a] Europe does not include the Russian Federation.
[b] Asia does not include China.

The relative weight of mining in total announcements also varied geographically during the period of analysis: mining accounted for 13% of total FDI project announcements in Latin America and the Caribbean, 11% in Africa, 8% in Oceania, 7% in Asia (excluding China), 7% in the Russian Federation, 5% in North America, 3% in China and 2% in Europe (excluding the Russian Federation). Still, a more detailed analysis again shows that the mining sector's share of total FDI in Latin America and the Caribbean shrank between the first decade and the second, from 16% in 2005–2014 to 9% in 2015–2024.

This trend varies by subsector and mineral group. In the first decade analysed, Latin America and the Caribbean attracted 47% of global announcements in the copper, nickel, lead and zinc subsector (led by Chile and Peru) and 52% of announcements for gold and silver (see figure II.16). Asia (excluding China) and Oceania were also top destinations, accounting for 39% of aluminium announcements and 22% of iron announcements, respectively. In the second decade, there was an overall decline in the value of announcements in all subsectors except non-ferrous metals and non-metallic minerals. The share of Latin America and the Caribbean in global FDI announcements decreased by 11 percentage points (to 36%) for the copper, nickel, lead and zinc subsector and by 10 percentage points (to 42%) for the gold and silver subsector. However, in both subsectors, the region remained the top destination for FDI announcements, and it had the second-largest share of announcements in the non-ferrous metals and non-metallic minerals subsector, which increased by 13 percentage points (to 23%). The largest share went to Asia (excluding China), with 33% of global announcements. Africa, meanwhile, was the top destination for iron announcements, with 70% of the total. The Democratic Republic of the Congo improved its relative position significantly, with its share in global announcements in the copper, nickel, lead and zinc subsector expanding from 5% in the first decade to 14% in the second, owing to the country's growing activity in the copper market.

Figure II.16
Selected regions and countries: FDI project announcements in mining, by minerals and metals subsectors, 2005–2014 and 2015–2024
(Billions of dollars and percentages)

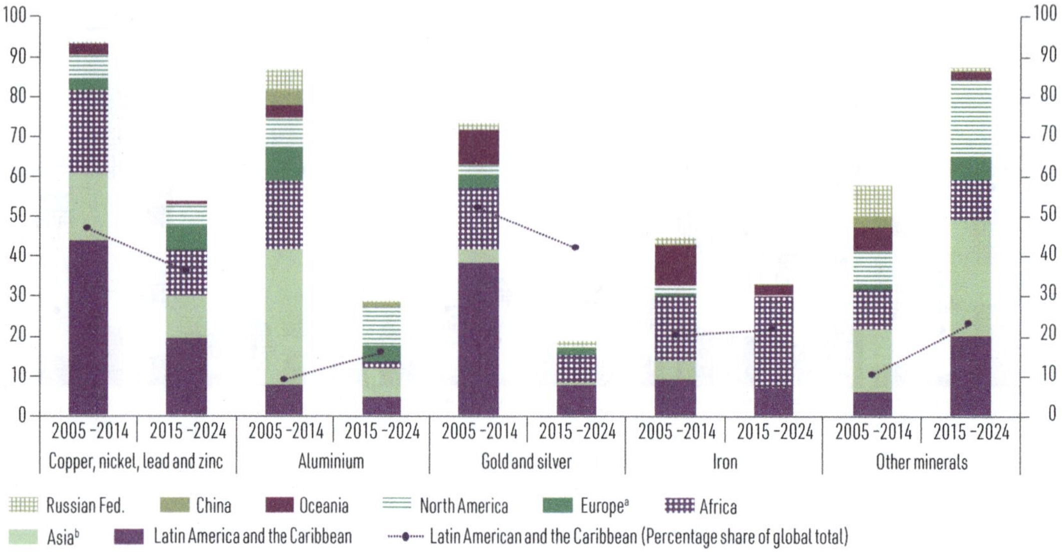

Source: Economic Commission for Latin America and the Caribbean, on the basis of *Financial Times*. fDi Markets. https://www.fdimarkets.com/.
Note: FDI project announcements in mining correspond to the minerals and metals sectors as defined in the source. "Other minerals" refers to the announcements in these sectors that pertain to the production and processing of other non-ferrous metals and the extraction of non-metallic minerals.
[a] Europe does not include the Russian Federation.
[b] Asia does not include China.

3. FDI trends in critical mineral mining in Latin America and the Caribbean

Between 2005 and 2024, 1,152 investment projects were announced in the minerals and metals sectors of Latin America and the Caribbean, amounting to US$ 230.065 billion for an average US$ 11.503 billion annually.[11] Critical minerals accounted for 23.5% of the announcements and 41.6% of their total value. Investment announcements in the region followed a volatile downward trajectory over the period (see figure II.17). However, since 2018 (with the exception of 2020 and 2021), FDI announcements in minerals and metals have been on the rise, in particular announcements in critical minerals, which despite being less numerous represent larger annual sums than those in other minerals and metals. For context, at the global level, critical minerals are estimated to have accounted for 52% of FDI announcements in extractive activities during the second decade considered in the analysis, according to available data. Latin America and the Caribbean has emerged as the top region of interest, accounting for 34% of global announcements, followed by Africa (29%), Asia (13%), North America (12%), Europe (10%) and Oceania (2%).

[11] These totals are marginally different from those presented in the previous section, in which they were being compared with totals for the other regions, owing to the different periods of analysis and the filter criteria applied to the data for this section's analysis of investment announcements in critical minerals in the region.

Figure II.17
Latin America and the Caribbean: value and number of FDI announcements in mining, by mineral, 2005–2024
(Billions of dollars and number)

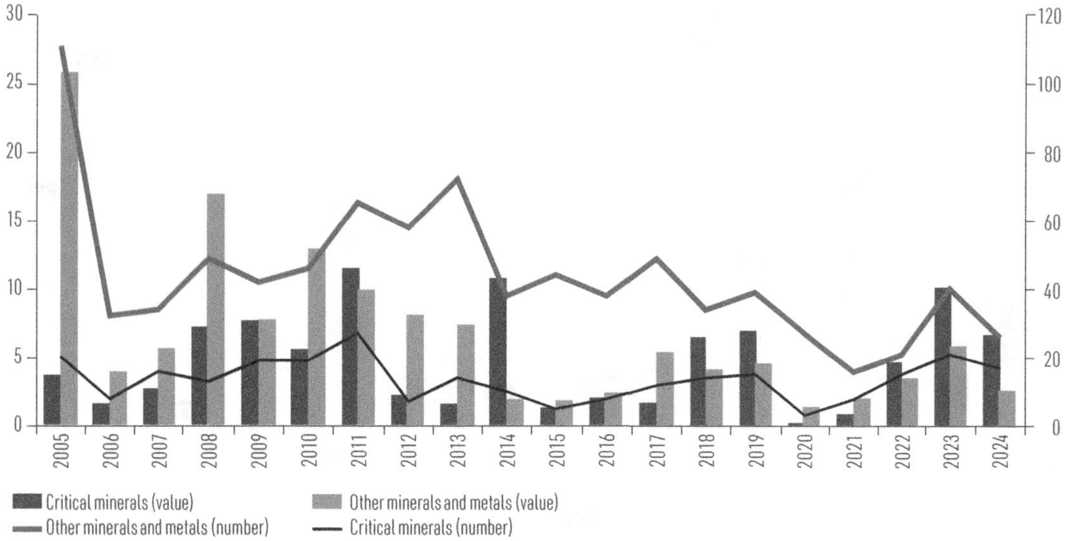

Source: Economic Commission for Latin America and the Caribbean, on the basis of *Financial Times*. fDi Markets. https://www.fdimarkets.com/.

Note: FDI project announcements in mining correspond to the minerals and metals sectors as defined in the source. The "critical minerals" category includes selected announcements pertaining to bauxite, alumina and aluminium; cobalt; copper; graphite; lithium; nickel; and rare earth elements. The "other minerals and metals" category corresponds to announcements in minerals and metals not included by the authors in the first category, including steel, iron, gold and silver.

Copper accounts for the lion's share of FDI announcements in Latin America and the Caribbean, with Chile and Peru as major destinations. However, the total value of copper investment announcements is declining, despite a post-pandemic recovery, and has exhibited a high degree of volatility throughout the period of analysis, owing to international prices and to the nature of the data (see figure II.18). Indeed, copper's share has been as high as 90% in some years and as low as 0% in others. More recently, there has been growing interest in lithium and, to a lesser extent, nickel —both critical minerals for the production of rechargeable batteries. Since 2016, FDI announcements in lithium have increased more than ninefold relative to the previous decade, in particular in Argentina (the top destination), followed by Chile, Brazil and, less closely, the Plurinational State of Bolivia. Nickel announcements have also increased since the pandemic, although they decreased overall between the first decade of analysis and the second. Brazil is a leading destination for nickel announcements as the region's top producer. Meanwhile, investment announcements in the aluminium group, despite relative stability since 2018, registered the largest contraction relative to the first decade of analysis. Cobalt and rare earth elements have followed a similar trend to nickel, increasing sharply since the pandemic. Brazil is also a leader in these metals, while Colombia and Mexico hold a lesser yet significant position in rare earth elements.

Figure II.18
Latin America and the Caribbean: FDI project announcements in critical minerals, 2005–2024
(Billions of dollars)

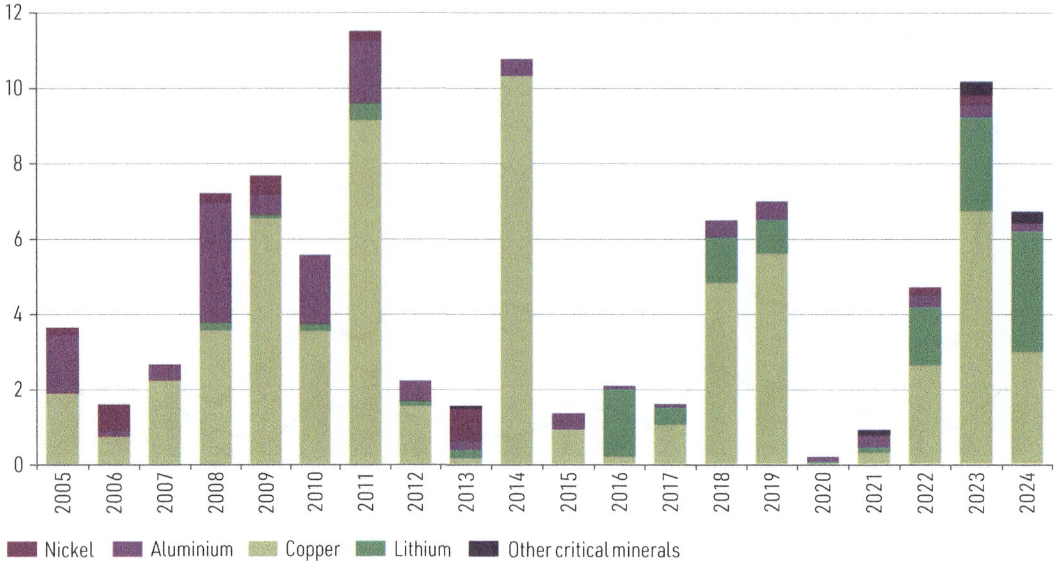

Source: Economic Commission for Latin America and the Caribbean, on the basis of *Financial Times*. fDi Markets. https://www.fdimarkets.com/.

Note: FDI project announcements in critical minerals correspond to the subset of announcements in the minerals and metals sectors (as defined in the source) that pertain to minerals designated as "critical". The aluminium category includes announcements pertaining to bauxite, alumina and aluminium, and the "other critical minerals" category includes those pertaining to cobalt, graphite and rare earth elements.

In terms of countries of origin, in the period 2005–2024, Canada accounted for 20% of critical minerals FDI, making it the top source of FDI for Latin America and the Caribbean, with First Quantum Minerals in Panama, Lundin Mining in Argentina and Chile, Quadra Mining (acquired by Poland's KGHM in 2012) in Chile, Hudbay Minerals in Peru and Amerigo Resources in Chile, among other investments (see figure II.19). The United Kingdom also accounted for about 20%, with investments including Anglo American in Chile and smaller ones in Brazil and Rio Tinto (also headquartered in Australia) in Argentina.[12] China has the next-largest share of announcements (14%), mostly through State-owned enterprises like China Minmetals Corporation and Aluminium Corporation of China in Peru and Bosai Minerals Group in Guyana. Australia accounts for 11% of announcements, with a focus on Chile, Peru and Argentina, mainly through BHP. Announcements from Switzerland's Glencore are concentrated in Peru, and Poland's KGHM and Japan's Mitsui & Co. (Chile) Ltda., among others, have focused primarily on Chile and Peru. Lastly, Mexico has the largest intraregional share, with Grupo México announcements in Peru.

12 Antofagasta Minerals, listed on the London Stock Exchange, has maintained a significant share in announcements from the United Kingdom but is controlled by Grupo Luksic (Chile).

Figure II.19
Latin America and the Caribbean: FDI project announcements in selected critical minerals, by country of origin and country of destination, according to total value, 2005–2024
(Percentages)

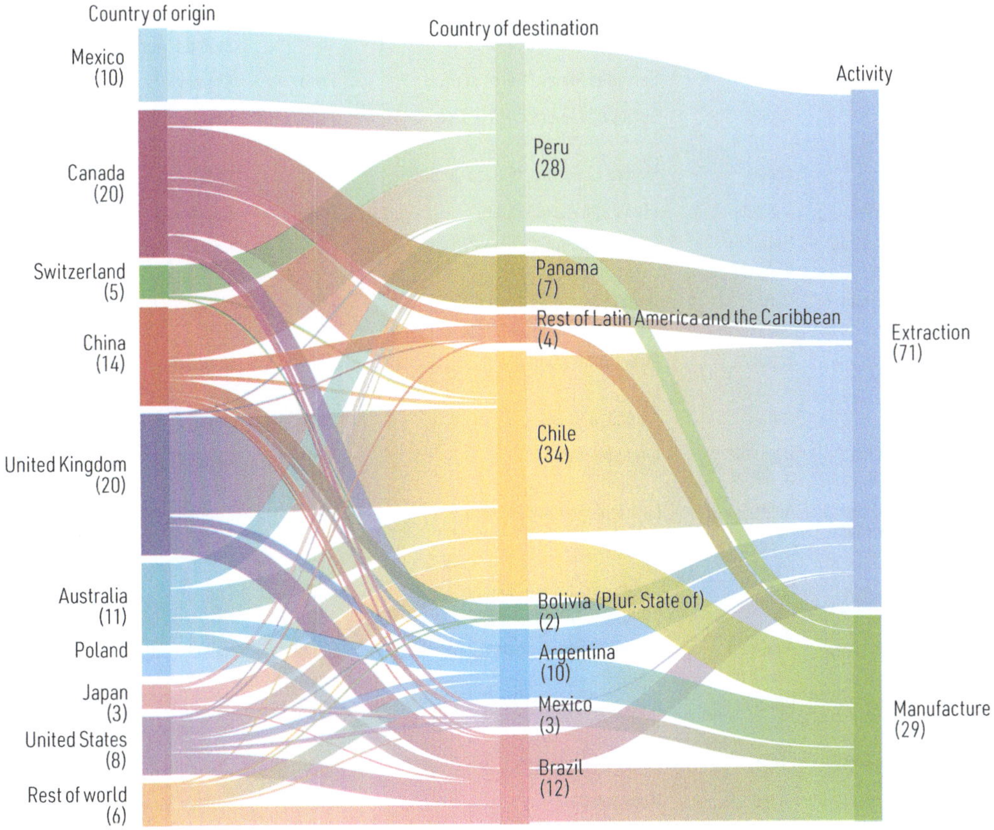

Source: Economic Commission for Latin America and the Caribbean, on the basis of *Financial Times*. fDi Markets. https://www.fdimarkets.com/.
Note: FDI project announcements in critical minerals correspond to the subset of announcements in the minerals and metals sectors (as defined in the source) that pertain to minerals designated as "critical".

The trend in FDI announcements in critical minerals in the region from 2005 to 2024 is consistent with the one observed in cross-border mergers and acquisitions involving firms active in critical mineral exploitation (see table II.4). These transactions were greater in number and value in the first decade of analysis than in the second, while in the second, they reflected a post-pandemic bump. The top destinations for mergers and acquisitions are Chile, Peru, Argentina and Brazil, where investments are concentrated in critical minerals like copper, lithium and aluminium. The region's natural advantage in these minerals has driven asset acquisitions by companies from countries including Australia, Japan, the United States and, in recent years, China. Most notable among these were the 2022 acquisition of the Sierra Gorda project by Australia's South32 for a sum of US$ 1.4 billion and two major transactions in Argentina's lithium sector involving Australian and Chinese firms.

Table II.4
Latin America and the Caribbean: 20 largest mergers and acquisitions in critical minerals, 2005–2024

Year	Firm	Country of origin	Assets acquired	Destination country	Mineral	Value *(Millions of dollars)*
2005	Southern Copper	United States	Minera México	Mexico	Copper, molybdenum	3 334
2005	Investor Group	Japan	Sociedad Minera Cerro Verde	Peru	Copper	300
2005	Sumitomo Metal Mining	Japan	Sociedad Minera Cerro Verde	Peru	Copper	265
2008	Marubeni	Japan	Minera El Tesoro, Minera Centinela	Chile	Copper	1 401
2011	Norsk Hydro	Norway	Aluminum Assets (Vale)	Brazil	Aluminium	5 270
2011	Korea Resources Corporation	Republic of Korea	Santo Domingo Copper-Iron-Gold Mine	Chile	Copper, iron, gold	219
2011	Solway Investment Group	Cyprus	Hudbay Minerals	Mexico	Nickel	140
2012	Mitsui & Co. (Chile) Ltda.	Japan	Inversiones Mineras Acrux	Chile	Copper	1 100
2012	Marubeni	Japan	Antucoya Project	Chile	Copper	541
2012	Korea Panama Mining Corp.	Republic of Korea	Inmet Mining	Panama	Copper	169
2014	MMG, CITIC Group, CNIC Corporation Limited	Australia	Las Bambas Copper Mine	Peru	Copper	7 005
2014	Lundin Mining	Canada	Candelaria Copper Mining Complex/Ojos del Salado	Chile	Copper	1 800
2014	Sirius Resources	Australia	Nova Bollinger (cobalt, copper and nickel)	Brazil	Nickel, copper and cobalt	164
2014	Noble Group	Hong Kong, China	Alcoa	Jamaica	Bauxite and alumina	140
2018	Empresas COPEC	Chile	Cumbres Andinas	Peru	Lithium	200
2021	Mitsubishi Materials	Japan	Mantoverde	Chile	Copper	184
2022	South32	Australia	Proyecto Sierra Gorda	Chile	Copper	1 400
2022	Ganfeng Lithium Group	China	LitheA	Argentina	Lithium	962
2022	Rio Tinto	Australia	Rincon Lithium Project	Argentina	Lithium	825
2024	Zijin Mining Group	China	La Arena copper-gold mine/ Perú, La Arena II/Perú	Peru	Copper and gold	245

Source: Economic Commission for Latin America and the Caribbean, on the basis of *Bloomberg*.

To sum up, for the past two decades, FDI project announcement trends in the minerals and metals sectors have fluctuated, reflecting changing geographical and sectoral patterns in global flows. Although Latin America and the Caribbean continues to be a significant destination for these announcements, in particular in critical minerals, its share has diminished relative to other regions. This trend comes with challenges in terms of competition and strategic positioning, but it also offers opportunities to attract quality investments through policies integrated with a productive development agenda that is driven by the critical minerals sector. It is therefore advisable to review existing and emerging policy frameworks in the region and their potential to improve the strategic participation of countries with a mining tradition in the sector's global value chains.

C. Policies for attracting investment and productive development in the mining sector

In 2024, the growing importance of critical minerals for developing countries led to the creation of the Secretary-General's Panel on Critical Energy Transition Minerals and the definition of a set of guiding principles and voluntary measures for governments, industries, communities and other stakeholders involved in these minerals' value chains (Secretary-General's Panel on Critical Energy Transition Minerals, 2024). The fourth of the Panel's guiding principles indicates that, in countries that are rich in these resources, development must be fostered through benefit-sharing, value addition and economic diversification. In other words, in addition to working towards responsible exploitation that takes into account environmental sustainability and the interests of Indigenous Peoples and local communities, countries should leverage their natural resources to boost their productive and technological capacities and diversify their economies, pursuing technology and knowledge transfer, value addition, research and development (R&D), and innovation.

Critical mineral abundance represents a major opportunity to attract FDI to this and related sectors in the region. Chile, Peru and Argentina, which have considerable copper and lithium reserves, have recently received increased interest from international investors involved in exploiting these resources. These FDI inflows have the potential to drive economic growth and job creation in the critical minerals sector. They can also foster productive linkages, new activities, technological advances and innovations, and increased productivity in this and related sectors.[13] As has been stressed throughout this chapter, Latin America and the Caribbean has a major opportunity to use critical minerals to boost and expand productive development, moving beyond its specialization in natural resource production and exports.

However, history shows that realizing this type of virtuous linkage —between FDI in natural resource exploitation and productive development— requires proactive measures. This means implementing appropriate productive development policies that define and align FDI attraction initiatives with productive development efforts so that the critical minerals and related sectors effectively contribute to productive transformation, increase productivity and, ultimately, achieve a more diversified, inclusive and sustainable system of production (see Salazar-Xirinachs and Llinás, 2023; ECLAC, 2024b; 2024d).

Linking FDI attraction policies with productive development policies would address significant challenges, including the need to resolve conflicting interests: for example, FDI attraction policies, like the ones advocated in international investment agreements, often limit the possibility of implementing characteristic instruments of productive development policies in order to alleviate the uncertainty of potential investors. However, these policy instruments, such as securing commitments for the transfer of technology from foreign firms to local firms, are crucial for optimizing investment impact, both directly and indirectly (see box II.2).

13 This idea alludes to the concept of "Schumpeterian efficiency", or the capacity of an economic system to generate and disseminate technological and organizational innovations that drive growth and competition in the entire production structure (Dosi, 1988).

Box II.2

Towards a new generation of international investment agreements in Latin America and the Caribbean

For many developing countries, attracting foreign direct investment (FDI) is a means of fostering economic growth, improving productivity, encouraging technology transfer, building infrastructure, creating jobs and gaining access to international markets. International investment agreements —bilateral or multilateral agreements that establish a framework for the protection of investments made by investors from one country in another country— are one of the most widely used tools for attracting FDI.

The first agreements of this kind were forged in the 1950s, but multiplied from the 1990s onward. According to the United Nations Conference on Trade and Development ([UNCTAD] 2024), there were 3,324 international investment agreements in effect worldwide in March 2025.[a] Of these, 2,844 were bilateral investment treaties and 480 were treaties with investment provisions.[b] Latin America and the Caribbean accounts for 16% of these agreements, including 445 bilateral investment treaties and 106 treaties with investment provisions. Within the region, Chile had the most agreements (67), followed by Argentina (63), Peru (50), Uruguay (48) and Mexico (46). As an alternative means of fostering FDI, several countries have passed national laws to attract investment that incorporate protection mechanisms. In 2024, there were 132 such laws, mainly in developing countries (UNCTAD, 2024; Mehranvar et al., 2024).

Attracting FDI through international investment agreements brings several benefits, such as access to external financing, technology transfer and entry into new markets, but may simultaneously limit some countries' ability to implement productive development policies, including local content requirements or technology transfer commitments, to strengthen the impact of FDI on the local production system. Brazil, which has a long tradition of productive development policy implementation, only has three bilateral investment treaties in effect (the last signed in 2019).[c] Given this potential constraint, along with the risks associated with some claims submitted to international arbitral tribunals by foreign investors, some countries have been proposing reform or adaptation of the global rules for international investment agreements since the late 2000s (UNCTAD, 2012, 2013, 2020; Gaukrodger, D. 2021; OECD, 2024a and 2024b; Valenti, 2018).

Critics of the current system highlight: (i) limitations to States' sovereignty with regard to regulating and directing policies in line with national interests, including productive development policies; (ii) the lack of guarantees or certainty that investment flows to States are not speculative; (iii) the exposure and financial risk faced by the State with regard to dispute settlement mechanisms; (iv) legal asymmetry in treatment of foreign and local investors (in favour of the former); and (v) the lack of binding obligations for investors (Commission for the Comprehensive Citizen Audit of Investment Protection Treaties and the International Arbitration System on Investment Matters, 2017; Olivet and Ghiotto, 2021; Brauch et al., 2024; Mehranvar et al., 2024). As of July 2024, there were 1,368 investment disputes in international arbitration, of which 368 involved Latin American and Caribbean countries. Within this group, the largest number of claims was made against Argentina (65), the Bolivarian Republic of Venezuela (64), Mexico (52), Peru (34) and Ecuador (29).

UNCTAD has played a key role in the debate on the need to reform global governance of investment protection (Nuñez, 2016; UNCTAD, 2017 and 2024). It has encouraged the development of a new generation of international investment agreements to replace the conventional ones and incorporate as fundamental elements the steering of investment towards sustainable development, with climate commitments, requirements for investors relating to environmental protection, labour rights, human rights and the rights of communities, reform of dispute settlement mechanisms, and above all, States' recovery of capacity for regulation and implementation of public policies, including productive development policies. Likewise, the Organisation for Economic Co-operation and Development (OECD) has expressed concern about the limitations to regulatory authority and the alignment of international investment agreements with sustainable development policies (OECD, 2024a and 2024b).

These concerns are paramount in mining, including in the critical minerals subgroup. Indeed, many of the policy instruments and models applied in several cases outlined in this section may be unfeasible under the agreements currently governing FDI in a number of developing countries, including several countries of the region. Against this backdrop, some countries, many with a strong mining tradition, have begun taking steps to end these agreements in advance: Plurinational State of Bolivia (2006), Ecuador (2008), South Africa (2010), Indonesia (2014), India (2015) and Honduras (2024).

Given the current geopolitical context and the growing interest in critical minerals, Latin American and Caribbean countries should try to adopt a united stance on the new generation of international investment agreements that takes into account regional needs, the policy priorities of each State, including —especially if they cover the mining sector— a greater focus on sustainable development and the rights of Indigenous Peoples and local communities, and that expands policy space for implementation of productive development policies. Always within the limits of institutions and local capacity, a new generation of international investment agreements could strike a fairer balance between FDI protection and promotion and investor obligations and rights, on the one hand, and between the reduction of risk for the State regarding dispute settlement mechanisms, regulatory authority and public policy in pursuit of development objectives, on the other.

Source: United Nations Conference on Trade and Development. (2024). *Investment Policy Monitor*. (2017). *UNCTAD's reform package for the international investment regime*; Mehranvar, L., et al. (2024). *Breaking free: Strategies for governments on terminating investment treaties and removing ISDS provisions*. Columbia Center on Sustainable Investment; United Nations Conference on Trade and Development. (2012). *World Investment Report 2012: Towards a New Generation of Investment Policies*; United Nations Conference on Trade and Development. (2013). *World Investment Report 2013: Global Value Chains: Investment and Trade for Development*; United Nations Conference on Trade and Development. (2020). *World Investment Report 2020: International Production Beyond the Pandemic*; Gaukrodger, D. (2021). The future of investment treaties: possible directions. *OECD Working Papers on International Investment, 2021*(03); Organisation for Economic Co-operation and Development. (2024a). *Strengthening sustainable investment through international investment agreements*; (2024b). *Promoting responsible business conduct in trade and investment: Latin America and the Caribbean* (OECD Business and Finance Policy Papers, No. 61); Valenti, M. (2018). New trends in international investment law treaty practice: Where does Latin America stand? *Seqüência: Estudos Jurídicos e Políticos, 39*(79), 9-26; Commission for the Comprehensive Citizen Audit of Investment Protection Treaties and the International Arbitration System on Investment Matters. (2017). *Comprehensive citizen audit of investment protection treaties and the arbitration system on investment matters in Ecuador: Executive summary*; Olivet, C., and Ghiotto, L. (2021). *Parallel justice: How the investment protection system threatens judicial independence in Latin America*. Public Services International and Transnational Institute; Brauch, M. D., et al. (2024). *An international law framework for climate-aligned investment governance* (Working Paper). Columbia Center on Sustainable Investment; Nuñez, E. (2016). *Developing countries and international investment negotiations: Ecuador's strategy*. Universidad Andina Simón Bolívar.

[a] Includes agreements in effect and agreements that have been signed but are not in effect. Excludes agreements that have ended or that are being negotiated.

[b] Aside from their specificities, both types of agreement contain a definition of investment, national treatment, fair and equitable treatment, most favoured nation, prohibition of direct or indirect expropriation, dispute settlement mechanism and survival.

[c] The bilateral investment treaty signed in 2019 with the United Arab Emirates entered into force in 2023. The other two bilateral investment treaties in effect in Brazil were signed with Angola and Mexico, both in 2015. Since 2019, Brazil has signed four bilateral investment treaties with the following countries: Morocco (2019), Ecuador (2019), India (2020) and Sao Tome and Principe (2023), none of which has entered into force.

[d] On 24 February 2024, Honduras notified the World Bank of its denunciation of the Convention on the Settlement of Investment Disputes between States and Nationals of Other States.

For various reasons, not many countries have attracted investments in mining and at the same time developed new productive and technological capacities and, as a result, diversified their economies. Beyond the best and worst performance in each case, it is interesting to note the different strategies adopted by countries according to their geographical, economic and institutional characteristics. Some have focused on: (i) developing and improving extraction technologies (upstream activities), (ii) promoting development of goods and services providers specializing in the mining sector (backward linkages) and (iii) adding value further along the value chain (forward linkages).

1. Notable international examples

The productive development policies of Australia and Canada have played a key role in absorbing and building capacity at the three strategic levels, in mining and related sectors, and have encouraged diversification (Daly et al., 2022; Anzolin and Pietrobelli, 2021). These countries have strengthened their productive and technological capacities in mining in a way that complements their policies to attract investment, instead of harming them.[14]

Australia and Canada have created a wide range of incentives to attractive investment in their mining sectors, which tend to focus on: (i) upstream activities, (ii) backward linkages and, to a lesser extent, (iii) forward linkages. The most common instruments are tax and financial incentives to mitigate the inherent risks of investing in mining with a view to becoming the most attractive option for foreign investors.

For example, reliable geological information is a prerequisite of mining project investment. Investment in exploration, which is high-risk, is therefore essential, and many available development instruments focus on creating incentives for this activity. Australia's Junior Minerals Exploration Incentive provides tax credits for small minerals exploration companies. Similarly, the Exploring for the Future programme (implemented from 2016 to 2024) supported the collection of precompetitive geoscientific information. The new Resourcing Australia's Prosperity initiative (2024–2059) aims to continue this type of incentive, by supporting exploration to gather crucial information on mineral and groundwater resources. These initiatives all reduce the high risk associated with the early development stages of mining projects, such as exploration and the gathering of geological information.

In Canada, meanwhile, exploration companies can issue flow-through shares, which allow them to access capital by transferring exploration costs to the investors who purchase these shares and can then deduct 100% of the cost of their investment from pre-tax income. Canada also offers a minerals exploration tax credit and a critical minerals exploration tax credit.

Another form of attracting investment is lowering mining companies' tax burden. In Canada, the capital cost allowance enables accelerated depreciation of equipment by mining companies, while Canadian development expense claims allow them to deduct the costs of mining project development and preparation and provincial taxes when determining the amount of federal tax owed.

The adoption or creation of clean technologies is also linked to the development and improvement of extraction technologies and is another means of attracting mining investment. Canada offers clean economy investment tax credits for adopting or creating clean technologies and established the Strategic Innovation Fund to provide financial support for projects that foster a low-carbon economy. It also created the Critical Minerals Infrastructure Fund to underpin development of the clean energy and transport infrastructure needed for the expansion and sustainable development of the critical minerals industry.

Productive and technological capacities are necessary to enhance extractive activities' competitiveness and appeal to foreign investors. In that regard, Australia designated mining equipment, technology and services a strategic sector. Under the Industry Growth Centre Initiative, it created the Mining Equipment, Technology and Services Growth Centre (METS Ignited), which fostered growth of advanced automation and mineral processing technologies, for example, with a focus on developing technological service providers through the formation of several clusters serving as innovation ecosystems. Australia also offers an R&D tax incentive, along with State-run programmes such as TechVouchers in New South Wales, the Innovation Voucher Program in South Australia and the

[14] FDI in mining in Australia notably accounted for 34.4% of total FDI in 2023.

Knowledge Transfer Partnerships in Queensland, which provide tax credits to companies investing in R&D. The Cooperative Research Centres Program has also helped to establish various research centres, including four in the mining sector.

Through the Strategic Innovation Fund, Canada created the Centre for Excellence in Mining Innovation for the development and commercialization of innovative low-carbon technologies. In addition, the Critical Minerals Research, Development and Demonstration Program supports development of innovative processing technologies for the critical minerals industry.

Australia and Canada also promote critical mineral processing and refining (forward linkages) through specific incentives, albeit to a lesser extent than they do with regard to development of extraction technologies and of specialized goods and services providers. For example, the critical minerals production tax incentive in Australia is a refundable tax credit designed to advance such processes in the country.

Australia and Canada are trying to position themselves in the most sophisticated segments of global mining value chains, concentrating on improving productive and technological capacities by fostering local R&D, while continuing to focus on a fundamental segment, extraction, to maintain or improve productive performance. Through a combination of financial and fiscal instruments and R&D investments (upstream activities and backward linkages), these countries are prioritizing improvement in extraction technologies and development of specialized suppliers. At the same time, they offer a more favourable and predictable investment climate and incentives to direct investment towards related activities that represent higher value added and that are more knowledge-intensive.

Other less developed countries with a mining tradition, such as Indonesia and South Africa, are also implementing policies to attract investment in coordination with productive development policies. Both of these countries established special economic zones to create attractive investment conditions. While Indonesia offers preferential loans and subsidies for the development of industrial parks, South Africa has two programmes to build productive capacity and infrastructure. The Industrial Development Corporation, through the Mining and Metals Strategic Business Unit, offers financing for mining projects across the value chain. The Critical Infrastructure Programme finances between 10% and 30% of the cost of critical infrastructure projects.

Indonesia has been one of the countries most focused on adding value further along the value chain (forward linkages). In 2014, it banned nickel ore exports, and introduced local content requirements for companies investing in smelters, as well as tax incentives to attract foreign investment. These measures complemented greater cooperation with China in financing, project facilitation and the establishment of special industrial zones. As a result, Indonesia has become the world's largest nickel producer and income from exports of this metal jumped from US$ 1 billion in 2015 to US$ 20.9 billion in 2021 (United Nations, 2025a; Tritto, 2023). Indonesia's current strategy, which is based on tax incentives, import duty exemptions, infrastructure development and R&D subsidies, is focused on developing the entire electric vehicle supply chain, from precursor materials to battery packs and electric vehicles.[15]

Through the Support Programme for Industrial Innovation, South Africa also reinforces forward linkages with two non-repayable grants for local companies specializing in technological development: the Product Process Development Scheme and the Matching Scheme. The National Research Foundation also supports R&D through the Technology and Human Resources for Industry Programme, co-financing projects in collaboration with educational institutions. South African Mining Extraction Research, Development and Innovation (SAMERDI) Research Centres have also been established to

[15] The Democratic Republic of the Congo, Ghana, Malaysia and Namibia also recently banned exports of several critical minerals to increase local value added through processing and refining of these minerals (United Nations, 2025a).

maximize sustainable development of the country's mineral resources through collaborative research, development and innovation. The Mandela Mining Precinct, a public-private partnership between the Department of Science, Technology and Innovation and the Minerals Council of South Africa, was created to implement the SAMERDI strategy, with the government providing twice the amount of financing contributed by the private sector.

In conclusion, some mining countries such as Australia, Canada, Indonesia and South Africa have introduced various policies and incentives to attract FDI in the mining sector and develop local capacities. These countries have taken a proactive approach to attracting foreign capital and promoting innovation and productive diversification in the sector, through tax incentives, financial subsidies, support for R&D and the building of specialized infrastructure.

2. Attracting investment and implementing productive development policies in Latin America and the Caribbean

In Latin America and the Caribbean, most investments in the mining sector are in extractive (upstream) activities. Policies to attract investment are also based mainly on tax incentives that ensure tax stability for defined periods. In some countries, these incentives are not specific to mining.[16] Although these policies vary across countries, they generally do not include requirements relating to local content, supplier development or technology transfer.

The few productive development policies in effect in the region's mining sector focus on lithium. Generally, the countries that possess this resource have designated it a strategic mineral for their development and foster its exploitation and, to varying degrees, value added.

Chile's National Lithium Strategy (see box II.3), which is based on a public-private ownership model, is noteworthy. An important previous step was the renegotiation of contracts between Chile's Production Development Corporation (CORFO) and two companies which exploit lithium in Salar de Atacama, Albemarle (2016) and SQM (2018), providing CORFO with resources from lithium income to finance initiatives focused on value added and R&D. Under this framework, companies were prohibited from selling any concentration of extracted lithium brine and were required to offer a share of their lithium compounds (lithium carbonate, lithium hydroxide and lithium chloride) at a better price to companies that add value in Chile, producing precursors, active materials and battery cathodes, for example. The entire SQM share was allocated to two Chinese companies, BYD Chile (BYD) and Yongqing Technology (Tsingshan Holding Group), although by May 2025, these companies had withdrawn their plans, citing market and contractual conditions.[17] Albemarle's share is currently being allocated and is expected to be available up to 2043.[18]

Regarding technology, under the terms of the above-mentioned renegotiation, Albemarle would gradually increase its annual contributions to one or more R&D centres, such as the Technological Centre for the Circular Economy and the Centre for Sustainable Acceleration of Electromobility, from US$ 6 million to US$ 12.4 million up to 2034, and SQM would contribute US$ 10.7 million to US$ 18.9 million up to 2030 to the Institute of Clean Technologies and to green hydrogen projects.

---

16 Argentina, for example, adopted an incentive system for large investments (more than US$ 200 million) in domestic and foreign investment projects in specific sectors, including mining, in 2024.

17 For example, the sharp drop in lithium prices since 2022 and the limitation of preferential prices only up to 2030.

18 Implementing this type of policy is highly complex. For example, Chile had to amend its Interim Trade Agreement with the European Union to allow preferential access in order to increase local value added. In 2018, CORFO selected Molymet, Posco-Samsung SDI and Sichuan Fulin to develop projects in Chile with access to lithium at favourable prices, under a contract with Albermarle. However, the three projects failed to materialize, for various reasons.

Box II.3
Chile's National Lithium Strategy

The National Lithium Strategy presented by the Government of Chile in 2023 is an example of a comprehensive approach to lithium exploitation to ensure the economically, environmentally and socially sustainable development of this industry. It recognizes that development of the lithium industry offers an opportunity to create various productive linkages and drive technological development and innovation, both upstream and downstream, including in advanced corporate and scientific activities. It also acknowledges that salt flats and surrounding areas are unique and complex ecosystems that contain water reserves in the desert and are home to Indigenous Peoples and cultures that must be respected and protected.

The Strategy's aims include sustainable development of productive potential, social and environmental sustainability, technological and supply chain development, and allocation of a share of lithium income to the country.

The main objectives of the Strategy linked to productive development are as follows:

- Create a strategic committee for lithium and salt flats to drive implementation of the National Lithium Strategy and advance policies for scientific, technological and productive development to create new forward and backward linkages and add value.
- Create the State-owned National Lithium Company which, in partnership with the private sector, promotes exploration, exploitation and value adding projects as well as technological development throughout the value chain.
- Create a public technology and research institute focused on lithium and salt flats to build knowledge and technologies that improve extraction, production, value adding, application and recycling processes, as well as increasing the understanding and protection of salt flats.
- Involve the State in lithium exploitation through coordination of the public and private sectors, with the State holding a majority share in partnerships.

The National Lithium Strategy has been well-received by investors. In 2024, the Government of Chile launched a public call for applications to develop lithium exploration and exploitation projects. It received 88 expressions of interest from 54 companies and consortiums from 10 countries.

At the same time, and in line with the National Lithium Strategy, in May 2024 the National Copper Corporation of Chile (CODELCO) signed a public-private partnership agreement with SQM to ensure advance participation of the State in lithium exploitation in Salar de Atacama, given that the contract between CORFO and SQM expires in 2030. Under the National Lithium Strategy, the agreement will ensure that the State holds a majority stake and is in full compliance with the existing contract. The agreement entails a partnership for the production of refined lithium in Salar de Atacama until 2060. It will include two phases: until 2030, SQM will be responsible for overall management and its current rental contract with CORFO will continue, as well as existing agreements with communities and other social organizations; from 2031 to 2060, CODELCO will assume management responsibilities. The State, through CODELCO, CORFO and tax authorities, will receive approximately 70% of the operating margin generated by new production between 2025 and 2030, and 85% from 1 January 2031.

Source: Government of Chile. (2023). National Lithium Strategy, 2023. https://www.gob.cl/litioporchile/en/.

Also in Chile, the National Strategy for Capacity-building in Smelting and Refining was introduced in 2023. Its three objectives are: (i) to develop enabling initiatives to strengthen the smelting and refining industry; (ii) to bolster the State's smelting and refining capacities through CODELCO and the National Mining Corporation (ENAMI) and (iii) to develop new smelting and refining projects. Of the three smelters for which an increase in capacity was recommended, until now the only progress made has been the initiation of a feasibility study by ENAMI on the Hernán Videla Lira Smelter. There has been no progress in the two smelters managed by CODELCO, while in the evaluation of a new smelter administered by the Chilean Copper Commission, the Ministry of Mining has yet to define either the location or potential investors.

In Argentina, regulations for lithium are similar to those applicable to other minerals. Although it has been designated a strategic mineral in several provinces where mining resources are located, policies to encourage investment in lithium have followed territorially decentralized market-based models to accelerate the development of mining projects, not to pursue comprehensive productive development.[19] Investment has focused primarily on lithium exploration, extraction and export, although the establishment of the National Plant for Technological Development of Lithium Cells and Batteries (UniLiB) is notable. This joint project of Y-TEC and the National University of La Plata, supported by the National Council for Scientific and Technological Research, is geared towards the production of lithium cells and batteries. Its estimated annual capacity is 13 MWh, equivalent to 1,000 batteries for renewable energy storage or roughly 50 batteries for electric buses, although at the time of writing, the plant had not begun operating.

In Mexico and the Plurinational State of Bolivia, lithium exploitation and value added are the responsibility of the State, through Litio para Mexico (LitioMx) and Yacimientos de Litio Bolivianos (YLB), respectively. Neither currently produce lithium on an industrial scale.[20] [21] YLB has a pilot plant for cathode materials and a pilot plant for batteries that produces lithium battery cells using cathode materials developed in-house, with lithium iron phosphate and nickel, manganese and cobalt, using the lithium carbonate produced in Salar de Uyuni. With regard to research and development, YLB has the Centre for Research in Science and Technology of Materials and Evaporite Resources of Bolivia located in La Palca, Potosí, which is at the heart of research, science and technology in support of Bolivian lithium industrialization.

Brazil differs from the other countries as its policies focus not only on lithium, but on productive chains for a broader group of critical minerals for the energy transition. The country recently advanced several initiatives to support exploration and extraction projects as well as projects to increase innovation, value added and decarbonization.[22] In February 2024, for example, the Ministry of Mining and Energy and the National Bank for Economic and Social Development established the Strategic Minerals Investment Fund, which is expected to mobilize up to 1 billion reais for small and medium-sized companies selected following a public call for applicationsto boost the sector and attract investment in the minerals value chain (Ministry of Mining and Energy of Brazil, 2024a).

In early 2025, the National Bank for Economic and Social Development and the Research and Projects Funding Authority, through the New Industry Brazil programme, launched a public call for applications for investment in productive capacity and research, development and innovation to transform strategic minerals and produce transformed materials or manufactured products for the energy transition and decarbonization. The initiative focuses on Brazilian companies that are either part of the productive chains for these minerals or that specialize in research, technological development and innovation.

19 For example, there are State-owned companies in the three provinces where lithium is exploited, namely: Recursos Energéticos y Mineros de Salta (REMSa), Jujuy Energía y Minería Sociedad del Estado (JEMSE) and Catamarca Minera y Energética (CAMYEN). In terms of scale, these companies are not comparable to CODELCO in Chile, as the production of minerals or energy is not their primary activity.

20 In December 2023, YLB opened its lithium carbonate industrial-scale plant with potential annual capacity of 15,000 metric tons. However, partial functioning of evaporation ponds limited the quality of the raw material. Hence, in 2024 the plant began stabilizing operations, also focusing on improving ancillary services such as water and energy supply.

21 LitioMx is just beginning to develop its policies. In collaboration with the National Council for Humanities, Sciences and Technologies, it has advanced in the metallurgical process of extracting high-purity lithium carbonate from clay. There are plans to build a pilot plant to extract lithium from lithium-enriched clays. However, the country's recent productive development policy, the Mexico Plan, currently does not include mining or critical minerals among its strategic sectors.

22 In 2024, the Ministry of Mining and Energy launched the 2025–2034 Plan for Basic Geological Mapping and Mineral Surveys (PlanGEO), a strategic initiative in collaboration with the Geological Service, to identify new deposits of critical minerals for the energy transition and food security. It also seeks to provide detailed information on the location and exploitation potential of these resources (Ministry of Mining and Energy of Brazil, 2024b).

To sum up, with the exceptions of Brazil and Chile, productive development policies for the mining sector in Latin America and the Caribbean are still emergent.[23] Unlike the experiences elsewhere in the world, the region appears to be concentrating (through action or omission) on the process of attracting FDI as an end in itself, as reflected in multiple international investment agreements and similar instruments (see box II.2). As shown in Australia, one of the world's major recipients of FDI in mining, attracting FDI is not incompatible with the implementation of productive development policies.

D. Conclusions and recommendations

Although FDI in mining has historically been significant in the countries of Latin America and the Caribbean with a mining tradition, it has declined in the past 20 years, unlike in other regions. Despite an improvement since 2017 and in the wake of the COVID-19 pandemic, levels have not returned to the peaks seen during the international commodity price boom (see section B). This is also the case for some critical minerals, which made the region the most attractive destination for FDI in mining extraction activities between 2015 and 2024, as seen in the smaller share of global production (see section A).

In any case, the region remains globally relevant with regard to reserves, production and exports of critical minerals, particularly copper and lithium. These minerals provide an unprecedented opportunity to attract new FDI and at the same time to implement productive development policies that foster development of productive and technological capacities, value added, research, development and innovation, and economic diversification. Leveraging this opportunity will require strengthening what ECLAC has defined as the technical, operational, political and prospective (TOPP) capabilities of government institutions. This in turn will require financing, sustained efforts to develop and maintain the necessary levels of training, and the creation of governance systems that encourage collaboration between crucial State and non-State stakeholders. Analysis and planning instruments must also be developed to monitor the policies implemented and manage different future scenarios.

These capacities are especially vital in mining, owing to the nature of investment in this sector. In additional to suitable institutions and TOPP capabilities, these investments require enabling conditions that are not always guaranteed in the countries of the region, from basic transport and communications infrastructure to basic geographical information and skilled human resources.

To increase the multiplier effect of mining investment from an economic, social and territorial perspective, policies to attract investment to the sector must be coordinated with productive development policies, as indicated by the experiences of countries such as Australia and Canada, which have done so effectively. Greater coordination in the design and implementation of these policies can have a much more meaningful impact on the countries of the region, allowing socioeconomic effects to transcend extractive activities. Table II.5 outlines some of the TOPP capabilities that must be strengthened to achieve greater synergy between policies to attract mining investment, including for critical minerals, and productive development policies.

---

[23] In late 2023, Colombia introduced a productive development policy, the Reindustrialization Strategy, that includes mining among its efforts to ensure a just energy transition and underscores, with regard to increasing participation in global value chains, that mining clusters and supply chains will be strengthened with a focus on reindustrialization for the transition. A strategy will also be developed to bolster productive chains that add value to strategic minerals (such as copper and nickel), in line with the National Mining Policy, which has yet to be finalized, and with the new mining law being drafted.

Table II.5
Technical, operational, political and prospective (TOPP) capabilities to strengthen attraction of foreign investment and productive development policies in mining

Technical	Operational	Political	Prospective
Gathering of precompetitive geoscientific information (geological, geochemical, geophysical) on critical minerals for the energy transition.	Development of geoscientific information, management and dissemination systems for critical minerals and provision of access to these systems for the public.	Coordination and agreement on sectoral policies and investment incentives relating to geological information and exploration, mining projects, suppliers and value chains for critical minerals.	Strategic long-term vision of critical mineral mining for the energy transition.
Research and development of technologies for sustainable extraction of critical minerals and reinjection of lithium brine.	Strengthening of public capacities for regulation, oversight and auditing.	Coordination and coherence between policies to attract investment and productive development policies.	Technological monitoring of the development of critical mineral extraction and refining technologies and of energy transition technologies and their use of critical minerals.
Research, development and innovation in mineral processing, smelting and refining.	Greater transparency, access to information and accountability of information relating to geological, productive, tax, social and environmental matters in the mining sector.	Participatory governance and management with regard to cluster initiatives for the mining sector and forward and backward linkages.	Definition of suitable economic sectors for productive diversification and steering of R&D in future industries relating to critical mineral value chains.
R&D in technology for the circular economy in mining (valuation of waste, recycling and reuse).	Use of new information and communications technologies to reduce disaster risk in mining projects and associated infrastructure.	Creation or strengthening of mechanisms for participation of key stakeholders and for public and private sector coordination.	Production of market intelligence for critical minerals.
Design and implementation of productive development policies and innovation in critical mineral value chains.	Production of real-time information on indicators of the productive, social and environmental performance of mining projects.	Regulation and application of methodologies to ensure participation and free and informed consultation of Indigenous Peoples and communities, in accordance with the Indigenous and Tribal Peoples Convention, 1989 (No. 169) of the International Labour Organization.	Projection of critical mineral supply and demand scenarios with risk criteria relating to climate change, technology penetration, geopolitical tension, and sustainability targets and commitments, for example.
Design and implementation of sovereign investment funds and the creation of durable capital.		Prevention and management of socioenvironmental conflicts.	Estimation of supply and demand of inputs, equipment, machinery and professional and technical mining services in line with critical mineral supply and demand projections.
Design and negotiation of investment contracts with foreign and domestic companies.		Negotiation and mediation of conflicts with governments and foreign mining companies.	
Promotion of investments in infrastructure relating to mining and its value chains.		Prevention of corruption, regulatory capture and undue political influence.	
Development of training and supply of technical and professional resources for critical minerals and their value chains.			

Source: Economic Commission for Latin America and the Caribbean.

For example, with regard to technical and operational capabilities, having workers with the skills and experience to manage information systems and precompetitive geoscientific data that are reliable and accessible to the public can sharply reduce the risks associated with exploration, leading to greater investor trust and more informed decision-making in the exploration and development phases of mining projects. These conditions also allow for more transparency by ensuring that all potential investors have access to the same information, facilitate strategic planning, confirm government support for the mining sector and foster more efficient and sustainable exploration and exploitation of mining resources, guaranteeing high environmental and social standards (Scott and Jones, 2014).

Another example relates to the technical and political capabilities for designing and implementing productive development policies with a view to fostering innovation in critical mineral value chains. All stages of mining are included, from production of inputs, equipment and machinery, and mining services (upstream) to the transformation of minerals in semi-finished and finished goods (downstream). The aim is to create quality jobs and forge ties with related industries, such as metalworking, chemicals and miscellaneous (e.g. geological, information and communications technologies, and engineering) services.

From a political perspective, this requires coordination and consensus for sectoral policies that incentivize investment and technology transfer. Participatory governance based on cluster initiatives or other forms of productive coordination in the mining sector —which allows work on strategic agendas with the participation of key stakeholders— is fundamental to ensure coherence between policies to attract investment and productive development policies.[24]

With regard to prospective capabilities, there is need of a long-term strategic vision for critical mineral mining, technological monitoring and market intelligence. The development of future scenarios and the inclusion of climate change risk criteria in planning are increasingly essential to anticipate and manage challenges in the sector.

Historically, the region has struggled to fully leverage the economic effects of exploitation of its abundant natural resources, especially in mining. Factors such as inadequate infrastructure, political instability and the resource curse associated with widespread rent-seeking have hampered the attraction of quality investment and implementation of tax, environmental and productive development policies to strengthen absorption capacity and foster new productive and technological capacities.[25] Latin America and the Caribbean is currently in an excellent position to adopt these policies as part of a more robust productive development strategy to capitalize on its strategic critical mineral resources. Leveraging this opportunity will require strengthening TOPP capabilities and encouraging dialogue between stakeholders, as proposed by ECLAC. Only with sustained efforts to achieve that goal will the region be able to benefit fully from the exploitation of its rich and strategic critical mineral resources.

Bibliography

Anzolin, G., y Pietrobelli, C. (2021). Local content policies: Why mining needs consistent policy packages to support capabilities development. *The Extractive Industries and Society, 8*(1), 395–399. https://doi.org/10.1016/j.exis.2020.12.005

Balaram, V. (2019). Rare earth elements: A review of applications, occurrence, exploration, analysis, recycling, and environmental impact. *Geoscience Frontiers, 10*, 1285–1303. https://doi.org/10.1016/j.gsf.2018.12.005

Brauch, M. D., Klonsky, E., Everard, F. M., Guanglin, Q., Alviano, T., Cuddihey, J., and Wang, M. (2024). *An international law framework for climate-aligned investment governance* (Working Paper). Columbia Center on Sustainable Investment. https://scholarship.law.columbia.edu/cgi/viewcontent.cgi?article=1028&context=sustainable_investment

Casella, B. and Formenti, L. (2022), *Mining Foreign Direct Investments and Local Technological Spillovers*, Cambridge University Press.

Chilean Copper Commission. (2024a). *Analysis of critical and/or strategic minerals*. https://www.cochilco.cl/web/analisis-de-minerales-criticos-y-o-estrategicos/

Chilean Copper Commission. (2024b). *Mining investment in Chile: Project portfolio 2024–2033*. https://www.cochilco.cl/web/download/965/2024/13094/inversion-en-la-mineria-chilena-cartera-de-proyectos-2024-2033.pdf

Commission for the Comprehensive Citizen Audit of Investment Protection Treaties and the International Arbitration System on Investment Matters. (2017). *Comprehensive citizen audit of investment protection treaties and the arbitration system on investment matters in Ecuador: Executive summary*.

Daly, A., Valacchi, G., and Raffo, J. D. (2022). Recent trends of innovation in the mining sector. In A. Daly, D. Humphreys, J. Raffo, and G. Valacchi (Eds.), *Global challenges for innovation in mining industries* (pp. 25–51). Cambridge University Press.

24 There are some mining cluster initiatives in the region, but they are in earlier development stages than those in Australia (Labó Fossa, 2022). They include Corporación Clúster Minero Región de Antofagasta in Chile, SAMMI-Clúster Minero Andino (in the south of Peru) and, more recently, the Cajamarca mining cluster in Peru.

25 See Di John (2011) for the historical and empirical relevance of the resource curse.

Di John, J. (2011). Is there really a resource curse? A critical survey of theory and evidence. *Global Governance, 17*(2), 167–184.

Dosi, G. (1988), Sources, procedures and microeconomic effects of innovation. *Journal of Economic Literature, 26*(3).

Dunning, J. H. (1993). *Multinational enterprises and the global economy*. Addison Wesley.

Dunning, J. H. (1998). *Explaining international production*. Unwin Hyman.

Economic and Social Commission for Asia and the Pacific. (1992). *Mineral investment conditions in selected countries of the Asia-Pacific region*. https://hdl.handle.net/20.500.12870/3900

Economic Commission for Latin America and the Caribbean. (2024a). *Development Traps in Latin America and the Caribbean: Vital Transformations and How to Manage Them. Summary* (LC/SES.40/4).

Economic Commission for Latin America and the Caribbean. (2024b). *Panorama of Productive Development Policies in Latin America and the Caribbean, 2024* (LC/PUB.2024/15-P/Rev.1).

Economic Commission for Latin America and the Caribbean. (2024c). *Natural Resources Outlook in Latin America and the Caribbean, 2023* (LC/PUB.2024/4).

Economic Commission for Latin America and the Caribbean. (2024d). *Foreign Direct Investment in Latin America and the Caribbean, 2024* (LC/PUB.2024/8-P).

Gaukrodger, D. (2021). *The future of investment treaties: possible directions* (OECD Working Papers on International Investment, No. 2021/03). https://doi.org/10.1787/75d0fd8d-en

Government of Chile. (2023). *National Lithium Strategy, 2023*. https://www.gob.cl/chileavanzaconlitio/

International Energy Agency. (2021). *The role of critical minerals in clean energy transitions*. https://www.iea.org/reports/the-role-of-critical-minerals-in-clean-energy-transitions

International Energy Agency. (2024a). *Global Critical Minerals Outlook 2024*. https://www.iea.org/reports/global-critical-minerals-outlook-2024

International Energy Agency. (2024b). *Energy Technology Perspectives 2024*. https://www.iea.org/reports/energy-technology-perspectives-2024

International Energy Agency. (2024c). *Critical minerals data explorer*. https://www.iea.org/data-and-statistics/data-tools/critical-minerals-data-explorer

International Energy Agency. (2024d). *Energy Technology Perspectives 2024*. https://www.iea.org/reports/energy-technology-perspectives-2024

International Energy Agency. (2024e). *Global EV Outlook 2024*. https://www.iea.org/reports/global-ev-outlook-2024

Jara, J. J. (2017). Determinants of country competitiveness in attracting mining investments: an empirical analysis. *Resources Policy, 52*, 65–71. https://doi.org/10.1016/j.resourpol.2017.01.016

Kelley, K. D., Huston, D. L., and Peter, J. M. (2021). Toward an effective global green economy: The Critical Minerals Mapping Initiative (CMMI). *SEG Newsletter, 48*(1), 1–5.

Labó Fossa, R. (2022). Governance of mining clusters: the cases of Australia, Chile and Peru. *Project Documents* (LC/TS.2022/33). Economic Commission for Latin America and the Caribbean.

Mehranvar, L., Brauch, M. D., Achyuth, A., Kloppe, A. S., Clover Alcolea, L., and Songy, M. (2024). *Breaking free: Strategies for governments on terminating investment treaties and removing ISDS provisions*. Columbia Center on Sustainable Investment. https://ccsi.columbia.edu/sites/ccsi.columbia.edu/files/content/docs/publications/ccsi-breaking-free-investment-treaties.pdf

Ministry of Energy and Mines of Peru. (2024). *Cartera de proyectos de inversión minera*. https://cdn.www.gob.pe/uploads/document/file/6150647/5325671-cpim-2024.pdf?v=1712348649

Ministry of Mining and Energy of Brazil. (2024a, 27 February). *MME e BNDES lançam fundo de R$ 1 bi para investimentos em projetos de minerais estratégicos para a transição energética*. https://www.gov.br/mme/pt-br/assuntos/noticias/mme-e-bndes-lancam-fundo-de-r-1-bi-para-investimentos-em-projetos-de-minerais-estrategicos-para-a-transicao-energetica

Ministry of Mining and Energy of Brazil. (2024b, 27 November). *MME cria PlanGEO para impulsionar mapeamento geológico e o levantamento de recursos minerais no Brasil*. https://www.gov.br/mme/pt-br/assuntos/noticias/mme-cria-plangeo-para-impulsionar-mapeamento-geologico-e-o-levantamento-de-recursos-minerais-no-brasil

Nuñez, E. (2016). *Developing countries and international investment negotiations: Ecuador's strategy*. Universidad Andina Simón Bolívar.

Olivet, C., and Ghiotto, L. (2021). *Parallel justice: How the investment protection system threatens judicial independence in Latin America*. Public Services International and Transnational Institute. https://www.tni.org/files/publication-downloads/justiciaparalela_eng.pdf

Organisation for Economic Co-operation and Development. (2024a). *Strengthening sustainable investment through international investment agreements*. https://www.oecd.org/investment/strengthening-sustainable-investment.htm

Organisation for Economic Co-operation and Development. (2024b). *Promoting responsible business conduct in trade and investment: Latin America and the Caribbean* (OECD Business and Finance Policy Papers, No. 61). https://doi.org/10.1787/672fbe56-en

S&P Global Commodity Insights. (2024). *Exploration Insights: CES 2024 Summary Report.*

S&P Global Market Intelligence. (2024). *World Exploration Trends 2024. PDAC Special Edition.*

Salazar-Xirinachs, J. M., y Llinás, M. (2023). Transforming growth and development strategy in Latin America and the Caribbean: The role of productive development policies. *CEPAL Review* (141) (LC/PUB.2023/29-P/-*). Economic Commission for Latin America and the Caribbean.

Scott, M., and Jones, M. (2014). *Gestión de datos geocientíficos públicos.* International Mining for Development Centre. https://im4dc.org/wp-content/uploads/2014/01/Management-of-public-geoscience-data-Spanish-version.pdf

Secretary-General's Panel on Critical Energy Transition Minerals. (2024). *Resourcing the energy transition: principles to guide critical energy transition minerals towards equity and justice.* https://www.un.org/sites/un2.un.org/files/report_sg_panel_on_critical_energy_transition_minerals_11_sept_2024.pdf

Tritto, A. (2023). *How Indonesia used Chinese industrial investments to turn nickel into the new gold.* Carnegie Endowment for International Peace. https://carnegieendowment.org/2023/04/11/how-indonesia-used-chinese-industrial-investments-to-turn-nickel-into-new-gold-pub-89484

United Nations Conference on Trade and Development. (2012). *World Investment Report 2012: Towards a new generation of investment policies.*

United Nations Conference on Trade and Development. (2013). *World Investment Report 2013: Global value chains – Investment and trade for development.*

United Nations Conference on Trade and Development. (2017). *UNCTAD's reform package for the international investment regime.* https://investmentpolicy.unctad.org/uploaded-files/document/Reform_Package_web_18%20Dec.pdf

United Nations Conference on Trade and Development. (2020). *World Investment Report 2020: International production beyond the pandemic.*

United Nations Conference on Trade and Development. (2024). *Investment Policy Monitor.* https://unctad.org/system/files/official-document/diaepcbinf2024d7_en.pdf

United Nations. (2025a). *Harnessing the potential of critical minerals for sustainable development. In World Economic Situation and Prospects 2025* (chap. 2).

United Nations. (2025b). *World Economic Situation and Prospects 2025.* https://desapublications.un.org/publications/world-economic-situation-and-prospects-2025

Valenti, M. (2018). New trends in international investment law treaty practice: Where does Latin America stand? *Seqüência: Estudos Jurídicos e Políticos, 39*(79), 9–26.

Vivoda, V. (2017). Determinants of foreign direct investment in the mining industry. In T. O'Callaghan and G. Graetz (Eds.), *Mining in the Asia-Pacific* (pp. 25–45). Springer. https://doi.org/10.1007/978-3-319-61395-6_2

CHAPTER

III

Digital transformation and foreign direct investment: trends, challenges and opportunities for Latin America and the Caribbean

Introduction

Digital transformation has become a key driver of development in the twenty-first century. Advanced technologies —such as artificial intelligence (AI), cloud computing, big data analytics, the Internet of things and blockchain technology, among others— are gaining increasing prominence. Their impact is disruptive, as they are reshaping production models, service delivery, consumption patterns and business operations. The application of these technologies holds the potential to enhance productivity, efficiency and resilience across sectors, while also contributing to improved quality of life, greater environmental sustainability and increased social inclusion. In this context, digitalization opens new opportunities to promote innovation-driven economic growth and boost competitiveness, while supporting progress towards achieving the 2030 Agenda for Sustainable Development.

Digitalization is redefining the strategies of transnational firms and boosting foreign direct investment (FDI) flows, which can serve as an important source of financing to foster progress in this domain and promote productive transformation in developing countries. However, this potential can only be realized when FDI is complemented by strong institutions, comprehensive digital policy frameworks and targeted productive development policies, which collectively shape the absorptive capacity of a host economy. In their absence, the effects of FDI may be limited and could even exacerbate existing gaps.

The global FDI landscape related to digital transformation is evolving rapidly. In recent years, semiconductors and data centres have seen significant growth, particularly in announcements of large-scale investment projects. This stems from a combination of technological, economic and geopolitical factors. The rise of technologies such as artificial intelligence, fifth-generation mobile networks (5G) and cloud computing has spurred global demand for advanced chips that are essential for large-scale data processing. The acceleration of digitalization in productive sectors and the expansion of digital service provision are increasing the demand for more robust and resilient infrastructure, increasing the need for computing power and data centres. As a result, data centres and semiconductor manufacturing have become strategic assets for technological leadership, digital sovereignty and national security. Consequently, several governments have identified these industries as priorities and implemented incentives and regulations that are reshaping investment patterns and the organization of production worldwide.

However, the benefits of this trend are not being distributed evenly across regions. Although Latin America and the Caribbean has made progress in digitalization, significant gaps remain in terms of technology adoption and enabling conditions, which contribute to the region's limited share of global FDI flows linked to digital transformation. The evolution of digital policies in the region over recent decades shows that, despite notable progress, challenges remain in terms of institutional coordination and alignment with productive development policies. It is therefore essential to explore how countries in the region can better position themselves in this evolving landscape, attract FDI and maximize its positive impacts as a foundation for digital and productive transformation, while also mitigating potential negative effects.

This chapter analyses FDI trends associated with digital transformation in Latin America and the Caribbean between 2005 and 2024. Following this introduction, section A examines the role that FDI can play in supporting a digital transformation that promotes sustainable, inclusive and productive development. Section B discusses key factors that attract foreign investors. Section C explores international FDI trends linked to digital transformation in the context of global change, while section D reviews the evolution of these flows in the region, focusing on two types of investments: announcements of new projects and cross-border mergers and acquisitions. Section E addresses policy options for attracting FDI for digital transformation and the alignment of such policies with productive development strategies, highlighting the role of investment promotion agencies. Section F concludes with policy considerations and recommendations to guide national and subnational efforts in this area.

A. The role of foreign direct investment in digital transformation and productive development

Digital transformation is broadly understood as the process by which advanced digital technologies are integrated into all aspects of economic and social life. This is a global phenomenon that entails a profound reconfiguration of how value is created and captured, affecting economies, societies, institutions and the environment (Economic Commission for Latin America and the Caribbean [ECLAC], 2022a). Given its cross-cutting, dynamic and synergistic nature, digital transformation does not occur in isolation within a single economic sector. Instead, it relies on increasing interconnections across sectors, supported by digital infrastructure (ECLAC, 2021). The process involves adaptation and experimentation and brings with it structural, cultural and organizational changes. In this context, it is essential to ensure the effective adoption of digital technologies and appropriate governance to fully leverage their potential in multiple domains (ECLAC, 2025), thereby helping to address the three development traps faced by the region (ECLAC, 2024a).[1]

From an economic perspective, digitalization can enhance productivity and competitiveness by enabling access to global markets, fostering productive sophistication and encouraging innovation, diversification and efficiency in key sectors (ECLAC, 2025). From a social standpoint, digital technologies should promote inclusion, well-being and advancement of people and societies, ensuring the respect, protection and promotion of human rights (United Nations, 2024). From an institutional and governance perspective, digitalization can increase transparency, efficiency and citizen participation by strengthening trust, enabling social dialogue and improving the quality of public services to better meet the population's needs (ECLAC, 2025). From an environmental perspective, digitalization is a tool for the green transition, as it supports the changes needed in production and consumption patterns to foster healthier, safer and more sustainable environments, and it facilitates progress towards circular economy models (ECLAC, 2022a). Ultimately, digital technologies have the potential to drive more productive, inclusive and sustainable development, provided they are deployed in ways that respond to the specific challenges and needs of each context.

Advancing in this direction requires the mobilization of multiple actors and financing sources, among which investments by transnational corporations can play an important role. However, like other forms of financing, FDI is not neutral. Its impacts on recipient economies and their digitalization processes can be both positive and negative and may be manifested in quantitative or qualitative terms (Padilla Pérez and Gomes Nogueira, 2015).

Quantitative impacts include increased productivity, gross capital formation —such as investment in communications infrastructure, connectivity, innovation and emerging technologies—, improved balance of payments owing to digital goods or service exports, and job creation in digital or related industries. Qualitative impacts may involve changes in the productive and technological environment, such as technology transfer, the strengthening of local capacities and training of specialized human talent.

Such impacts may be transmitted to host economies through various channels. Among the most significant are the creation of productive linkages between multinational and local firms, the integration of domestic enterprises into collaborative networks within digital and productive ecosystems, and a range of spillover effects stemming from these interactions (ECLAC, 2024b).

However, the uptake of these effects is not automatic and largely depends on the absorptive capacity of the host economy. This capacity is shaped by macroeconomic, institutional and governance

[1] According to ECLAC (2024a), the region is facing three development traps: low capacity for growth; high inequality and low social mobility and cohesion; and weak institutional capacities and governance.

factors, as well as the existence of a robust innovation system, learning capabilities and policies that foster their development. These include FDI promotion, regulation and management policies, in addition to productive development policies (ECLAC, 2024b).

Despite its enabling potential, foreign investment in digitalization can also generate adverse effects. Economically, it can contribute to market concentration, crowd out local firms and capabilities, weaken endogenous technological development and encourage export models reliant on imported inputs and the remittance of profits abroad (ECLAC, 2024b). In the labour sphere, the adoption of advanced technologies and automation presents important challenges, as it may lead to job displacement —though the net effects remain uncertain— and deepen job polarization. This highlights the importance of expanding access to reskilling and upskilling opportunities, especially for vulnerable groups (ECLAC, 2022a).

FDI can also generate negative effects in environmental, territorial and sovereignty-related dimensions. The expansion of digital infrastructure poses environmental risks, including high energy consumption in data centres and growing volumes of electronic waste owing to the rapid obsolescence of devices (United Nations Conference on Trade and Development [UNCTAD], 2024a). These risks and challenges are more pronounced in countries that attract FDI in lower value-added segments, such as digital component manufacturing or raw material extraction, which limits the benefits and exacerbates inequalities (Organisation for Economic Co-operation and Development [OECD], 2025). At the territorial level, FDI tends to be concentrated in major urban or technology hubs, which may widen digital and income divides and deepen regional disparities (ECLAC, 2024b; OECD, 2025). Lastly, there are growing concerns about digital sovereignty and data security, particularly regarding the control and use of data (ECLAC, 2018; UNCTAD, 2021a).

The foregoing underscores the need for appropriate strategies and policy frameworks to unlock the potential of FDI for digital transformation and productive development. As previously mentioned, this involves not only attracting investment, but also strengthening absorptive capacities, infrastructure and institutional frameworks to facilitate its effective use. In settings where these conditions are lacking, both the inflow and the impact of FDI tend to be limited, and existing inequalities within or among countries may be exacerbated.

Conversely, when FDI is aligned with policy frameworks that guide its integration, foster the development of local capacities and mobilize complementary investments, its impact can be significantly enhanced. When aligned with sectors and technologies that are prioritized in digital and productive development policies within a comprehensive approach, FDI can serve as a catalyst and amplify the effects of these policies on productivity.

Achieving this goal requires tailoring policies to the characteristics of each context and considering the factors that determine the location of digital technology investments —factors that vary by sector, company and type of project. These issues are analysed below.

B. Key determinants of the location of investments related to digital transformation

A company's decision to internationalize through FDI is influenced by a combination of sector- and firm-specific factors, along with broader strategic considerations. While the digitalization process is increasingly blurring the traditional boundaries between industries, the sectors and activities associated with digital transformation can be broadly classified into three main areas (see diagram III.1).

Diagram III.1
Digital transformation: areas, key sectors and types of firms

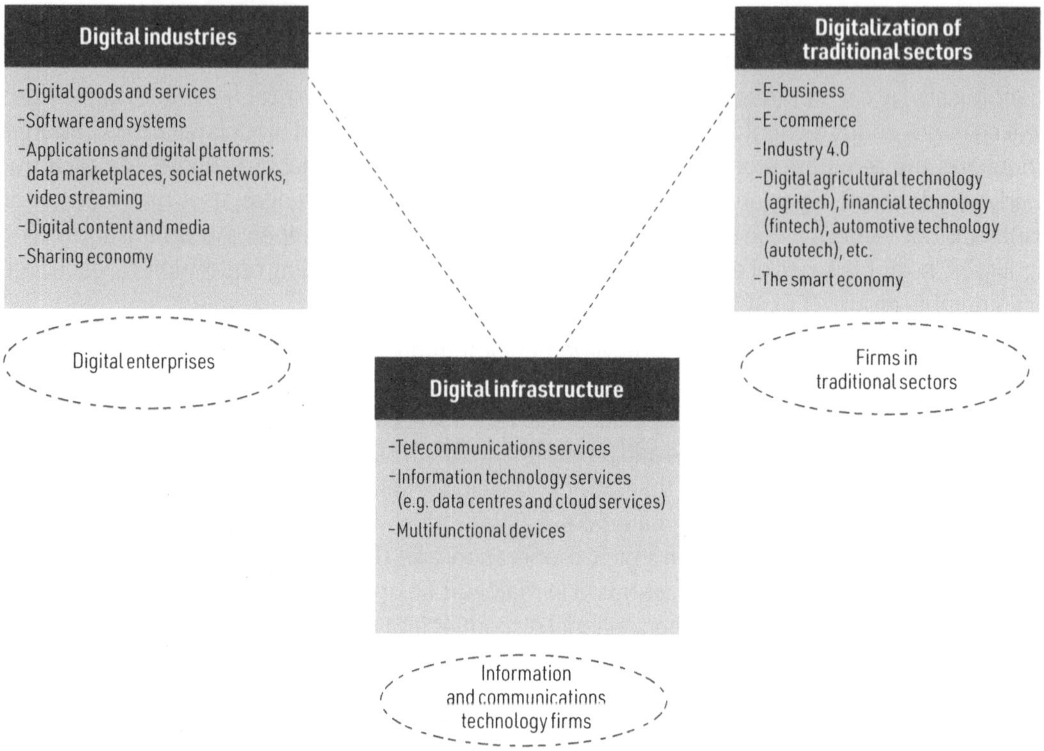

Source: Economic Commission for Latin America and the Caribbean, on the basis of Economic Commission for Latin America and the Caribbean. (2021). *Foreign Direct Investment in Latin America and the Caribbean, 2021* (LC/PUB.2021/8-P).

Digital infrastructure forms the physical and logical foundation of digital transformation. It includes fixed and mobile broadband networks, data centres, cloud services and connected devices. The communications, hardware (microprocessors, semiconductors and integrated circuits, among others) and software sectors and associated firms play a fundamental role in this area.

Digital industries generate economic output through digital business models based on digital goods and services and online platforms (Bukht and Heeks, 2017). Since 2017, these industries have undergone rapid transformation, driven by the expansion of software and cloud computing services and, more recently, by the widespread adoption of AI-based solutions, including generative AI applications in production processes, services and content. Alongside established tech giants such as Alphabet, Amazon, Apple, Microsoft and Meta, new players have emerged specializing in software development, foundation model training, data analytics and cognitive automation. These actors are reshaping traditional sectors such as retail trade and logistics, tourism, financial services and healthcare. Such data-intensive activities rely on shared digital infrastructure, connecting supply and demand on a global scale and forming what is commonly referred to as the "digital ecosystem": a complex and evolving network composed of digital infrastructure and platforms (intermediation, distribution and development) associated with the delivery of content and services over the Internet, alongside a web of public and private actors that interact along a highly interdependent, technologically dynamic and increasingly integrated transnational value chain.

The third area concerns the transformation of traditional economic sectors by modifying processes, products and business models through advanced digital technologies. Traditional firms with international operations are incorporating digital tools to enhance efficiency and competitiveness (McKinsey, 2023). These advances range from the automation of productive tasks to the digitalization of marketing, sales and after-sales service channels, thereby reshaping global value chains. In this context, firms investing —or with the potential to invest— in digitalization processes span a broad array of sectors, including natural resource-intensive industries such as mining, as well as manufacturing and services.

According to a survey by the World Economic Forum, investors assign varying levels of priority to the key factors that influence investment decisions related to digital infrastructure, new digital activities and the adoption of technology (Stephenson, 2020). Each decision is governed by its own logic and conditioning factors (see table III.1).

Table III.1
Examples of key factors influencing investment decisions in the digital sector

Areas	Digital infrastructure	Digital industries	Adoption of digital technologies
Policy environment	Ease and efficiency of licensing Clear rules for network deployment and spectrum use International standards and regional coordination for investment	Intellectual property protection and data security	Regulations that incentivize adoption (e.g. tax incentives)
Local capabilities	Availability of skilled technicians and engineers	Support for entrepreneurial talent and research and development capacity	Digital training and reskilling programmes
Physical infrastructure and support	International, national and urban connectivity	Data centres, digital logistics, access to financing	Access to basic digital services (e.g. e-payments and cloud services)

Source: Economic Commission for Latin America and the Caribbean, on the basis of Stephenson, M. (2020, September). *Digital FDI: policies, regulations and measures to attract FDI in the digital economy*. White paper. World Economic Forum.

These factors are merely illustrative and underscore that investment decisions in the digital sector are strongly influenced by both basic and technological infrastructure requirements, the quality of connectivity, the availability of digitally skilled talent and the regulatory and policy frameworks specific to each sector.

Such aspects must be integrated into the strategic framework that guides investment decisions aimed at market-seeking, resource-seeking, efficiency-seeking and risk diversification, as well as the acquisition of strategic assets, as adapted from Dunning's classification (2002). Given the highly technological and data-intensive nature of these investments, intangible assets —especially knowledge— are of critical importance. Resource-seeking in this context involves access to digital infrastructure and to essential services, such as electricity, under reliable and cost-effective conditions. Market-seeking requires digital payment mechanisms, logistics capabilities, a sufficient market size and adequate user growth prospects. Efficiency-seeking and risk diversification highlight the need for clear and favourable regulatory environments and raise considerations related to data, property rights and tax matters, among others. These elements are reflected in the motives and determinants of FDI location cited by multinational enterprises and their representatives when announcing or launching a new project (see figure III.1).

Naturally, this does not imply that traditional investment attraction factors have ceased to be relevant. Investment protection frameworks, stability and predictability of business environments, openness to foreign capital and non-discrimination, as well as legal certainty, among others, continue to be important considerations for technology and digital firms, alongside cost advantages (Kallmer, 2024). In the current context, marked by high levels of uncertainty, these factors may become even more significant.

Figure III.1
Main motives and determinants of global foreign direct investment location in digital technology-related sectors, 2005–2024
(Percentages of total projects for which data are available)

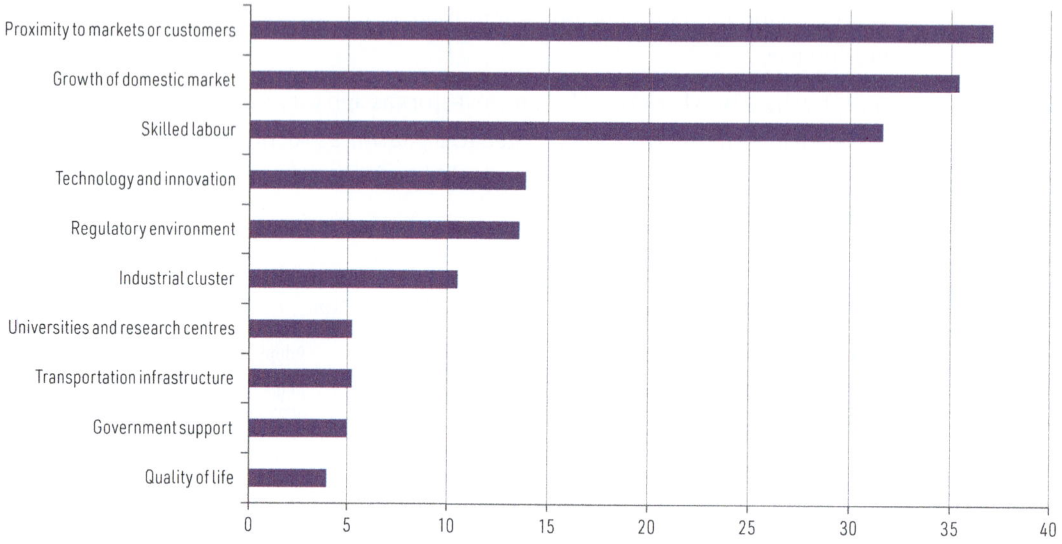

Source: Economic Commission for Latin America and the Caribbean, on the basis of *Financial Times*. fDi Markets. https://www.fdimarkets.com/.
Note: Data are based on company-reported information for 15,513 FDI project announcements out of a total of 79,430 in the following sectors: communications, software and information technology services, semiconductors, electronic components, consumer electronics and business machines and equipment. Motives and determinants are not mutually exclusive, as more than one may be recorded for a single project.

Indeed, the rise of business models based on digital services, data and platforms is reshaping global value chains and adding complexity to the investment landscape, even as these models coexist with the traditional economy. These digital models allow companies to expand globally with lower levels of physical investment, which presents regulatory and governance challenges and makes it difficult to measure and qualify the actual impact of foreign investment. In this context, analysing FDI trends linked to digital transformation is essential to understand the region's position in the face of global market shifts and to identify strategic opportunities.

C. Global trends in foreign direct investment in sectors linked to digital technologies

The expansion of the digital economy presents methodological challenges when measuring and analysing FDI flows. The traditional approach, based on the balance of payments, records cross-border financial flows; however, in many countries it does not provide a sectoral breakdown and does not distinguish between investments that increase productive capacity and those that do not lead to the creation of new physical assets, such as mergers and acquisitions. These limitations are particularly relevant in the case of the digital economy, where companies can internationalize without a significant physical presence; furthermore, the cross-cutting nature of digital technologies makes it difficult to accurately classify investment flows. Nevertheless, sectoral analysis remains useful for identifying patterns of productive transformation in digital FDI.

Given these constraints, an alternative is to use complementary sources, such as data on cross-border mergers and acquisitions or investment project announcements.[2] Although this approach does not fully capture all dimensions of digital transformation, particularly digitalization processes in traditional sectors or smaller-scale investments, it makes it possible to identify investment trends and characteristics, such as amounts, associated employment, sector, type of activity and geographical distribution within host countries, thereby providing an approximation of potential impacts. This section and the one that follows draw on the analysis of investment project announcements and cross-border mergers and acquisitions between 2005 and 2024. The findings should be interpreted with caution, as some project announcements may not materialize or may be modified.

1. Sectoral reconfiguration and value chain shifts

Over the past decade, sectors linked to digital technologies have become increasingly important. Taken together, digital infrastructure and the digital industry have grown at roughly three times the pace of the overall economy in the countries of the Organisation for Economic Co-operation and Development (OECD), recording an average growth rate of 7.6% in 2023 (OECD, 2024).[3] That same year, global exports of digital services totalled US$ 4.5 trillion, accounting for 56% of total global services exports —nearly double the US$ 2.3 trillion recorded in 2013 (UNCTAD, 2024b). According to the same source, developing economies surpassed the US$ 1 trillion threshold in digital services exports, while Latin America and the Caribbean exported nearly US$ 90 billion in 2023, compared to approximately US$ 57 billion 10 years earlier, marking a 58% increase. Nevertheless, the region's share in total global exports remained low and fell from 2.5% in 2013 to 2.0% in 2023, reflecting a relative loss of positioning compared to more dynamic regions, despite absolute growth.

In the global investment landscape, the advance of digital technologies is reflected in the increased prominence of sectors that are directly linked to them: communications, electronic components, consumer electronics, business machines and equipment, semiconductors, and software and information technology services. As highlighted in chapter I, the communications and semiconductors sectors grew significantly and in 2024 became the second- and third-largest sectors in terms of investment amounts, respectively. That same year, electronic components and software and information technology services remained among the top destination sectors (ranking ninth and tenth, respectively). Collectively, these technology-linked sectors accounted for 18% of total investment announcement amounts between 2005 and 2024. The total global amount directed to these sectors more than quadrupled during this period, reaching a peak of US$ 384 billion in 2024.

The recent surge in digital FDI is driven by the rapid advancement of technologies such as AI and cloud computing, alongside the growth in the trade in digital services.[4] This is further reinforced by the reconfiguration of corporate internationalization strategies amid rising geopolitical tensions, in a context of global FDI stagnation (UNCTAD, 2024c).

Artificial intelligence stands out owing to its disruptive potential in the current landscape. The global AI market is projected to grow from US$ 189 billion in 2023 to US$ 4.8 trillion by 2033, a 25-fold increase over 10 years (UNCTAD, 2025). Moreover, the share of artificial intelligence in the advanced technology market is expected to rise from 7% to 29%, consolidating its dominant role in the sector. This trend explains the growing demand for data processing and storage capacity and why the largest amounts of announced FDI in the digital economy continue to be concentrated in more consolidated sectors,

2 Another potential approach is to make progress in defining new indicators to analyse the internationalization process, including trade in services and intangible and digital goods. In this regard, see UNCTAD (2021b).

3 This study uses the concept of information and communications technologies.

4 Although the coronavirus disease (COVID-19) pandemic is now in the past, its effects were decisive in the worldwide acceleration of digitalization processes, such as those associated with e-commerce, remote work and the provision of online services. These structural changes laid the foundations for the subsequent growth of digital investments, although in recent years some segments have shown signs of slowing or decline.

such as communications. These not only provide connectivity but also play a central role in supporting critical infrastructure for AI, such as data centres and high-speed networks (see figure III.2). This sector has maintained its leadership both before and after the pandemic, although more recently with a renewed focus on large-scale and strategically significant projects, such as data centres. In 2024, data centres accounted for the largest share of announced investment amounts, with a global total over US$ 144 billion. According to McKinsey (2024), global demand for data centre capacity is expected to grow by 19% to 22% annually through 2030, requiring between 171 and 219 gigawatts per year.

Figure III.2
Value of global foreign direct investment project announcements related to digital technologies, by period average and sector, 2005–2024
(Billions of dollars)

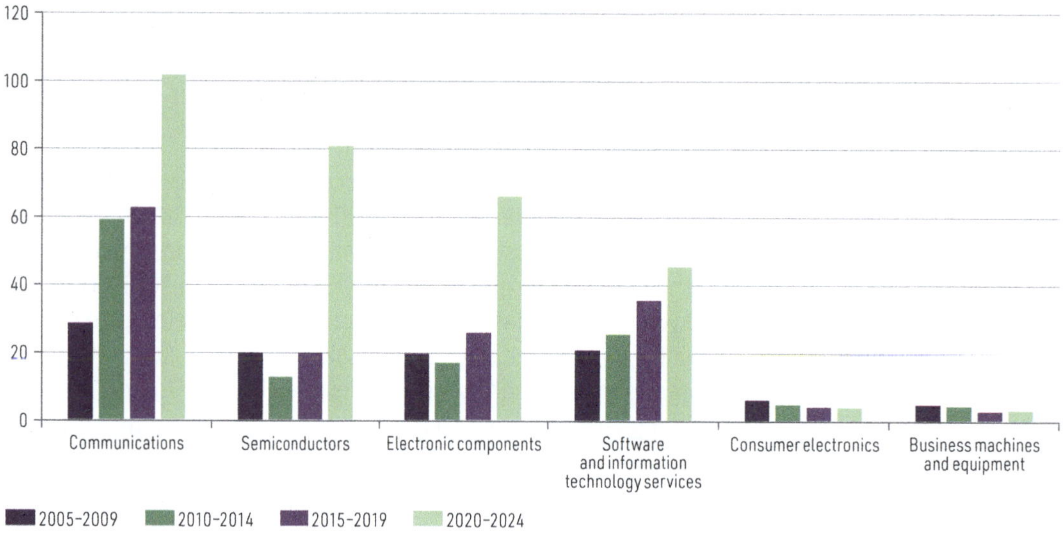

Source: Economic Commission for Latin America and the Caribbean, on the basis of *Financial Times*. fDi Markets. https://www.fdimarkets.com/.

The distribution of the value of announced projects across the remaining sectors has shifted over time. Up to 2019, the software and information technology services sector ranked second, followed by electronic components. However, in the period 2020–2024, semiconductors emerged as the second-largest sector, growing by more than 300% compared to 2015–2019. The expansion of investment in this area reflects its rising strategic importance —both technological and political— as companies increasingly benefit from targeted incentives to build new facilities in the United States, Singapore, Japan and several European Union countries (ECLAC, 2022b). Under these circumstances, software and information technology services were pushed to fourth place, although the sector continues to lead in terms of the number of projects announced in the period 2005–2024, accounting for 14% of announcements worldwide.

This sectoral trend is also evident in the distribution of FDI projects across different segments of the value chain. Across all segments, more projects were announced in 2020–2024 than in 2010–2019. However, the strongest growth occurred in the production segment (269%) and in infrastructure and capacities (76%), pointing to a shift in investment —both to meet the rising demand for digital products and services and to support the sector's expansion— toward enabling infrastructure, within a context of favourable public policies and government incentives. Activities related to production and infrastructure and capacities also attracted the highest amounts of announced investment, accounting for 40% and 35%, respectively, of the cumulative total between 2005 and 2024 (see figure III.3).

Figure III.3
Value of global foreign direct investment project announcements related to digital technologies, by value chain segment, 2005–2024
(Billions of dollars)

Source: Economic Commission for Latin America and the Caribbean, on the basis of *Financial Times*. fDi Markets. https://www.fdimarkets.com/.

Note: The sectors included are communications, software and information technology services, semiconductors, electronic components, consumer electronics, and business machines and equipment. Each segment is composed of the following business activities: infrastructure and capacities (education and training, electricity, information and communications technology (ICT) and Internet infrastructure); pre-production (headquarters, research and development); production (construction, extraction, manufacturing, recycling); services (business services, customer contact centre, logistics, distribution and transportation, maintenance and servicing, retail, sales, marketing and support, shared services centre, technical support centre).

The recent increase in investments in the production segment appears to be largely driven by the reconfiguration of global supply chains and the prioritization of strategic sectors and assets such as hardware manufacturing, semiconductors and critical infrastructure. The disruption caused by the COVID-19 pandemic and rising geopolitical tensions have accelerated diversification and relocation strategies, driving investment in new manufacturing plants and hubs in several regions. According to new project announcements, key industries for the digital transformation appear to be following a different trajectory than the broader, long-term trend of a gradual deglobalization of manufacturing observed in overall FDI flows (UNCTAD, 2024c). This raises important questions, such as whether digital FDI is concentrated in low value-added stages or whether it also encompasses strategic and more sophisticated functions, and whether its expansion may replicate —or even exacerbate— the growing marginalization of developing economies observed in FDI flows of the economy as a whole. This marginalization carries the risk of widening existing gaps affecting developing countries, particularly where productive and technological capabilities are weaker, unless governments adopt a clear stance and implement appropriate strategies and policies.

2. Geographical reconfiguration and emerging actors

The strategic nature of investments related to digital technologies is also reflected in the geographical distribution of project announcements. Between 2005 and 2024, Asia and the Pacific, Western Europe and North America were the main destinations for announced investments, while Latin America and the Caribbean accounted for a limited share, accounting for just 7% of the total amount associated with announcements (see figure III.4). The United States, China and India, in that order, have consolidated their positions as the leading destinations for investment announcements in the digital sector. This performance is closely tied to active policies that combine investment attraction with digital strategies and a focus on strengthening technological and productive capacities.

Figure III.4
Distribution of global foreign direct investment project announcements related to digital technologies, by destination region, 2005–2024
(Percentages)

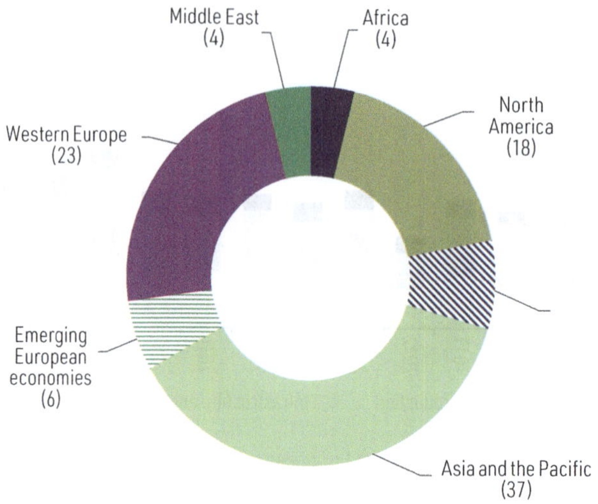

Source: Economic Commission for Latin America and the Caribbean, on the basis of *Financial Times*. fDi Markets. https://www.fdimarkets.com/.
Note: The sectors included are communications, software and information technology services, semiconductors, electronic components, consumer electronics, and business machines and equipment.

The case of India illustrates the importance of sound public policy design and sustained implementation. The country has encouraged digital transformation within the framework of a diversified economy and a well-established technology ecosystem focused on service delivery. Its success is attributed both to structural factors —such as market size, strong economic growth, availability of skilled human talent and a growing information and technology services industry— and to the adoption of active policies and strategies (see box III.1).

Box III.1
India: the central role of public policy in digitalization and technological development

Among the policies driving digitalization in India, the Digital India programme, launched in 2015 and still in effect, has been a cornerstone for the promotion of digital infrastructure, the digitalization of public services and technological literacy (India Brand Equity Foundation, n.d.). This has been complemented by policies encouraging local production (Make in India) and fostering the entrepreneurial ecosystem (Startup India), as well as specific measures targeting data centres and semiconductors. The presence of technology parks and service zones offering investment incentives has helped to establish a favourable environment for foreign direct investment and position the country as a global hub for technology services. In recent years, momentum has intensified around the development of data centres and advancements in artificial intelligence, reflecting India's ambition to become both a major consumer and exporter of this technology (Parkin and Hodgson, 2024).

Source: Economic Commission for Latin America and the Caribbean, on the basis of India Brand Equity Foundation. (n.d.). Digital India. https://www.ibef.org/government-schemes/digital-india and Parkin, B. and Hodgson, C. (2024, 17 June). India pulls in tech giants for its AI ambitions. *Financial Times*.

A combined analysis of the regions of origin and destination of announced investments highlights the role of Asia and the Pacific, where there is a strong tendency towards intraregional investment and economic integration is being reinforced. This is less evident in other regions and may suggest a possible path forward for Latin America and the Caribbean (see figure III.5). In addition to illustrating the growing influence of Asian investors in the global digital technology landscape, this trend also intensifies competition among the world's largest economies and geopolitical tensions. Against this background, the United States remains a key country of origin for digital FDI: between 2005 and 2024, companies based in the United States accounted for 33% of the total investment amount, followed by firms based in Taiwan Province of China (8%), the Republic of Korea (7%), China (6%) and Japan (5%), underscoring Asia's strategic importance once again.

Figure III.5
Global foreign direct investment project announcements related to digital technologies, by region of origin and destination, 2005–2024
(Proportions based on investment amounts)

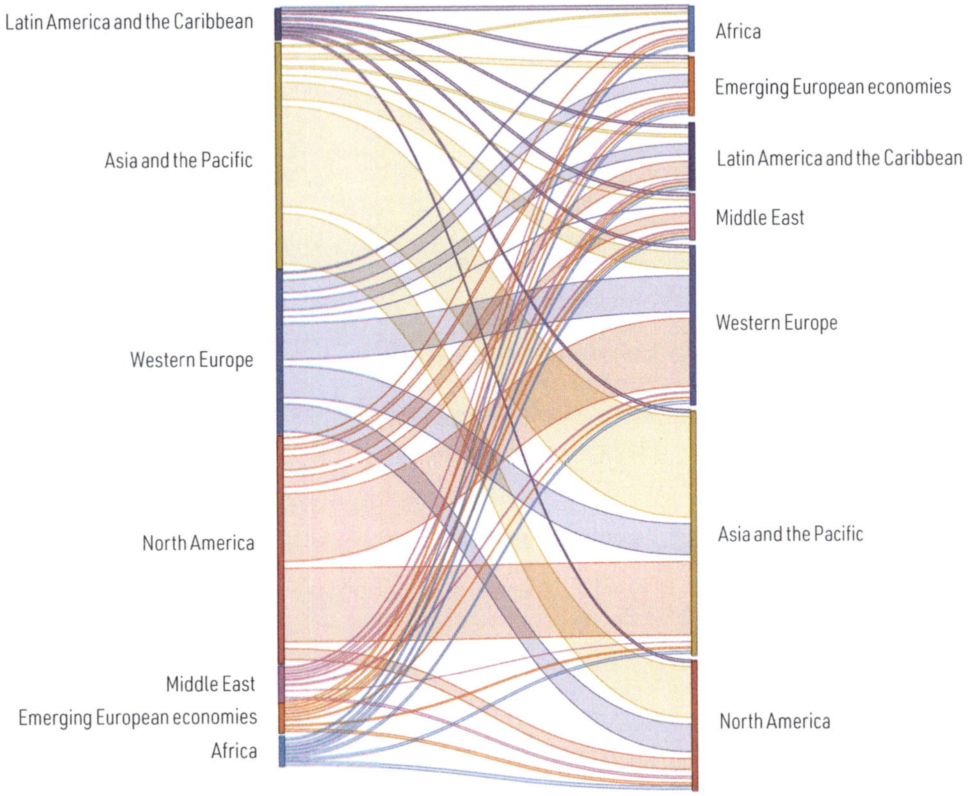

Source: Economic Commission for Latin America and the Caribbean, on the basis of *Financial Times*. fDi Markets. https://www.fdimarkets.com/.
Note: The sectors included are communications, software and information technology services, semiconductors, electronic components, consumer electronics, and business machines and equipment.

The companies leading investments in digital transformation play a central role in shaping FDI flows. Among the key players in global digital expansion are large, internationally active firms whose strategies combine greenfield investments with acquisitions. These firms leverage opportunities and resources across markets to develop innovations and solutions in AI, cloud computing, the Internet of things and 5G, while also expanding productive capacities in sectors such as semiconductors (see table III.2). In this pattern of growth, the acquisition of digital assets has becoming increasingly important (see box III.2).

Table III.2
Top 10 global investors in sectors related to digital technologies, by parent company and capital committed to project announcements, 2005–2024

Parent company	Country or territory of origin	Company profile and focus	Project announcements 2005-2024		Project announcements 2024
			Value (*Million of dollars*)	Number	Value (*Million of dollars*)
Samsung Group	Republic of Korea	Diversified conglomerate with investments in electronics, household appliances and telecommunications	132 908	482	30 375
Intel	United States	Technology firm specializing in the production of semiconductors, microprocessors and computing solutions	131 133	182	451
Taiwan Semiconductor Manufacturing Company (TSMC)	Taiwan Province of China	Leading semiconductor manufacturer	103 269	22	25 000
Amazon	United States	E-commerce giant with significant investments in cloud computing and artificial intelligence	78 049	304	21 250
Hon Hai Precision Industry (Foxconn)	Taiwan Province of China	World's largest electronics manufacturer	57 267	178	1 048
Microsoft	United States	Leading software company and cloud services provider	55 027	479	17 266
LG	Republic of Korea	Diversified conglomerate with investments in electronics, household appliances and telecommunications	52 118	242	879
Telefónica	Spain	Major telecommunications provider	42 421	250	19.2
Nippon Telegraph and Telephone Corporation (NTT)	Japan	Major telecommunications provider	33 566	297	1 868
Vodafone	United Kingdom	Major telecommunications provider	28 732	319	678

Source: Economic Commission for Latin America and the Caribbean, on the basis of *Financial Times*. fDi Markets. https://www.fdimarkets.com/ and company websites.

Box III.2

Artificial intelligence and digital infrastructure: trends in cross-border mergers and acquisitions

Recent trends in cross-border mergers and acquisitions by transnational corporations highlight the growing appeal of AI and the intensifying competition among major technology firms to consolidate their leadership in digital infrastructure (Institute for Mergers, Acquisitions & Alliances, 2024; Levy, 2025). Microsoft, Google, Amazon and Nvidia have pursued some of the most aggressive strategies in acquiring AI startups and expanding their capacities in cloud computing and high-performance chips (CBInsights, 2024a). Key cross-border transactions related to AI in 2024 include the acquisition of WalkMe by SAP, Run:ai by Nvidia and Silo AI by AMD (see table). Large technology companies continue to expand into sectors traditionally considered non-digital, such as energy and healthcare, where ongoing digitalization offers significant potential for growth and returns (CBInsights, 2024b, 2024c).

Three major cross-border mergers and acquisitions related to artificial intelligence, 2024

Acquiring firm	Country of origin	Firm acquired	Profile and focus of acquired firm	Country of assets	Value (Millions of dollars)	Purpose of the transaction
SAP	Germany	WalkMe	Leader in digital adoption platforms	Israel	1 500	Artificial intelligence for automation and user experience
Nvidia	United States	Run:ai	Artificial intelligence infrastructure start-up	Israel	700	Artificial intelligence infrastructure management
AMD	United States	Silo AI	Largest artificial intelligence laboratory in Europe	Finland	665	Talent and software to provide high-performance artificial intelligence solutions based on open standards

Source: Economic Commission for Latin America and the Caribbean, on the basis of Whiting, R. (2024, 24 December). *The 24 Biggest Tech M&A Deals of 2024*. CRN. https://www.crn.com/news/software/2024/the-24-biggest-tech-m-a-deals-of-2024?page=1.

Source: Economic Commission for Latin America and the Caribbean, on the basis of Institute for Mergers, Acquisitions & Alliances. (2024). *AI M&A Software Deals: Analysis of Numbers and Values*; Levy, B. (2025, 28 January). *M&A in 2025: big deals, winning hands, and wild cards*. PwC. https://www.pwc.com/gx/en/services/deals/trends.html; CBInsights (2024a, 12 March). *The Big Tech AI Arms Race: 75+ AI Startups Backed by Amazon, Google, Microsoft, and Nvidia*; CBInsights (2024b, 12 June). *Big Tech in Healthcare: How Amazon, Google, Microsoft, & Nvidia are Looking to Transform Drug R&D, Primary Care, and More*; CBInsights (2024c, 4 September). *Big Tech in Energy: How Amazon, Google, Microsoft, & Nvidia are Advancing the Global Energy Transition*; Whiting, R. (2024, 24 December). *The 24 Biggest Tech M&A Deals of 2024*. CRN. https://www.crn.com/news/software/2024/the-24-biggest-tech-m-a-deals-of-2024?page=1.

To sum up, during the period 2005–2024, the share of global FDI linked to the digital transformation has grown, and there has been a major mobilization of resources targeting strategic areas like digital infrastructure —in particular data centres— and semiconductors, primarily flowing to developed countries. This period has witnessed growing competition and a rapidly evolving global landscape, with leading countries and top technology firms jockeying for control over infrastructure and other strategic assets, and transnational corporations increasingly turning to external markets, primarily in Asia and the Pacific, North America and Europe, and to a lesser extent, Latin America and the Caribbean.

D. FDI in sectors linked to digital technologies in Latin America and the Caribbean: productive development opportunities and challenges

The transformative potential of digital technologies is a highly valuable resource in enabling the region to address its structural development challenges, and artificial intelligence is especially promising in that regard. Its estimated economic contribution in 17 selected countries of the region was over US$ 70 billion in 2023 (1.11% of GDP) and could reach US$ 565 billion in 2030 (1.03% of cumulative GDP for the period 2024–2030), according to conservative forecasts (Katz and Jung, 2024).

Despite this progress, the region's efforts to establish the enabling conditions for digital FDI continue to face substantial hurdles, including deficiencies in the following areas: adoption of technology (in multiple sectors but especially production); domestic demand for digital solutions; digital, energy and logistics infrastructure; productive and innovative capacity; digital labour and skills; and regulations and institutional capacities.

These gaps are also reflected in the region's share of international trade in digital goods and services, which remains marginal compared to other developing economies. Since 2005, growth in modern services exports has outpaced goods and other services exports. The share of digitally provided services in the region's services exports increased from 24% in 2005 to 37% in 2023 but remains below the global average of 54% (ECLAC, 2024c). In addition, the leading centres of innovation and the greatest concentration of digital skills in the region tend to be found in major cities or strategic locations, and the resulting low-technology export profile means that Latin America and the Caribbean is more of a consumer than a producer when it comes to strategic digital services and assets.

This situation curtails value addition and high-quality job creation and affects FDI attraction, as many investors seek not just consumer market access but also integration into digital ecosystems that have the capacity to produce, innovate and adequately scale up technological solutions, whether regionally or globally. The above context calls for a regional analysis of changing patterns of FDI related to digital technologies, the types of FDI projects in this sector and the extent to which these investments can galvanize productive transformation in Latin America and the Caribbean.

1. Relative weight and location of digital FDI in the region

FDI project announcements linked to digital technologies in the region increased between 2005 and 2024, albeit with notable fluctuations (see figure III.6). In terms of value, these announcements were on a decidedly upward trajectory until 2011, which marked the beginning of a period of stability that lasted until 2020. On the back of a sustained recovery initiated in 2020, the value of announcements registered 36% year-on-year growth in 2024, for a 10-year high of US$ 20.253 billion. This trend reflects renewed interest in the region amid the acceleration of digitalization worldwide.

Figure III.6
Latin America and the Caribbean: FDI announcements related to digital technologies, 2005–2024
(Number of projects and billions of dollars)

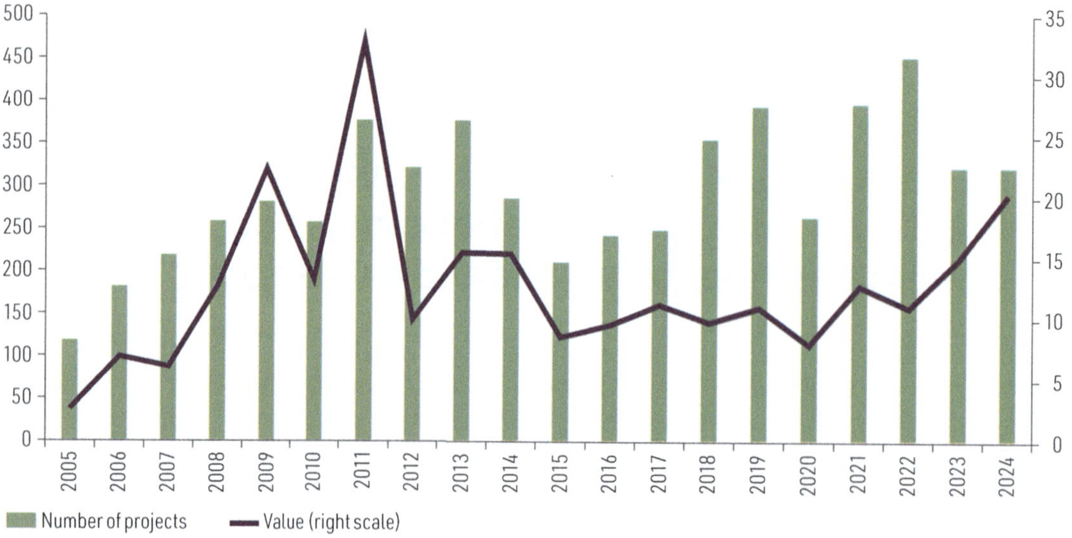

Source: Economic Commission for Latin America and the Caribbean, on the basis of *Financial Times*. fDi Markets. https://www.fdimarkets.com/.

Note: The sectors included are communications, software and information technology services, semiconductors, electronic components, consumer electronics, and business machines and equipment.

The decoupling of the number of project announcements from their value is notable, suggesting a higher number of announcements in less capital-intensive sectors (e.g. digital services and software), while the highest values are associated with larger one-off projects in areas such as network infrastructure, connectivity and data centres.

Although FDI linked to the digital transformation has gone up in recent years, its share in the total value of project announcements in the region has averaged approximately 15% since 2010. At the same time, since 2005, the number of cross-border mergers and acquisitions[5] in the sector has grown significantly, accounting for 11% of total transactions in 2005 but 26% in 2024 following a record high of 28% in 2022 (see figure III.7).

Figure III.7
Latin America and the Caribbean: cross-border mergers and acquisitions related to digital technologies as a share of total transactions, 2005–2024
(Percentages)

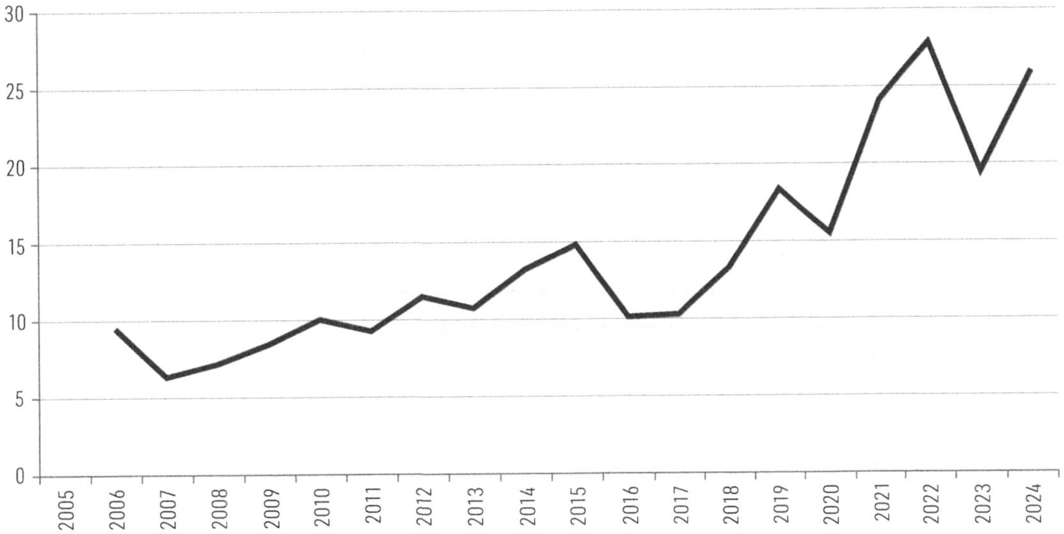

Source: Economic Commission for Latin America and the Caribbean, on the basis of Bloomberg.

Digital technology FDI is unevenly distributed among the countries of the region and especially concentrated in the larger economies (see figure III.8A). Mexico and Brazil accounted for a respective 32% and 29% of the cumulative value of project announcements between 2005 and 2024; these countries, together with Argentina, Chile and Colombia, accounted for more than 80% of the total. In the past five years, Mexico's average annual growth rate was the highest (50%) in the region, peaking at US$ 9.251 billion in 2024. This performance suggests that Mexico is an increasingly attractive destination for digital FDI. In 2024, Brazil was the second-largest destination in the region, with a total value of US$ 5.854 billion. Colombia came in third, with a record US$ 2.672 billion, driven by data centre projects and investments in wireless telecommunications operators (see figure III.8B).

5 Includes all transactions in which the acquiring or acquired entity is involved in industrial sectors, groups or subgroups related to digital technologies.

Figure III.8
Latin America and the Caribbean: value of FDI announcements related to digital technologies, by country, 2005–2024
(Billions of dollars)

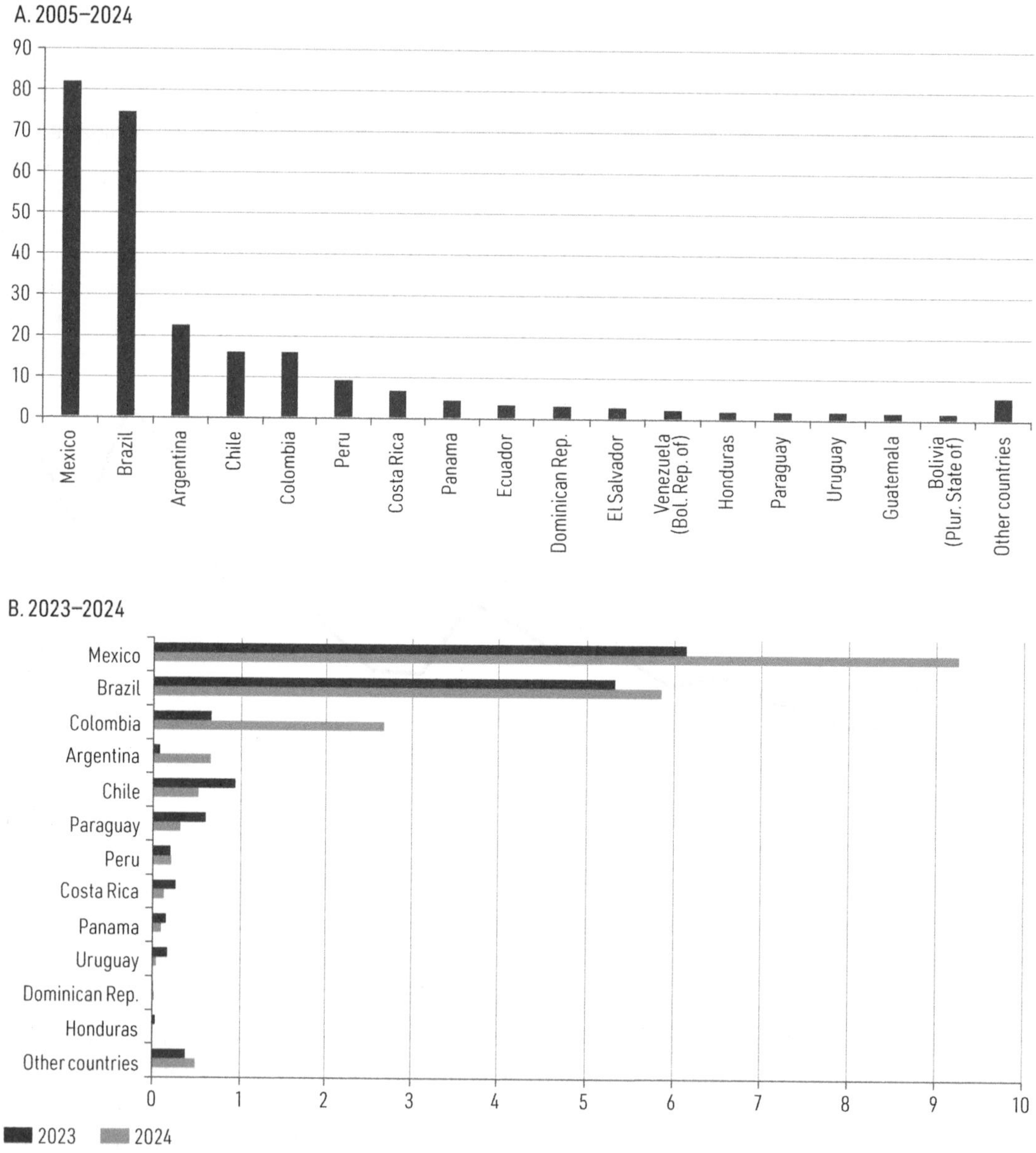

Source: Economic Commission for Latin America and the Caribbean, on the basis of *Financial Times*. fDi Markets. https://www.fdimarkets.com/.

Note: The sectors included are communications, software and information technology services, semiconductors, electronic components, consumer electronics, and business machines and equipment. Also included are parent companies that announced investment projects worth more than US$ 1 billion in countries of the region and recipient countries with announcements worth more than US$ 300 million in 2015-2019 and more than US$ 100 million in 2020-2024.

The factors explaining this concentration of new project announcements vary by country, according to the specific context of each. For example, Mexico's main advantages include its geographical proximity to the United States; the Agreement between the United States of America, the United Mexican States, and Canada; its burgeoning technology sector; the availability of skilled labour;

and the proliferation of digital hubs in Querétaro, Nuevo León and Jalisco, among other states (Yepes, 2024; Oropeza, 2024). In these centres, digital cluster initiatives of varying sizes and phases of consolidation have helped to cultivate a conducive environment for FDI.[6]

Brazil boasts a domestic market of over 210 million people, rapid growth in e-commerce and a strategic geographical position providing access to other South American countries (Agência Brasil, 2024; Valor Econômico, 2024). It also has long-term national plans and policies in place, such as the Action Plan for Neoindustrialization 2024–2026 (Ministry of Development, Industry, Trade and Services, 2024) and the New Industry Brazil programme, the fourth objective of which is to digitally transform industry, with incentives for investing in technology sectors and strengthening local capacities, including support for small and medium-sized enterprises to adopt Industry 4.0 technologies (Office of the President of the Republic, 2024). Brazil has also made progress on digital policy, with a comprehensive strategy and a specific and ambitious artificial intelligence agenda that aim not only to attract but also to steer investment, so that its impact aligns with strategic development objectives.

Argentina is known for its highly skilled workforce in sectors like computer science, data science and engineering, its leadership in software and digital services exports and its capacity for continuous innovation. Incentive policies and the consolidation of technology clusters have further strengthened the country's digital ecosystem (Argentine Investment and International Trade Agency, 2022).

Chile's combination of advanced infrastructure, well-defined regulations and a collaborative ecosystem make it an attractive destination for investment in digital technologies, encouraging firms to establish and grow their presence in the sector (InvestChile, 2025).

Colombia has been working to strengthen its digital infrastructure through the gradual adoption of technology and investment in telecommunications. The country seeks to boost its competitive edge in the region through strategic tax incentives and firm government support for digitalization (Mazo González, 2024).

While this analysis is focused on investment project announcements, it is worth noting that its findings are partly mirrored by cross border mergers and acquisitions. Brazil accounts for nearly 50% of these transactions, followed by Mexico (14%), reaffirming both economies' attraction as growing digital hubs. However, it should also be noted that the factors that motivate firms' investment decisions differ from those motivating mergers and acquisitions. A description of these strategies and the key players involved is provided later in this chapter.

2. FDI distribution by sector and position in the value chain

The sectoral distribution of the value of FDI announcements related to digital technologies in the region has changed over time. Since 2005, communications has accounted for the largest share of total value, but recently the software and information technology services sector and the electronic components sector have gained ground (see figure III.9). Consumer electronics, meanwhile, never regained its 2005–2009 share of 9%, and shares have shrunk in the case of semiconductors and remained marginal throughout the period in the case of business machines and equipment.

6 Cluster initiatives are sets of deliberate actions that firms, governments and supporting institutions take with a view to improving value chain productivity in specific geographical areas, which may or may not correspond to areas that private interests and market forces have made de facto centres of economic activity. ECLAC developed a platform that seeks to boost awareness and cooperation regarding cluster and other territorial productive articulation initiatives in Latin America and the Caribbean, which includes an interactive map that allows users to locate all such initiatives that have a digital focus. See [online] https://www.cepal.org/en/node/60739.

Figure III.9
Latin America and the Caribbean: distribution of value of FDI announcements related to digital technologies, by sector, 2005–2024
(Percentages)

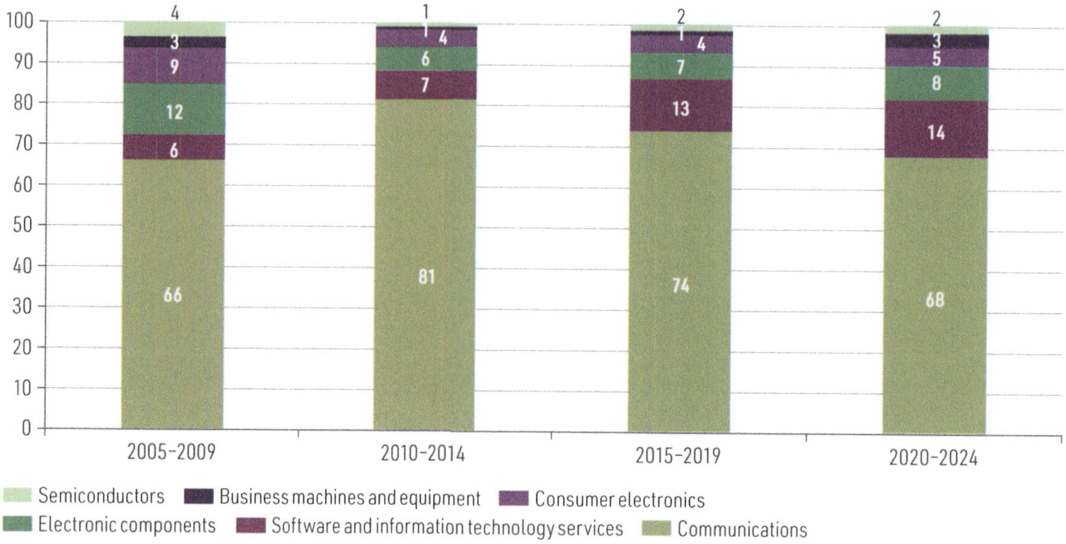

Source: Economic Commission for Latin America and the Caribbean, on the basis of *Financial Times*. fDi Markets. https://www.fdimarkets.com/.

Analysing the number of projects in addition to their value offers greater insight into trends and the intensity of activity in each sector. More than half of project announcements were in the software and information technology services sector (52% of announcements since 2010), and that figure is trending upward. Communications, with the second-largest number of announcements (27% of the total), has remained relatively steady since 2010. Strong growth in electronic components from 2005 to 2011 levelled off between 2012 and 2024, settling around 12% of the total.

An analysis of the distribution of announcements according to where they fall in the value chain shows that, between 2005 and 2024, the greatest concentration of value was in infrastructure and capacities. Although infrastructure projects, such as telecommunications networks and data centres, are fewer in number, they represent major capital outlays (see figure III.10). In contrast, services projects are higher in number but significantly lower in value, as many of them involve developing software and applications and require less capital up front. The picture emerging from these findings is of a digital ecosystem experiencing strong growth in services, which have lower financing requirements than infrastructure— a key feature of new business models. There was also increased investment in the production segment in 2022 and 2023.

This pattern of investment is somewhat of a departure from the global trend. While global investment is generally concentrated in production (40%), the majority of announcements in Latin America and the Caribbean are in infrastructure (66%), and production accounts for a significantly smaller share (14%). This considerable gap limits the potential of FDI to strengthen local capacities and leads to increased dependency on digital goods and services produced abroad, making the region more vulnerable to external disruptions.

Considering its sectoral orientation and its position in the value chain, digital FDI in the region has two components that are notable for their relative weight, recent growth and strategic value: digital infrastructure, which for many economies is the main point of entry for investment; and software and information technology services, which has the most FDI announcements.

Figure III.10
Latin America and the Caribbean: value of FDI announcements related to digital technologies, by segment of the value chain, 2005–2024
(Billions of dollars)

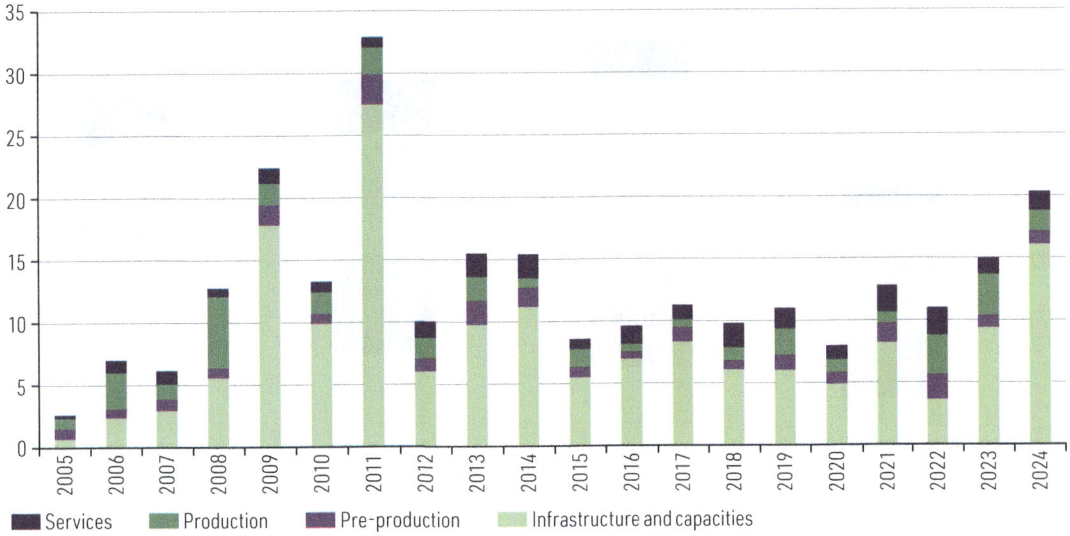

Source: Economic Commission for Latin America and the Caribbean, on the basis of *Financial Times*. fDi Markets. https://www.fdimarkets.com/.

Note: The sectors included are communications, software and information technology services, semiconductors, electronic components, consumer electronics, and business machines and equipment. Each segment is composed of the following business activities: infrastructure and capacities (education and training, electricity, information and communications technology (ICT) and Internet infrastructure); pre-production (headquarters, research and development); production (construction, extraction, manufacturing, recycling); services (business services, customer contact centre, logistics, distribution and transportation, maintenance and servicing, retail, sales, marketing and support, shared services centre, technical support centre).

(a) Digital infrastructure and the shift from connectivity to data centres to drive investment

In recent years, digital infrastructure has undergone a significant transformation, as focus has shifted away from traditional telecommunications infrastructure to the development of computing infrastructure and services. This trend is reflected in FDI, with the data processing and hosting subsector taking on a dominant role in both the number and the value of announcements. Up to 2010, there were 36 announcements of data centres in the region; by 2019, that number had increased to 195, and an additional 165 announcements since then have brought the total to 360.

The number of projects in the communications sector rose until 2014, when it fell slightly (see figure III.11). However, the sector has maintained a high level of activity, spurred on by investments in data centres (in the data processing, hosting and related services subsector): 77 in 2024 and 74 in 2023. Meanwhile, FDI trends for fixed broadband operators and mobile broadband operators have diverged: the former experienced a moderate and relatively uniform contraction (down 29% for the entire period), while the latter cycled through more pronounced periods of expansion and contraction, with an initial boom (85% growth between the 2005–2009 period and the 2010–2014 period) followed by a 77% fall in 2020–2024 relative to its highest point. This is consistent with the market consolidation of wireless network and the structural challenges facing fixed networks in terms of expanding coverage or updating technology, for example through the deployment of fibre-optic networks.

Figure III.11
Latin America and the Caribbean: FDI announcements in communications, by subsector, 2005–2024
(Number of projects and billions of dollars)

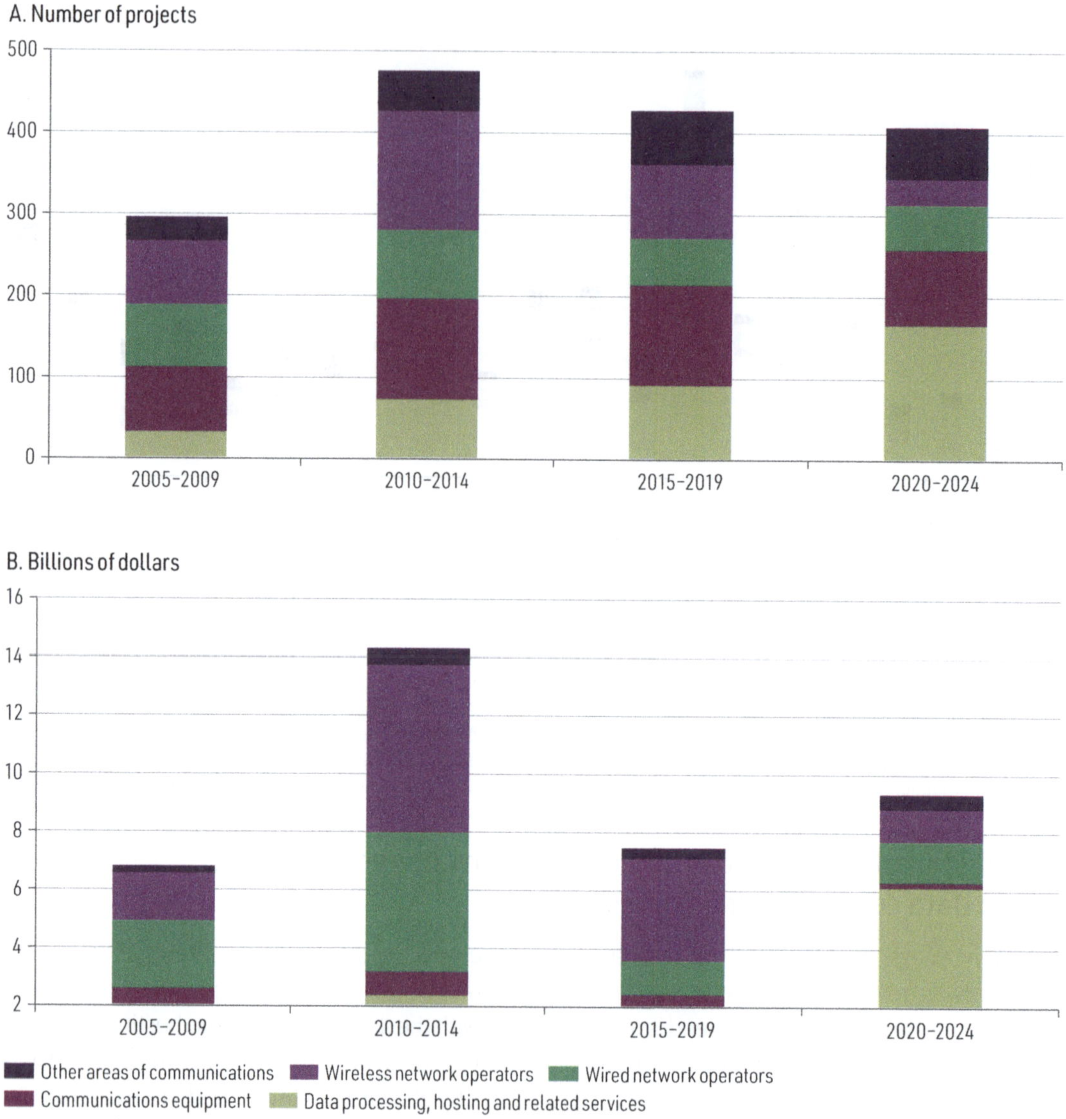

Source: Economic Commission for Latin America and the Caribbean, on the basis of *Financial Times*. fDi Markets. https://www.fdimarkets.com/.

Note: The "other areas of communications" category includes cable programming and other subscription services, motion pictures and sound recording, navigation equipment, radio and television broadcasting, and satellite telecommunications.

Investment figures for data centre show a move towards the more structural components of the digital ecosystem, in particular a diminished focus on connectivity and a greater focus on data infrastructure, which is crucial for the feasibility of adopting technologies like artificial intelligence, big data analytics and the Internet of things.

The data centre market in Latin America is projected to double in size over the next four years, with growth of approximately US$ 5 billion in 2023 and US$ 10 billion in 2029 (Menski et al., 2024). This rapid growth is mainly attributable to structural factors related to the global expansion of advanced digital infrastructure and the growing demand for computing power for intensive applications, including artificial intelligence and analytical processing.

The geographical concentration of data centre project announcements in Latin America and the Caribbean is very high, at the country and territorial levels alike, making it difficult to achieve more equitable development. This has given rise to digital clusters, where computing power and the sector's critical infrastructure are most highly concentrated. At the country level, Brazil had the most project announcements (33% of the regional total), thanks to rising demand for technology services and its energy mix, followed by Mexico (16%), Colombia (13%), Chile (12%) and Argentina (6%); together, these countries accounted for 80% of the regional total (see figure III.12). This distribution is giving shape to a digital ecosystem characterized by the formation of specialized hubs and is aligned with the region's overall pattern of digital FDI inflows.

Figure III.12
Latin America and the Caribbean: FDI announcements in the data processing, hosting and related services subsector, by country, 2005–2024
(Number of projects)

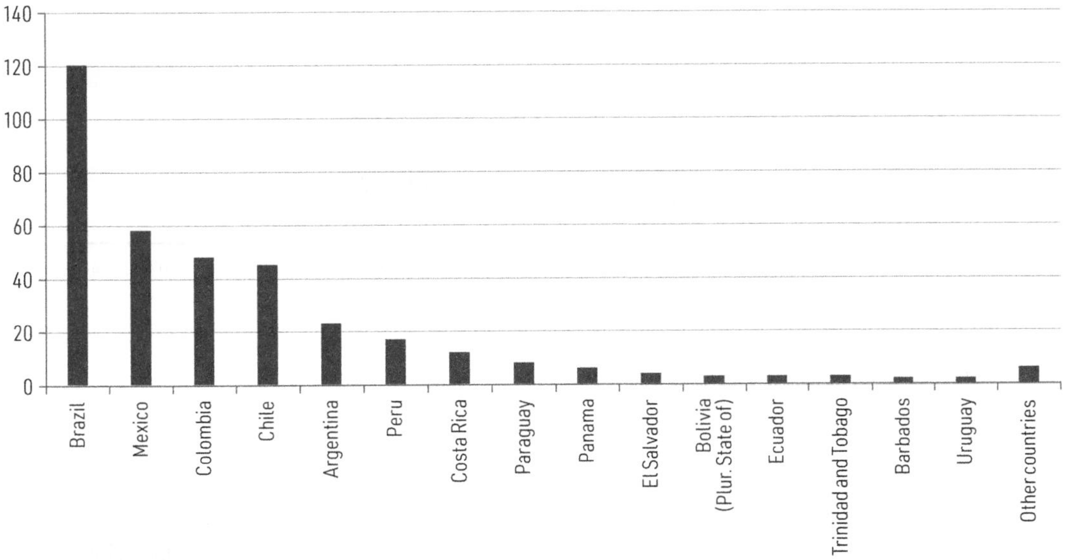

Source: Economic Commission for Latin America and the Caribbean, on the basis of *Financial Times*. fDi Markets. https://www.fdimarkets.com/.

The emergence of new FDI destinations outside the existing centres, such as Peru (17 announcements), Costa Rica (12) and Paraguay (8), suggests an incipient move towards diversification. Peru's strong performance of late is linked to growing demand in the digital sector, connectivity improvements, the availability of renewable energy sources and a proactive government strategy to attract foreign capital (BITNESS, 2024). Paraguay has secured large investments in the computing power of digital assets, leveraging its low-cost renewable hydroelectric energy.

The concentration of FDI at the subnational level is even more pronounced. São Paulo accounts for 64% of announcements in Brazil; the Metropolitan Region of Santiago accounts for 84% of Chile's announcements; the Capital District of Bogotá accounts for 46% of Colombia's announcements; and Querétaro and Mexico City account for 45% of announcements in Mexico. Many of these locations are existing digital hubs or are supported by cluster initiatives, helping to consolidate their role as strategic nodes within the digital infrastructure network and their potential to create local capacity linkages. Despite their high degree of concentration in a relatively small number of countries and territories, investments vary significantly by size and type.

(b) The software and information technology services sector as a major source of jobs

Software and information technology services, another strong sector in the region, is notable for receiving the most project announcements while being less capital-intensive than data centres, making its development a more viable option in many countries (see figure III.13).

Figure III.13
Latin America and the Caribbean: FDI announcements in software and information technology services, by subsector, 2005–2024
(Number of projects and value)

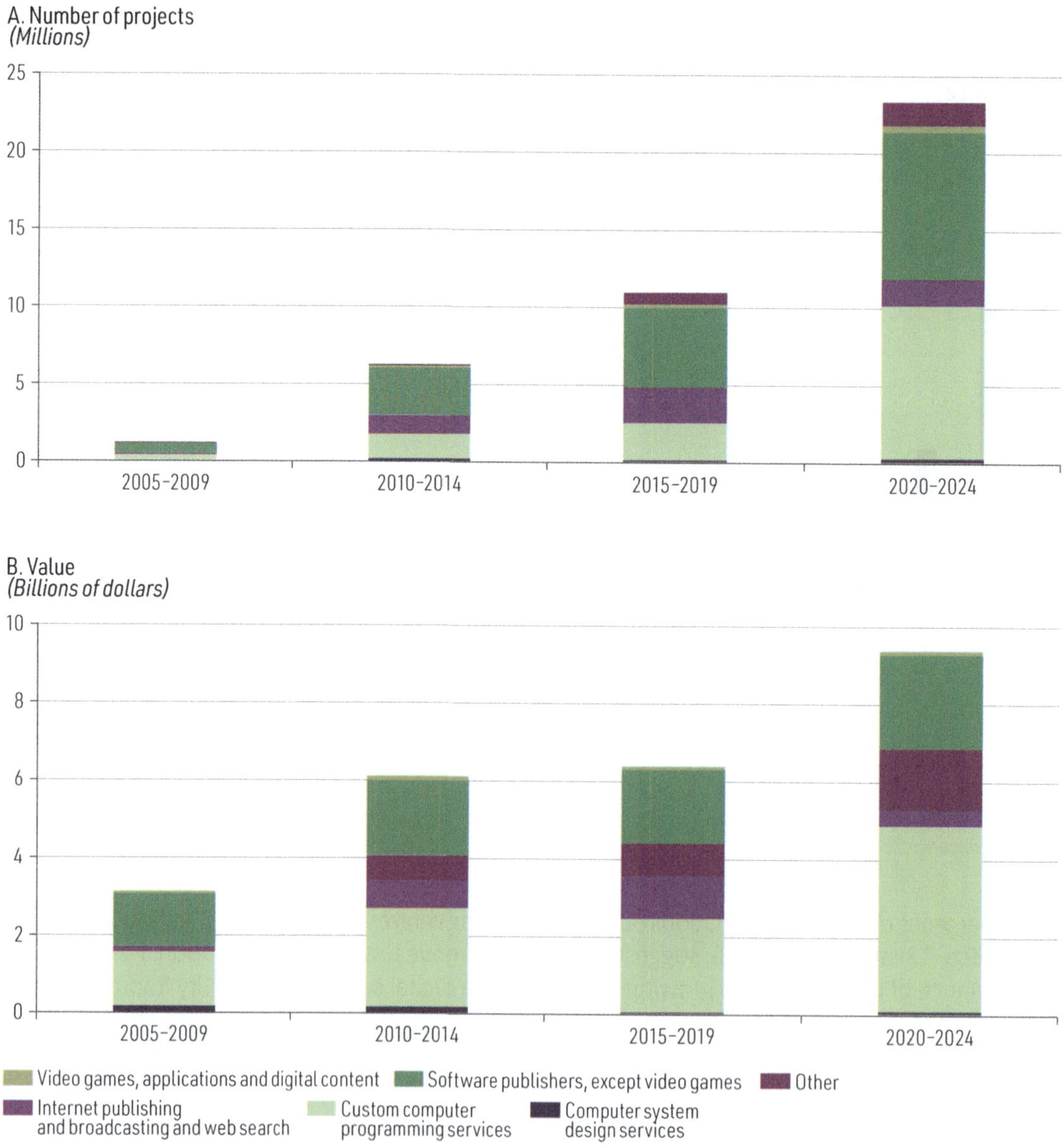

Source: Economic Commission for Latin America and the Caribbean, on the basis of *Financial Times*. fDi Markets. https://www.fdimarkets.com/.
Note: The "other" category comprises all other information services, information facilities management services, computing services and services related to software and information technology services.

An analysis of variation in the value of FDI announcements across the sector's different components provides useful insight. The value of announcements rose in custom computer programming services, information technology services and other computing services, while it held steady in the software publishers component and remained low in information system design services. This pattern has implications for digital development, productive specialization and positioning within digital value chains. The increase in the value of FDI announcements in custom computer programming services is a sign of increased interest in for-hire developer services, including in the form of outsourcing or custom services for foreign or domestic clients, which suggests that the region's labour force is equipped with programming skills but not necessarily with the innovative skills to design its own products. This observation is supported by the stability of investment in software publishing and the near total absence of investment in system design, indicating that product creation, strategic design, technological innovation, and leadership in devising digital solutions are among the region's weak points. This translates into a diminished capacity to generate value added and is indicative of functional specialization rather than strategic positioning.

However, it is equally useful to assess the software and information technology services sector —including its limitations— in the broader context of the digital industries, where it is the leading generator of skilled jobs (see figure III.14). During the COVID-19 pandemic, rising digital demand propelled significant job growth in the sector. Even after the trend levelled off, job growth remained high, positioning software and information technology services as a steady source of job creation.

Figure III.14
Latin America and the Caribbean: distribution of estimated added jobs linked to digital FDI announcements, by sector, 2005–2024
(Percentages)

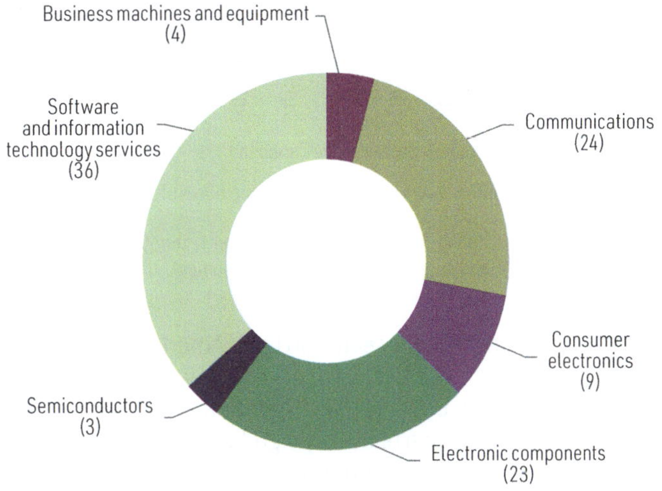

Source: Economic Commission for Latin America and the Caribbean, on the basis of *Financial Times*. fDi Markets. https://www.fdimarkets.com/.

The sector's clear potential could be harnessed through strengthened policies to boost digital industries. Its combination of low physical capital intensity and high demand for skilled labour represents a strategic opportunity for skilled job creation, local capacity-building and digital services exports. At the same time, the aim of ensuring that those new jobs are ultimately located in the FDI recipient countries poses a challenge. This calls for the implementation of policies to develop the labour force and other enabling factors to support the sector's growth.

3. Top investors and investment strategies

As with all sectors (see chapter I), the United States and the European Union were the leading investors in sectors related to digital technologies in the region for the period 2005–2024, accounting for a respective 36% and 33% of total value. Each held the top spot at various points throughout the period, but since 2018, the United States has strengthened its lead, with steady growth in the value of announcements, while the value of announcements from the European Union has trended down (see figure III.15). China was also a major investor, especially in 2024, when its digital investments increased by 72% compared to the previous year.

Figure III.15
Latin America and the Caribbean: value of digital FDI announcements from selected countries or regions, by origin, 2005–2024
(Billions of dollars)

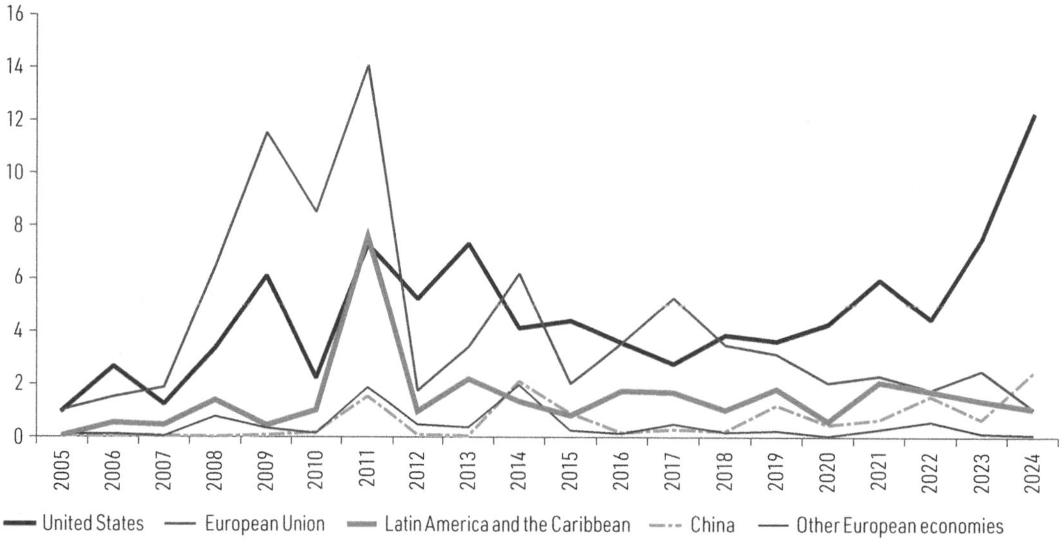

Source: Economic Commission for Latin America and the Caribbean, on the basis of *Financial Times*. fDi Markets. https://www.fdimarkets.com/.

Note: The sectors included are communications, software and information technology services, semiconductors, electronic components, consumer electronics, and business machines and equipment.

Intraregional investment in digital technology sectors in Latin America and the Caribbean amounted to US$ 29.473 billion for the period 2005–2024, or 12% of the total value announced. Most of this capital came from Mexico (55%), followed by Brazil (11%), Argentina (8%), Colombia (7%) and Chile (6%). Given that intraregional flows account for a relatively significant share of the total, they offer a strong foundation for closer cooperation and further regional integration, with a view to achieving more favourable conditions to boost FDI and its positive effects.

In addition to changes in the geographical origin of cross-border capital and subsectoral trends in communications, the types of firms that invest have also changed. Once led by telecommunications companies, investment in the sector is now led by major technology firms. The 2020–2024 period was a turning point in that regard, as companies specializing in data processing and cloud computing services—namely Aligned Energy, CloudHQ, Amazon and Microsoft— became the largest investors, each announcing upward of US$ 3.4 billion (see figure III.16). The infrastructure and governance of the digital ecosystem are entering a new phase; with greater economic reliance on cloud computing, advanced analytics and artificial intelligence comes the redefinition of needs in digital skills-building and the emergence of technological dependency challenges. At the same time, these companies' expanded presence in the region's communications sector may lead to new opportunities to develop related digital services, including cybersecurity, infrastructure maintenance and artificial intelligence support services. More complex cross-sectoral regulatory frameworks are needed to navigate this ongoing restructuring of the digital landscape.

Figure III.16
Latin America and the Caribbean: value of digital FDI announcements, by investing firm and destination country, 2015–2024
(Billions of dollars)

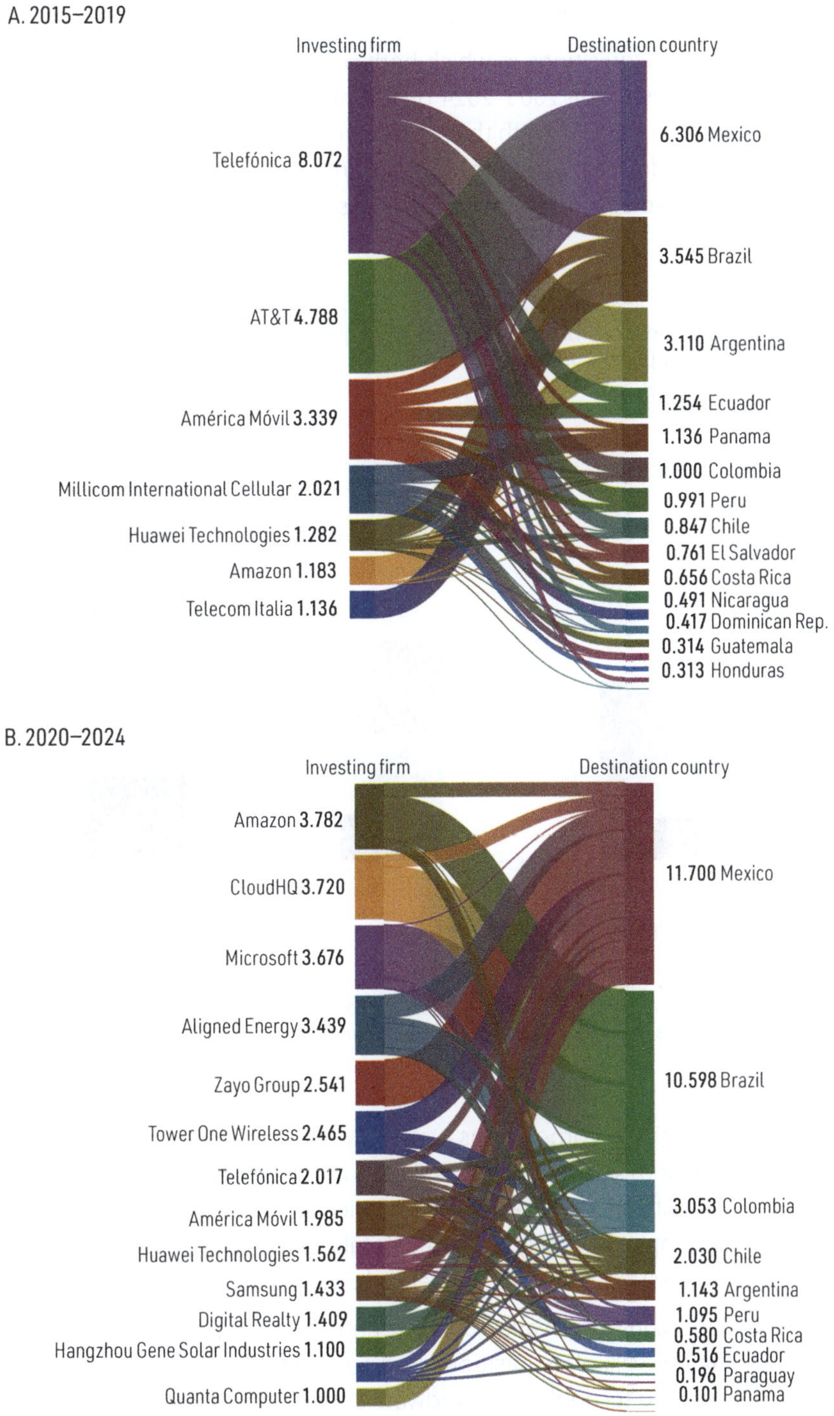

Source: Economic Commission for Latin America and the Caribbean, on the basis of *Financial Times*. fDi Markets. https://www.fdimarkets.com/.

Note: The sectors included are communications, software and information technology services, semiconductors, electronic components, consumer electronics, and business machines and equipment. Also included are parent companies that announced investment projects worth more than US$ 1 billion in countries of the region and recipient countries with announcements worth more than US$ 300 million in 2015–2019 and more than US$ 100 million in 2020–2024.

A similar shift is apparent in recent cross-border mergers and acquisitions, where the roster of top investors and their market strategies have undergone changes. These transactions can be grouped into at least three categories according to the parties' main commercial activity and sector: (i) digital firms acquiring other digital firms; (ii) digital firms acquiring firms in traditional sectors; and (iii) traditional sector firms acquiring digital firms.

In Latin America and the Caribbean, acquisitions in which both parties are digital firms were the most common of the three categories in the 2005–2024 period and accounted for 10% of total transactions in the past five years. The category with the highest growth was acquisitions of digital firms by traditional sector firms, quadrupling its share of total transactions (see figure III.17). The share of acquisitions of traditional sector firms by digital firms also grew significantly during the period, from 2% to 5%.

Figure III.17
Latin America and the Caribbean: trends in cross-border mergers and acquisitions involving digital firms, by type of transaction and five-year period, 2005–2024
(Percentage share of total number of transactions)

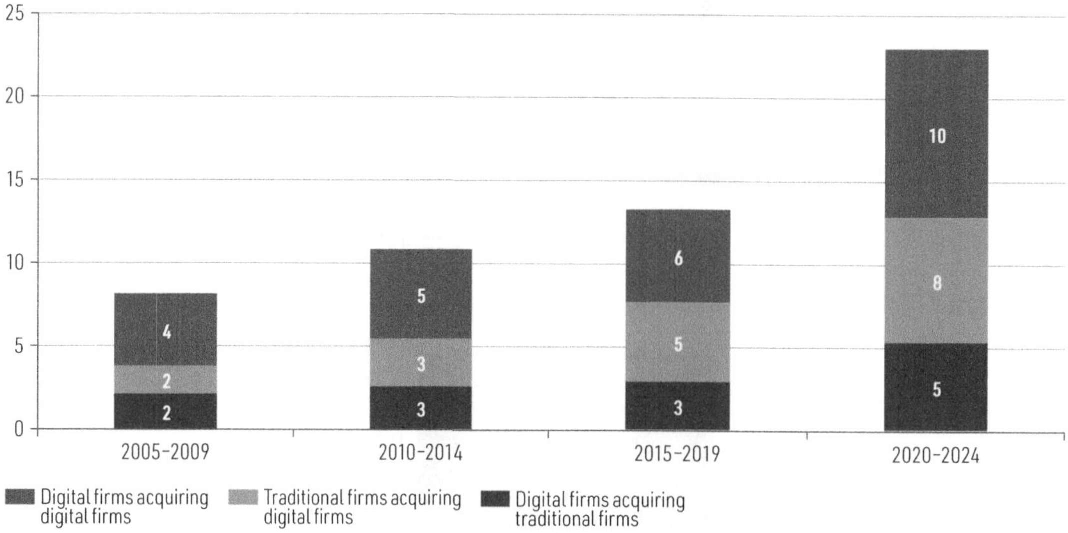

Source: Economic Commission for Latin America and the Caribbean, on the basis of Bloomberg.
Note: For each five-year period, the percentage remaining to complete total transactions refers to transactions between traditional firms.

In recent years, digital sector transnational corporations have shown growing interest in acquiring digital assets in the region. There were 18 such transactions in 2005 and double that number in 2024 (following a record high in 2022). Software and technology services have emerged as the main target of acquisitions, accounting for approximately 50% of the total, which highlights their strategic importance for companies seeking to strengthen their presence in the digital sector.

The type of digital firms behind these acquisitions varies. Software and technology services companies are the largest group, accounting for 34% of acquisitions (see figure III.18), followed by firms in communications, Internet services, and technological hardware and semiconductors, which have remained more or less stable.

Figure III.18
Latin America and the Caribbean: distribution of cross-border mergers and acquisitions between digital firms, by sector of acquiring firm, 2005–2024
(Percentage share of total number of transactions)

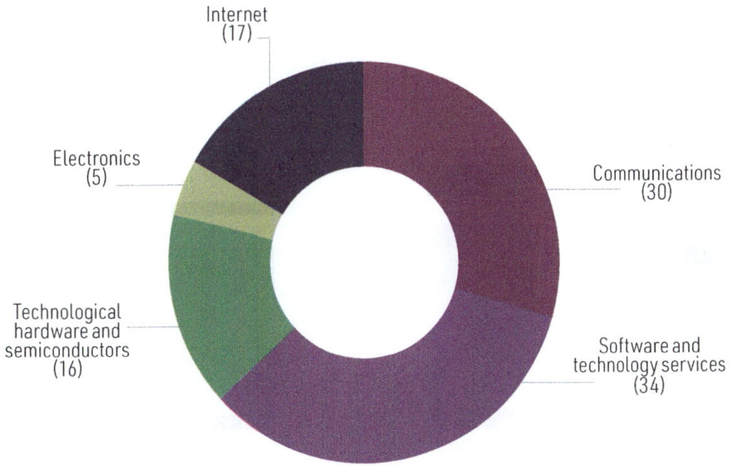

Source: Economic Commission for Latin America and the Caribbean, on the basis of Bloomberg.

The challenge for digital firms acquiring other digital firms is not so much assimilating digital skills but rather becoming bigger, better positioned and more agile players in a highly competitive environment. To that end, their strategies aim to rapidly expand their market share, gain access to new client segments or regions and eventually reduce direct competition by absorbing potential rivals.

These transactions illustrate both the transformative potential of global technological capital and the policy and regulatory issues involved in building a diverse and competitive digital ecosystem in the region. It is important to be mindful of the potential risk associated with these mergers and acquisitions; for example, an acquiring firm's motivation could be to discontinue its competitor's goods or services, in a manoeuvre known as a strategic (or killer) acquisition (Ivaldi et al, 2024; Da Silva and Núñez, 2021). Thus, building local capacities for innovation should be accompanied by appropriate regulation to prevent stifled growth and market concentration.

Digital firms have also shown an interest in acquiring firms in traditional sectors to expand into new areas of value addition, accelerate growth through skills absorption and diversify their operations, taking advantage of physical infrastructure and consolidated supply chains.

There were 231 such transactions in the region between 2005 and 2024. Firms in the industrial sector were the largest target, accounting for 36% (see figure III.19). Nearly two thirds of transactions in this sector involved industrial services, such as logistics and commerce support services, which indicates a tendency to integrate key functions within the value chain. The financial sector was also a significant target of these transactions. This may be related to the growth of financial technology firms, especially in the most recent five-year period (ECLAC, 2022a).

Figure III.19
Latin America and the Caribbean: cross border mergers and acquisitions by digital firms targeting traditional firms, by sector and five-year period, 2005–2024
(Number of transactions)

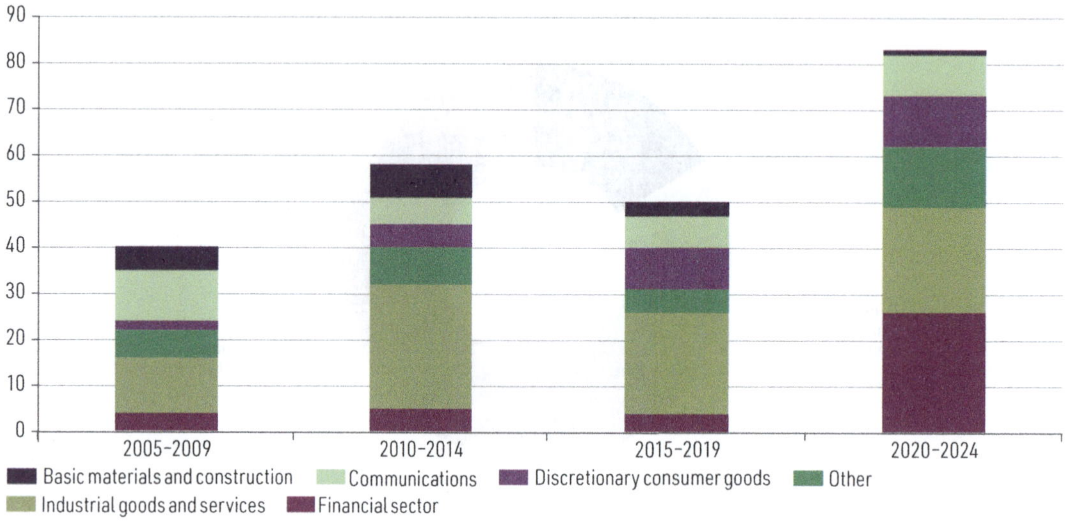

Source: Economic Commission for Latin America and the Caribbean, on the basis of Bloomberg.
Note: The "other" category includes health services, energy, real estate, consumer staples and utilities.

This type of transaction could offer opportunities to accelerate digitalization, introduce new technologies and modernize value chains in the region. However, it could also pose risks for the region's productive and technological development, such as the loss of sovereignty over strategic infrastructure and assets; dependency on external platforms and limitation of spillover effects and local value capture, without sufficient links to the productive sector; and the displacement of local firms. Such challenges should be addressed through comprehensive public policy, reconciling openness with strategic selectiveness to preserve local capacities while improving value chain integration.

4. Summary

In recent decades, Latin America and the Caribbean has attracted a considerable amount of FDI in key areas for the digital transformation. However, as mentioned, the region's share in global FDI flows to sectors linked to digital technologies remains limited, reflecting the structural challenges of digital value chain integration. Regional FDI was concentrated primarily in the infrastructure and capacities segment, while the production segment and the research and development segment received a much smaller share. This pattern of investment prevents greater capture of value added and underscores the need to direct investment towards activities that facilitate the development of local productive capacities and technologies.

Increased FDI geared towards the region's digital transformation can affect a range of factors, including infrastructure development, restructuring of the corporate landscape, jobs, innovation and environmental sustainability. However, these effects do not occur spontaneously or uniformly; they are determined in large measure by the type of investment, the institutional landscape, the characteristics of the local productive structure and the implementation of supporting policies.

Although instability, uncertainty and global tensions may have a dampening effect, investment such as it is will likely go to the regions and countries that offer the most favourable conditions, supported by strategies and policies that link productive development, digital development and FDI.

E. Policies, governance and institutional capacities for FDI attraction to support the digital and productive transformation

In general, one of the main policy challenges facing the region is to find areas in which strategic national development objectives and the interests of the private sector converge. Private investment decisions are influenced by a variety of factors, which in turn can be affected by public policy and other aspects, depending on the sector and type of project. The public sector needs to design and implement coordinated, long-term productive development policies and strategies, and governance structures are needed to ensure that those policies are coherent, legitimate and on-target. Naturally, this means developing adequate institutional capacities.

While many areas of public policy can influence FDI attraction, the focus of the present analysis is on policies that directly aim to increase and strengthen investment, in particular through investment promotion agencies (see table III.3). One of the main arguments in favour of using public resources to achieve this aim is that FDI has the potential to establish production linkages, foster knowledge transfer and support economic growth (ECLAC, 2010, 2023). In that regard, investment promotion agencies can not only facilitate inflows of foreign capital but also play a strategic role in reconciling public and private interests, helping to shape both the conditions that enable investment and the impact of that investment.

Table III.3
Policies, policy areas and instruments of FDI attraction to support the digital transformation

Policy type	Policy area	Instruments
Policies addressing institutional or structural determinants of the investment environment	Transparency and rule of law	- Legal frameworks - Independent judicial systems - Anti-corruption standards
	Macroeconomics	- Fiscal instruments - Monetary instruments - Exchange rate instruments
	Openness to investment and general investment regime	- International trade, tax, and investment promotion and protection agreements - National regulations governing the entry, operation, protection, and repatriation of capital and earnings - Investment screening or scrutiny mechanisms to identify risks or strategic interests - Investment contracts
	Sectoral regulation	- Data ownership and use - Privacy - Cybersecurity - Jurisdiction
	Infrastructure	- Public investment projects - Concessions and public-private partnerships
	Suitable workforce	- Provision of education, technical training and job skill certification - Incentives for continuous training
	Productive and technological development	Strengthening of innovation systems and productive coordination, including: - Incentives for research, development and innovation - Funding for technology start-ups - Technological linkage programmes - Technology transfer programmes - Provision of science and technology infrastructure - Promotion of clusters, cluster initiatives and institutional cooperation networks - Public procurement

Policy type	Policy area	Instruments
Incentive policies	Tax incentives	- Corporate income tax reduction - Income tax reduction or deduction - Tax holiday - Exemption from labour taxes - Exemption from import taxes on capital goods and equipment, among others - Tax relief on investment or investment tax credits
	Financial incentives	- Direct subsidies (investment subsidies) - Government guarantees - Government insurance at privileged rates or government investment bonds
	Promotion policies	Investment promotion agencies: - One-stop-shop facilities - Active search for strategic investors - Country image or brand building - Investment aftercare and monitoring programmes - Policy advocacy

Source: Economic Commission for Latin America and the Caribbean, on the basis of Economic Commission for Latin America and the Caribbean. (2024). *Foreign Direct Investment in Latin America and the Caribbean, 2024* (LC/PUB.2024/8-P).

With progress in digital transformation becoming a key issue on the government agenda for many countries, investment promotion agencies or institutions have not remained on the sidelines in this regard. Internationally, these agencies are including digital transformation as one of their priorities, by developing strategies and initiatives to attract FDI in this area. In this respect, the situation varies considerably at the international level, as countries and regions are at different stages in the development of the digital economy, the establishment of the institutional framework for investment promotion and the adaptation of their practices for attracting digital FDI (UNCTAD, 2017; Economic and Social Commission for Asia and the Pacific [ESCAP], 2023). Across OECD countries, for example, 40% of investment promotion agencies explicitly cite enabling the digital transformation of the economy as one of their goals, and more than 75% of these agencies allocate at least a quarter of their resources to mobilizing investment in digital sectors (OECD, 2021, 2025).

In the 2024 edition of this report, the role of the region's investment promotion agencies and how well-aligned these agencies were with productive development objectives were examined. One of the findings was that digital technologies and infrastructure are now emerging priorities (ECLAC, 2024b). With this year's edition, the aim is to better understand the role of these agencies in the digital transformation and how their strategies and activities align with digital policies and productive development policies. To this end, beginning in March 2025, primary data were collected from the investment promotion agencies (or institutions that fulfilled this function in the past) through an online questionnaire. At the time of writing for this chapter,[7] responses had been received from 10 countries: Argentina, Brazil, Chile, Colombia, Costa Rica, Dominican Republic, Guyana, Panama, Peru and Uruguay. Secondary sources were used to complement the analysis of the findings, which brought to light similarities and differences in the strategies and institutional capabilities for promoting, attracting and facilitating FDI in key sectors for digital transformation, for ensuring linkages between FDI policies and other policies, and governance.

1. Regional experiences with investment promotion agencies

In Latin America and the Caribbean, investment promotion agencies have significantly varying roles in and approaches to attracting FDI to advance the digital transformation. For some agencies, efforts to attract FDI in this field may be envisioned, but are not yet a priority. According to a recent survey, the priority sectors for 8 of the 10 Caribbean investment promotion agencies that responded were agriculture, aquaculture and agroprocessing, manufacturing and tourism (United Nations Industrial

[7] Early June 2025.

Development Organization and World Association of Investment Promotion Agencies [UNIDO and WAIPA], 2023). They did, however, recognize the need to redefine the priority sectors for investment promotion through a more strategic approach. One of the main drivers identified by investment promotion agencies is strengthening science, technology and innovation and digitalization to enhance countries' competitiveness and attractiveness. It is therefore likely that the digital transformation will be one of the goals that guide their actions in the future.

A number of investment promotion agencies and institutions in the region have already reported that they are giving priority to the digital sector or sectors related to digital transformation, some of which are cross-cutting, such as global services and technology, highlighting the importance of these sectors in the new global value chains and their potential contribution to the sustainable development of the countries (ECLAC, 2024b). In Argentina, the focus has been on promoting the installation of global hubs for services, mostly digital and technological transformation services, and Guyana has been successful in attracting investment in services for export. In Colombia, information technologies and creative industries are among the key sectors for ProColombia, while in Panama, the Investment Attraction and Export Promotion Authority (PROPANAMA) has prioritized digital hubs and Uruguay's XXI agency is focusing on information and communications technology (ICT) and other sectors.

In practice, both the approach and scope of the sectors that these institutions promote and prioritize vary. In many cases, FDI is targeted simultaneously from several stakeholders in the technology ecosystem, which is in line with the 'whole-of-ecosystem' approach (UNESCAP, 2023). Almost all of the countries surveyed have a multi-sectoral approach, which in some cases ranges from connectivity infrastructure and data centres to software development, digital commerce and e-commerce platforms, ICT-enabled services, artificial intelligence, machine learning or big data analytics, smart cities, advanced manufacturing and Industry 4.0. Infrastructure attracts significant interest. InvestChile, for example, is actively involved in attracting FDI in digital infrastructure through the national data centre plan, launched in 2024. This initiative has gone hand in hand with rapid growth in installed capacity, with more than 30 projects under development and a projected investment of more than US$ 4.1 billion, positioning the country as a regional data centre hub (Ministry of Science, Technology, Knowledge and Innovation, 2024). Meanwhile, PROPANAMA is providing support for the installation of the first Internet exchange point (IXP) in Panama, spearheaded by InteRed and the National Authority for Government Innovation. The aim of the initiative is to position the country as a key regional node and attract companies from the data centre, telecommunications, cloud services and video games sectors.[8]

For this broad-based approach to be effective, however, investment promotion agencies must work in coordination with a range of local and international stakeholders in the public and private sector —mature digital companies and start-ups, venture capital and seed capital funds, business accelerators and incubators, training and talent development institutions, law firms, public relations and communications firms, and market research and analysis companies— to create synergies and drive comprehensive digital development. Conversely, some investment promotion agencies have opted for more targeted strategies focused on specific sectors or niches (OECD, 2021). In any case, it is important for agencies to align their aspirations and objectives with the strengths of the host economy, as well as with its actual capabilities, as discussed below.

To attract digital FDI, countries use a variety of incentives and strategic tools which, in many cases, are not defined or implemented directly by investment promotion agencies. These tools include both fiscal incentives (e.g. tax exemptions and credits) and non-fiscal incentives (e.g. subsidies, financing and access to infrastructure). The tools most frequently used by promotion agencies, however, are related to the different phases of the investment cycle. These include, to varying degrees depending on

8 According to information provided online by PROPANAMA on 15 April 2025.

the context, the proactive search for and promotion of strategic investors and projects, "soft landing" support programmes to facilitate the establishment of foreign companies, assistance with regulatory procedures and requirements (access to one-stop shops, obtaining permits and compliance with sectoral regulations, among others), and services to support and retain existing investors.

Importantly, some investment promotion agencies also promote initiatives aimed specifically at building and strengthening the digital ecosystem, with a view to enhancing the impact of and leveraging FDI. This includes, for example, encouraging digital cluster initiatives, business incubators and technology centres, as in the case of Brazil, Colombia and Peru (see box III.3). Other increasingly significant efforts include participation in initiatives to strengthen digital talent, through partnerships with universities and training programmes that meet investor demand, as is the case in Uruguay and Costa Rica (see box III.4).

Box III.3
Boosting investment and digital ecosystems in the region

In Brazil, ScaleUp is one of the most successful programmes implemented by the Brazilian Trade and Investment Promotion Agency (Apex-Brasil) to attract and facilitate sustainable investment. The programme, which is in line with the Nova Indústria Brasil industrial strategy and focuses on digital transformation, seeks to attract international technology start-ups through an 18-month cycle of business acceleration (i.e. initial support to fuel their rapid and efficient growth), combining face-to-face and virtual activities. It provides specialized consultancy, mentoring, support for product validation, access to local investors and to potential customers, facilitating the effective entry of the companies into the Brazilian market. Since its inception, ScaleUp in Brazil has provided business acceleration services to more than 60 start-ups, facilitated more than 1,000 business meetings and helped at least 13 foreign companies to set up in Brazil. The programme, which was developed in partnership with the Brazilian Venture Capital and Private Equity Association (ABVCAP) and has assisted start-ups from Israel, Japan and Singapore, has received recognition from the United Nations Conference on Trade and Development (UNCTAD) for excellence in attracting sustainable FDI in agribusiness.

In Colombia, a venture capital immersion programme for digital sector companies developed capacity in 13 Colombian companies by offering intensive training in investment, investor pitching and negotiation, and connections in the United States venture capital ecosystem. More than US$ 20.5 million in investment opportunities were generated as a result, far exceeding initial expectations.

In Peru, as part of an initiative to strengthen the digital ecosystem, the Peruvian Export and Tourism Promotion Commission (PROMPERÚ) organized the Lima Tech Week, aimed at boosting investment in tech start-ups. A focal point of the programme was the Fourth High Technology Investment Meeting, which enabled the agency to bring ecosystem stakeholders together, increasing the participation of foreign investors and opportunities to connect with local entrepreneurs.

Source: Economic Commission for Latin America and the Caribbean, on the basis of information from Brazilian Trade and Investment Promotion Agency, ProColombia and Peruvian Export and Tourism Promotion Commission (PROMPERÚ) [Online consultation conducted on 1, 10 and 11 April 2025]; Brazilian Trade and Investment Promotion Agency (2022, 22 November). *Projeto da ApexBrasil em parceria com a ABVCAP e Israel Trade & Investment é premiado por órgão da ONU*. https://apexbrasil.com.br/br/pt/conteudo/noticias/projeto-da-apexbrasil-em-parceria-com-a-abvcap-e-israel-trade---.html; ProColombia (2024, 24 October). *Explora el ecosistema de inversión con el "Programa de Inmersión de Venture Capital"*. https://procolombia.co/sala-de-prensa/noticias/explora-el-ecosistema-de-inversion-con-el-programa-de-inmersion-de-venture-capital; and Peruvian Export and Tourism Promotion Commission (2024, 4 November). *PROMPERÚ trae a Lima fondos de inversión extranjeros interesados en invertir en startups peruanas de tecnología*. https://www.gob.pe/institucion/promperu/noticias/1051401-promperu-trae-a-lima-fondos-de-inversion-extranjeros-interesados-en-invertir-en-startups-peruanas-de-tecnologia.

Box III.4
Development of digital talent in the region

The agency Uruguay XXI, in partnership with the National Institute of Employment and Vocational Training (INEFOP), fosters the training of human talent in digital skills through initiatives such as Uruguay Bootcamp and Finishing Schools. These programmes offer intensive and specialized training to prepare participants for the labour market, with an emphasis on the export sector. Since their inception, more than 1,240 people have been trained, with a significant investment in projects that contribute to job creation. The agreement between the two institutions aims to facilitate the start-up of new businesses and enhance labour force quality, aligning the supply of training with market demands.

In Costa Rica, curriculum planning for technical training and university degree programmes, which is conducted in conjunction with foreign companies that have invested and are operating in the country and academia, as well as other stakeholders, aims to align the education supply with global market requirements, especially in sectors such as information technology, knowledge-intensive services and advanced manufacturing.

Source: Economic Commission for Latin America and the Caribbean, on the basis of Office of the President of Uruguay (2022, 15 December), *INEFOP y Uruguay XXI acuerdan capacitar a unas 1.200 personas para atraer nuevas inversiones*. https://www.gub.uy/presidencia/comunicacion/noticias/inefop-uruguay-xxi-acuerdan-capacitar-1200-personas-para-atraer-nuevas; Ministry of Public Education of Costa Rica (2024, 3 July), *Educación técnica profesional contribuye directamente a la innovación, las ciencias, la tecnología y el desarrollo humano*. https://www.mep.go.cr/noticias/educacion-tecnica-profesional-contribuye-directamente-innovacion-ciencias-tecnologia; and information from Uruguay XXI.

Empirical data at the international level suggests that investment promotion agencies operating at the local (subnational) level have been more active in developing talent attraction strategies, particularly in large cities with a high proportion of qualified individuals. However, national agencies are paying increased attention to the issue as well and are adopting placemaking[9] initiatives to develop their brand or highlight the quality-of-life advantages offered by areas with access to open space and nature, and solid infrastructure (World Association of Investment Promotion Agencies [WAIPA], 2023). While this trend is not yet pronounced in Latin America and the Caribbean, it shows investment promotion agencies the importance of more holistic approaches to help position their countries and regions as attractive destinations in which to invest, live and develop digital talent, and thus open up opportunities.

In this regard, investment promotion agencies highlight the importance of promoting a differentiated value proposition that highlights the country's attractiveness for investment (ECLAC, 2024b). Costa Rica, for example, has chosen to differentiate itself through aspects such as the development of human talent, the improvement of the business climate and a strategic narrative on its value proposition. The proposal is adjusted on an ongoing basis and currently focuses on high-growth sectors, in line with developing trends in key industries such as corporate services, advanced manufacturing and life sciences.[10]

Despite their strengths and attractiveness, economies face obstacles that can inhibit or slow the attraction of investment to advance and harness the digital transformation. When asked about the main challenges they face in attracting FDI in digital sectors, investment promotion agencies identified a range of issues of varying magnitude. Regulatory and legal challenges include the lack of clear and predictable regulatory frameworks for digital sectors, bureaucracy, complex and myriad procedures (including the red tape involved in obtaining permits), and outdated or restrictive regulations governing digital sectors, which hinder the development of adequate infrastructure and adaptation to new technological trends.

---

9 The concept of placemaking, which has its origins in urban planning and community development, has been adapted as a strategy for attracting talent and investment, especially in technology sectors. In this context, it refers to designing and fostering environments that enhance a community's attractiveness, functionality and competitiveness for knowledge economy professionals and companies. To this end, the focus is on measures such as quality of life, access to open and natural spaces, and robust infrastructure (International Economic Development Council, 2017).

10 According to information provided by the Costa Rican Investment Promotion Agency (CINDE) on 14 March 2025.

In terms of infrastructure and connectivity, some agencies have to contend with gaps in connectivity and broadband in key areas, as well as a lack of modern infrastructure to support digital sectors, which limits the potential for attracting investment. In the area of human talent, there is a significant skills gap between the workforce and the needs of investment firms, a critical obstacle that is likely to be exacerbated by the difficulty of attracting and retaining qualified digital technology professionals. There are also financial challenges related to limited access to financing for local start-ups and tech companies. This is compounded by intense international competition, as better incentives and more favourable conditions in other countries or regions help to consolidate their position as attractive investment destinations, potentially crowding out economies with lower margins for action.

These challenges, in turn, are part of a complex global dynamic that has an impact on the decision-making of countries and their investment promotion institutions, requiring increasingly sophisticated responses. In this context, there is a growing consensus on the importance of the quality —rather than just the quantity— of investment, and this is creating pressure to align investment attraction efforts with strategic national development objectives for productive development, social inclusion and environmental sustainability. In Latin America and the Caribbean, some agencies recognize the importance of these criteria and, while they have not yet undertaken specific measures in this regard, are evaluating how to incorporate them into digital sector policies and strategies. Others have already undertaken initiatives in this regard and, consistent with international trends, have adopted different approaches. This reflects, among other aspects, the significant variation in institutional capacities (WAIPA, 2023).

2. Institutional capacity for attracting investment to support digitalization

In Latin America and the Caribbean, there are marked organizational and institutional differences across investment promotion agencies. Some, such as Apex-Brasil, have robust structures, while others have more limited capacities. Similarly, agencies such as InvestChile, ProColombia and Apex-Brasil have an international presence, unlike those operating at the national level only (ECLAC, 2024b). Mandates also vary: some agencies focus exclusively on investment attraction, while others combine this function with export promotion, as is the case of the Argentine Investment and International Trade Agency and PROPANAMA.

These differences are explained by structural factors, such as the size of the country, its administrative structure and the position of the agency in the government hierarchy, all of which affect its capacity to design and implement digital and productive transformation strategies. These institutional characteristics can also have a direct influence on the effectiveness of FDI attraction. In this regard, Volpe Martincus and Sztajerowska (2019) find that there is a positive relationship between the size of agencies' budgets, the degree of specialization of their activities and the presence of offices overseas and higher FDI inflows, both in terms of the total stock value of FDI and the number of affiliates of multinational firms in the country.

In this context, just as a one-size-fits-all approach cannot be used for the digital and technological transformation of companies, which depends on company-specific factors such as size, investment appetite and pre-existing digital skills and competencies, specialized capabilities must be developed in investment promotion agencies to assist and guide this process. As outlined by ECLAC (2024a), these capabilities can be grouped into four broad categories: technical, operational, policy and prospective (see table III.4). Although there are examples of investment promotion agencies taking steps to address the needs in this area, available information suggests that many challenges remain at the global level, and the region is no exception (WAIPA, 2023; UNIDO and WAIPA, 2023).

Table III.4
Capabilities needed to attract foreign direct investment in the digital age: examples of investment promotion agencies

Capability	Description	Examples from selected countries
Technical	Expertise in digital sectors and understanding of specific investment needs, making it possible to identify opportunities and advise investors on emerging technologies and market trends.	The Estonian Investment Agency (Invest in Estonia) draws on strong sector knowledge to provide specialized consultancy services to investors in areas such as information and communications technology, cybersecurity, e-commerce and financial technology. Its strategic focus on digital sectors is aligned with the country's strengths in this area, allowing it to leverage Estonia's advanced digital ecosystem to provide strategic information and facilitate linkages with key stakeholders in the sector.
Operational	Qualified human resources and advanced technological systems are in place to effectively manage the promotion and facilitation of investments in the digital sector.	The Costa Rican Investment Promotion Agency (CINDE) is a private non-profit agency that has strengthened its internal capabilities by integrating online platforms and portals that provide information for investors and partners. It uses artificial intelligence, data analytics and machine learning tools to improve digital marketing and identify investment opportunities with greater precision, thanks to a combination of advanced technological systems and skilled technical teams.
Political	Ability to coordinate with various government entities, manage conflicts in the business sector and align investment promotion strategies with national and regional digital transformation and productive development policies.	IDA Ireland, the country's inward investment promotion agency, is a semi-State agency operating under the aegis of the Department of Enterprise, Trade and Employment. It works in coordination with several government entities (Enterprise Ireland, Science Foundation of Ireland (SFI) and local government, among others), through joint funds and initiatives. The agency's strategy for the period 2025-2029 includes clear aims to deepen partnership with other institutions and promote digitalization, in line with the 2022 national digital strategy.
Prospective	Ability to anticipate technological and market trends, adapting investment promotion strategies to leverage emerging opportunities in the digital economy.	The Singapore Economic Development Board (EDB) identifies and promotes investment in emerging sectors and technologies such as advanced manufacturing and artificial intelligence, among other key areas for digital transformation. In addition to anticipating trends, it devises incentives to position Singapore as a technology hub. This capability is complemented by the Centre for Strategic Futures, which advances systemic foresight in the field of public policy.

Source: Economic Commission for Latin America and the Caribbean, on the basis of World Association of Investment Promotion Agencies. (2023). *The New Laws of FDI Attraction: How to Attract, Measure and Sustain Quality FDI*; and information from Invest in Estonia, Ireland's Foreign Direct Investment Agency (IDA Ireland), Singapore Economic Development Board (EDB) and Centre for Strategic Futures (CSF).

In the particular case of Latin America and the Caribbean, investment promotion agencies often face —albeit to varying degrees— staffing and financial constraints which hinder not only the development of technical capabilities such as expertise and experience in the complex and dynamic field of digital transformation, but also the strengthening of operational capabilities for designing and implementing strategies and of prospective capabilities for anticipating technological trends and redefining the strategic sectors to be prioritized in the future. This is also true in the case of agencies with a longer and relatively successful track record in promoting investment in the digital economy. An example of this is Apex-Brasil, which notes that technical and operational capabilities are among those it most needs to strengthen to attract digital FDI.[11]

In the area of operational capabilities, the region's investment promotion agencies are in line with international trends and have been moving towards new ways of working online and using digital tools, as was done during the COVID-19 pandemic (UNCTAD, 2023). However, for many agencies digital innovation and digitalization of operations remain insufficient, limiting their ability to attract and facilitate investment in an agile and efficient manner, which is key in vibrant sectors such as digital-intensive industries. There are notable contrasts between countries in this respect, with some national agencies at a more nascent stage of digitalization, while others use a wider and relatively more sophisticated range of tools, including, for example, data analytics, maps or interactive online portals and marketing tools powered by artificial intelligence.

[11] According to information published online by Apex-Brasil on 1 April 2025.

The varying extent to which an investment promotion agency can enhance the digitalization of its operations depends largely on the development of the digital ecosystem of the country or territory in which it is located, as well as the availability of adequate digital infrastructure and skills (UNCTAD, 2023). Therefore, these elements need to be strengthened and agencies need to develop strategic and proactive approaches to enhance the innovative use of digital technologies to promote and facilitate investment linked with digital transformation. This can help to avoid the risk of widening the existing gaps between more technologically advanced agencies and those lagging behind, which exacerbate inequalities in access to, use and leveraging of these tools.

With regard to the political capabilities of investment promotion agencies, significant challenges remain in the area of coordination both between local and national levels of government and between institutions at the same level (ECLAC, 2024c). This becomes particularly complex when collaboration is required between stakeholders working on complementary policies —such as investment attraction, digital transformation and productive development— but whose priorities are not always aligned, which can reduce the effectiveness of measures. However, there are exceptions in the region. This is the case of Uruguay, which has a promotion agency that is noted for a high degree of inter-institutional cooperation and is therefore able to coordinate its investment strategies with other relevant public policies more effectively (Volpe Martincus and Sztajerowska, 2019). Beyond managing inter-institutional interests, it is also crucial to address challenges and tensions in the business sector. Although challenges remain, some countries have begun to take steps to improve policy coherence. Uruguay and Chile, for example, have adopted specific national strategies to attract FDI in the digital sector, linking them to other policy efforts.[12] One example in Chile is the partnership between the public and private sectors in the framework of the Public-Private Technical Committee for Services Exports, led by the Ministry of Finance, which aims to transform the country into a global services hub. In Brazil, the linkages between Apex-Brasil's strategy and the country's long-term national policies are noteworthy. The general trend of heterogeneity in the region also extends to the existing mechanisms for coordination in this area (ECLAC, 2024d). Where investment attraction and digital policy are concerned, these mechanisms may be formal (e.g. an inter-institutional body, working group or committee that facilitates institutional coordination), but they are often informal.

Alignment between investment promotion strategies and digital and productive development policy frameworks is key to improving the coherence and effectiveness of measures. However, even in OECD member countries, many agencies are still not actively involved in the formulation of such strategies (OECD, 2025).

In Latin America and the Caribbean, coordination of this kind is hampered by persistent obstacles. Although digital agendas have expanded in recent years to include multiple policy areas —from digital infrastructure, health and education to e-government, productive transformation, data protection and cybersecurity— limited coordination, lack of evaluation mechanisms and insufficient resources hinder their implementation (see map III.1) (ECLAC, 2025). In addition, there is often a disconnect between these agendas and productive development policies, including FDI attraction policies, making it difficult to fully harness the potential of foreign investment.

12 According to information provided online by Uruguay XXI on 18 March 2025 and by InvestChile on 24 March 2025.

Map III.1
Latin America and the Caribbean (18 countries):[a] level of development of national digitalization policies in digital agendas and strategies, 2023

Source: Economic Commission for Latin America and the Caribbean, Digital Development Observatory. https://desarrollodigital.cepal.org/en/home.

Note: The level of intensity in digital agendas and strategies is measured by three criteria: the existence of a current strategy, the scope of efforts to deal with major issues, and institutional aspects. The last include coordination, budgeting and monitoring mechanisms and gender mainstreaming. Each criterion is assessed on a scale of 0 to 3 and provides a clear picture of the development and effectiveness of digital policies in the countries.

[a] Argentina, Brazil, Chile, Colombia, Costa Rica, the Dominican Republic, Ecuador, El Salvador, Guatemala, Honduras, Jamaica, Mexico, Panama, Paraguay, Peru, the Plurinational State of Bolivia, Trinidad and Tobago and Uruguay.

Prospective capabilities are of great importance for underpinning the actions of investment promotion agencies in an uncertain and ever-changing global landscape marked by technological change. These capabilities allow them to identify emerging sectors, anticipate future needs for talent and infrastructure and inform investment attraction policies that are aligned with strategic objectives such as the digital transformation. In addition, by exploring possible futures, organizations can design strategies that are better adapted to existing conditions, thus building resilience. This implies a shift in attitude and approach, moving from a reactive to a proactive rationale in which the agency not only responds to opportunities, but also creates and shapes them, as part of a comprehensive long-term productive development strategy (ECLAC, 2007, 2024b; UNCTAD, 2023).

Despite their importance, prospective capabilities are nascent in most countries of the region and are not well institutionalized (Cuervo and Guerrero, 2018). Investment promotion agencies are no exception in this regard. As mentioned above, these agencies often do not actively participate in strategic planning, which limits their ability to contribute to long-term policies and align efforts with digital and productive transformation agendas. This stems, at least in part, from the lack of institutionalization of these capabilities in public bodies and the limited coordination among strategic planning bodies and other State agencies. Regional experience shows that institutionalizing these capabilities requires not only political will, but also institutional arrangements that are conducive to intersectoral work, collective learning and continuity of processes (Cuervo and Guerrero, 2018).

Consequently, for investment promotion agencies to integrate strategic intelligence, it will be necessary to strengthen inter-institutional coordination and create spaces for sustained interaction among promotion agencies, planning units and think tanks, universities or other actors specialized in foresight analysis.

Developing the technical, operational, political and prospective capabilities of institutions is a gradual and continuous process that agencies the world over are pursuing. Institutions in the region wishing to move in this direction must create an environment that encourages exploration, trial and error, and learning. This is a prerequisite not only for strengthening agencies' capacities, but also for improved engagement with different stakeholders from the public and private sector, and for the appropriate targeting of investment for the digital transformation.

F. Conclusions and policy guidelines

In recent years, digital sectors and assets have become increasingly strategic for countries, as reflected in trade flows, investment and active productive development policies. Governments are increasingly looking to harness the opportunities provided by digital transformation to boost economic growth, productivity and competitiveness, as well as to secure their geopolitical position.

For Latin America and the Caribbean, which must overcome the traps that hinder its development, the digital transformation is an imperative both for the present —as it strengthens resilience to external shocks amid great instability and uncertainty— and for the future. In this sense, it helps to drive innovation, learning and the development of capabilities that enable long-term, sustainable and inclusive growth. The region has a limited share as a destination for FDI announcements in the sectors linked to digital technologies, which are heavily influenced by challenges and bottlenecks in productive and technological capabilities. Between 2005 and 2024, investments went primarily to countries such as Brazil, Mexico, Colombia, Chile and Argentina, which have consolidated regional hubs. In value terms, announced FDI was largely concentrated in new digital infrastructure, while the software and information technology services sector accounted for the highest number of projects. Activities that generate greater value added, such as research and development (R&D) and production, have received less investment when compared with more advanced economies.

Against this backdrop, it is only by adopting productive development policies and active digital policies, with a comprehensive approach where the objectives of both are aligned, that the region's countries will be able to boost the potential of digital technologies. While this course of action poses its own challenges given the weak institutional capacities in countries, international experience and the experience of some countries in the region suggest that the following can contribute to a successful outcome:

- **Analysis**. A detailed analysis should be carried out of current capacities, investment gaps and potential to attract investment, with emphasis on infrastructure, digital industries and digitalization of traditional sectors. This should be the basis for subsequent strategic decisions and should be reviewed periodically.
- **Strategic definition**. A national strategy with a vision for the country and for the future that explicitly incorporates the role of FDI should be developed. This vision should guide both investment promotion agencies and productive sectors, ensuring coherence between national and sectoral objectives, such as those defined in the framework of cluster initiatives.

- **Policy alignment**. Effective linkages between digital, productive development and investment policies should be ensured through governance mechanisms that promote an integrated and complementary approach.
- **Institutional coordination and multilevel governance**. Collaboration among national and subnational public bodies should be promoted, through coordination mechanisms with clear functions (consultative, deliberative, executive) that ensure the effective implementation of the investment attraction strategy.
- **Targeted investment promotion**. FDI attraction efforts should be directed towards strategic niches previously identified in the analysis phase, prioritizing projects with high potential impact (on employment, innovation, added value and the environment) over the volume of investment.
- **Conditionalities for sustainable development**. The incorporation of requirements or incentives that channel FDI towards long-term objectives, such as the creation of quality employment, technology transfer, productive linkages and environmental sustainability, should be assessed.
- **Impact measurement and assessment**. Monitoring and evaluation systems should be designed and implemented to measure the impact of FDI on strategic objectives, using investment quality indicators that are comparable and aligned with national priorities.
- **Institutional strengthening**. Funding should be provided for the development of technical, operational, political and prospective capabilities of the institutions responsible for attracting investment, promoting the incorporation of expertise, the effective use of digital technologies, continuous learning and strategic intelligence.
- **Improved enabling conditions**. The structural and institutional factors that determine the location of FDI and the positive impacts thereof —including digital infrastructure, human talent, regulatory frameworks and productive linkages (e.g. through cluster initiatives)— should be strengthened.
- **Regional cooperation for digital governance and investment**. Regional-level dialogue and joint efforts to address common regulatory, investment and digitalization challenges should be fostered. The Digital Agenda for Latin America and the Caribbean (eLAC)[13] provides an example of how to promote common agendas that enable regulatory convergence and investment. Meanwhile, through the Platform for Cluster and Other Territorial Productive Articulation Initiatives in Latin America and the Caribbean,[14] the aim is to develop an agenda for the digitalization of production and enhance the competitiveness of digital industries through productive linkages in the region. These efforts highlight the value of regional spaces for collectively addressing challenges and opportunities that call for a regional approach, in a context of profound asymmetries —both among countries and in relation to the power of large companies.

13 https://elac.cepal.org.
14 https://www.cepal.org/en/node/60739.

Bibliography

Agência Brasil. (2024, 7 September). *El comercio electrónico brasileño totalizó R$ 196 mil millones en 2023.* https://agenciabrasil.ebc.com.br/es/geral/noticia/2024-09/el-comercio-electronico-brasileno-totalizo-r-196-mil-millones-en-2023#:~:text=El%20Observatorio%20del%20Comercio%20Electr%C3%B3nico,1%20mil%20millones%20en%202023

Argentine Investment and International Trade Agency. (2022). Software. *Informe Sectorial para Inversores Internacionales* (3).

BITNESS. (2024, 22 October). *Centros de datos en Perú para el crecimiento en LATAM: el Perú se consolida como destino clave para la expansión de centros de datos en América Latina.* https://bitness.pe/centros-datos-peru-crecimiento-latam

Brazilian Trade and Investment Promotion Agency. (2022, 22 November). *Projeto da ApexBrasil em parceria com a ABVCAP e Israel Trade & Investment é premiado por órgão da ONU.* https://apexbrasil.com.br/br/pt/conteudo/noticias/projeto-da-apexbrasil-em-parceria-com-a-abvcap-e-israel-trade---.html

Bukht, R. and Heeks, R. (2017, 3 August). Defining, conceptualising and measuring the digital economy. *Development Informatics Working Paper* (68). University of Manchester. https://dx.doi.org/10.2139/ssrn.3431732

CBInsights. (2024a, 12 March). *The Big Tech AI Arms Race: 75+ AI Startups Backed by Amazon, Google, Microsoft, and Nvidia.*

CBInsights. (2024b, 12 June). *Big Tech in Healthcare: How Amazon, Google, Microsoft, & Nvidia are Looking to Transform Drug R&D, Primary Care, and More.*

CBInsights. (2024c, 4 September). *Big Tech in Energy: How Amazon, Google, Microsoft, & Nvidia are Advancing the Global Energy Transition.*

Cuervo, L. M. and Guerrero, F. (Eds.) (2018). Prospectiva en América Latina: aprendizajes a partir de la práctica. *Seminars and Conferences Series* (88) (LC/TS.2018/38).

Da Silva, F. and Núñez, G. (2021). Free competition in the post-pandemic digital era: the impact on SMEs. *Project Documents* (LC/TS.2021/15). Economic Commission for Latin America and the Caribbean.

Dunning, J. H. (2002). European foreign direct investment in Latin America. In Z. Vodusek (Ed.), *Foreign Direct Investment in Latin America : The Role of European Investors.* Inter-American Development Bank.

Economic and Social Commission for Asia and the Pacific. (2023). *Policy Guidebook on Attracting and Promoting FDI in the Digital Economy* (ST/ESCAP/3075).

Economic Commission for Latin America and the Caribbean. (2007). *Foreign Direct Investment in Latin America and the Caribbean, 2006* (LC/G.2336-P).

Economic Commission for Latin America and the Caribbean. (2010). *Foreign Direct Investment in Latin America and the Caribbean, 2009* (LC/G.2447-P).

Economic Commission for Latin America and the Caribbean. (2018). *Data, algorithms and policies: Redefining the digital world* (LC/CMSI.6/4).

Economic Commission for Latin America and the Caribbean. (2021). *Foreign Direct Investment in Latin America and the Caribbean, 2021* (LC/PUB.2021/8-P).

Economic Commission for Latin America and the Caribbean. (2022a). *A digital path for sustainable development in Latin America and the Caribbean* (LC/CMSI.8/3).

Economic Commission for Latin America and the Caribbean. (2022b). *Foreign Direct Investment in Latin America and the Caribbean, 2022* (LC/PUB.2022/12-P).

Economic Commission for Latin America and the Caribbean. (2023). *Foreign Direct Investment in Latin America and the Caribbean, 2023* (LC/PUB.2023/8-P/Rev.1).

Economic Commission for Latin America and the Caribbean. (2024a). *Panorama of Productive Development Policies in Latin America and the Caribbean, 2024* (LC/PUB.2024/15-P/Rev.1).

Economic Commission for Latin America and the Caribbean. (2024b). *Development Traps in Latin America and the Caribbean: Vital Transformations and How to Manage Them* (LC/SES.40/3-P/-*).

Economic Commission for Latin America and the Caribbean. (2024c). *Foreign Direct Investment in Latin America and the Caribbean, 2024* (LC/PUB.2024/8-P).

Economic Commission for Latin America and the Caribbean. (2024d). Digital Development Observatory. https://desarrollodigital.cepal.org/en/home

Economic Commission for Latin America and the Caribbean. (2024e). *International Trade Outlook for Latin America and the Caribbean, 2024* (LC/PUB.2024/16-P).

Economic Commission for Latin America and the Caribbean. (2025). *Overcoming Development Traps in Latin America and the Caribbean in the Digital Age: The Transformative Potential of Digital Technologies and Artificial Intelligence* (LC/CMSI.9/3/Rev.1).

Gestrin, M. V. and Staudt, J. (2018). The digital economy, multinational enterprises and international investment policy. *OECD Business and Finance Policy Papers* (46). Organisation for Economic Co-operation and Development. https://doi.org/10.1787/0ba19bae-en

India Brand Equity Foundation. (n.d.). *Digital India*. https://www.ibef.org/government-schemes/digital-india

Institute for Mergers, Acquisitions & Alliances. (2024). *AI M&A Software Deals: Analysis of Numbers and Values.*

International Economic Development Council. (2017). Place Matters: The Role of Placemaking in Economic Development.

InvestChile. (2025, 20 January). *Chile: líder en inteligencia artificial en Latinoamérica*. https://blog.investchile.gob.cl/bloges/chile-lider-inteligencia-artificial-latinoamerica

Ivaldi, M., Petit, N. and Ünekbas, S. (2024). Killer acquisitions: evidence from European merger cases. *TSE Working Paper* (1420). Toulouse School of Economics.

Jonker, A. and Gomstyn, A. (2025, 21 de febrero). *What is an AI data center?* IBM. https://www.ibm.com/think/topics/ai-data-center

Kallmer, J. (2024). The FDI determinants for high-tech companies. *Columbia FDI Perspectives* (397). Columbia Center on Sustainable Investment.

Katz, R. and Jung, J. (2024). Impacto económico de la inteligencia artificial en América Latina. Economic Commission for Latin America and the Caribbean [unpublished].

Levy, B. (2025, 28 January). *M&A in 2025: big deals, winning hands, and wild cards*. PwC. https://www.pwc.com/gx/en/services/deals/trends.html

Mazo González, D. (2024, 10 August). *Ministerio de las TIC prepara incentivos fiscales para impulsar inversiones en inteligencia artificial*. Infobae. https://www.infobae.com/colombia/2024/08/10/ministerio-de-las-tic-prepara-incentivos-fiscales-para-impulsar-inversiones-en-inteligencia-artificial/

McKinsey. (2023, 14 July). *Five key questions to get a tech transformation right*. https://www.mckinsey.com/capabilities/mckinsey-digital/our-insights/five-key-questions-to-get-a-tech-transformation-right

McKinsey. (2024, 29 October). *AI power: expanding data center capacity to meet growing demand*. https://www.mckinsey.com/industries/technology-media-and-telecommunications/our-insights/ai-power-expanding-data-center-capacity-to-meet-growing-demand

Menski, M., Johnson, J. and De Feydeau, A. (2024, 18 November). *Data center boom in Latin America calls for accelerating infrastructure investment*. White & Case. https://www.whitecase.com/insight-our-thinking/latin-america-focus-2024-data-center-infrastructure-investment

Ministry of Development, Industry, Trade and Services. (2024). *Plano de Ação para a Neoindustrialização 2024-2026*. http://www.gov.br/mdic/pt-br/composicao/se/cndi

Ministry of Science, Technology, Knowledge and Innovation. (2024). *Data Centers 2024-2030: Plan Nacional*. https://minciencia.gob.cl/archivos/sharing/1733343018/3496/

Office of the President of the Republic. (2024, 26 January). *Brasil tiene una nueva política industrial con metas y acciones para el Desarrollo hasta el 2033*. https://www.gov.br/planalto/es/ultimas-noticias/2024/01/brasil-tiene-una-nueva-politica-industrial-con-metas-y-acciones-para-el-desarrollo-hasta-el-2033

Organisation for Economic Co-operation and Development. (2021). Investment promotion and the digital economy: a comparative analysis of investment promotion practices across the OECD. *OECD Business and Finance Policy Papers* (54). OECD Publishing. https://doi.org/10.1787/5c840788-en

Organisation for Economic Co-operation and Development. (2024). *Digital Economy Outlook 2024 (Volume 1): Embracing the Technology Frontier*. https://doi.org/10.1787/a1689dc5-en

Organisation for Economic Co-operation and Development. (2025). *FDI qualities: Investment policy framework for the digital transformation* [unpublished].

Oropeza, A. (2024, 8 August). *México se consolida como hub tecnológico, atrayendo inversión, talento e innovación*. Mexico Industry. https://mexicoindustry.com/noticia/mexico-se-consolida-como-hub-tecnologico-atrayendo-inversion-talento-e-innovacion

Padilla Pérez, R. and Gomes Nogueira, C. (2015). Determinants and home-country effects of FDI outflows: evidence from Latin American countries. *Studies and Perpectives Series-ECLAC Subregional Headquarters in Mexico* (LC/L.4060/Rev.1-LC/MEX/L.1187/Rev.1). Economic Commission for Latin America and the Caribbean.

Parkin, B. and Hodgson, C. (2024, 17 June). India pulls in tech giants for its AI ambitions. *Financial Times*.

Peruvian Export and Tourism Promotion Commission. (2024, 4 November). *PROMPERÚ trae a Lima fondos de inversión extranjeros interesados en invertir en startups peruanas de tecnología*. https://www.gob.pe/institucion/promperu/noticias/1051401-promperu-trae-a-lima-fondos-de-inversion-extranjeros-interesados-en-invertir-en-startups-peruanas-de-tecnologia

ProColombia. (2024, 24 October). *Explora el ecosistema de inversión con el "Programa de Inmersión de Venture Capital"*. https://procolombia.co/sala-de-prensa/noticias/explora-el-ecosistema-de-inversion-con-el-programa-de-inmersion-de-venture-capital

Stephenson, M. (2020, September). *Digital FDI: policies, regulations and measures to attract FDI in the digital economy*. White paper. World Economic Forum

United Nations. (2024). *The Pact for the Future. Resolution adopted by the General Assembly on 22 September 2024* (A/RES/79/1).

United Nations Conference on Trade and Development. (2017). *World Investment Report 2017: Investment and the Digital Economy*.

United Nations Conference on Trade and Development. (2021a). *Digital Economy Report 2021. Cross-border Data Flows and Development: For Whom the Data Flow* (UNCTAD/DER/2021).

United Nations Conference on Trade and Development. (2021b). *Manual for the production of statistics on the digital economy 2020. Revised edition* (UNCTAD/DTL/STICT/2021/2).

United Nations Conference on Trade and Development. (2023, January). *The digital transformation of investment promotion agencies. The IPA Observer* (12) (UNCTAD/DIAE/PCB/INF/2022/9).

United Nations Conference on Trade and Development. (2024a). *Digital Economy Report 2024: Shaping an Environmentally Sustainable and Inclusive Digital Future* (UNCTAD/DER/2024).

United Nations Conference on Trade and Development. (2024b, 6 December). *Developing economies surpass $1 trillion mark in digitally deliverable services exports*. https://unctad.org/news/developing-economies-surpass-1-trillion-mark-digitally-deliverable-services-exports.

United Nations Conference on Trade and Development. (2024c). *Global economic Fracturing and Shifting Investment Patterns: A Diagnostic of 10 FDI Trends and their Development Implications* (UNCTAD/DIAE/2024/1).

United Nations Conference on Trade and Development. (2025). *Technology and Innovation Report 2025: Inclusive Artificial Intelligence for Development* (UNCTAD/TIR/2025).

United Nations Industrial Development Organization and World Association of Investment Promotion Agencies. (2023). *Investment Promotion and Facilitation in the African, Caribbean and Pacific (ACP) region: State-of-play, Challenges and Opportunities*.

Valor Econômico. (2024, 6 November). *Brasil ganha destaque como destino para investidores estrangeiros*. https://valor.globo.com/conteudo-de-marca/apex-brasil/noticia/2024/11/06/brasil-ganha-destaque-como-destino-para-investidores-estrangeiros.ghtml

Volpe Martincus, C. and Sztajerowska, M. (2019). *How to Solve the Investment Promotion Puzzle: A Mapping of Investment Promotion Agencies in Latin America and the Caribbean and OECD Countries*. Inter-American Development Bank.

Whiting, R. (2024, 24 December). *The 24 Biggest Tech M&A Deals of 2024*. CRN. https://www.crn.com/news/software/2024/the-24-biggest-tech-m-a-deals-of-2024?page=1

World Association of Investment Promotion Agencies. (2023). *The New Laws of FDI Attraction: How to Attract, Measure and Sustain Quality FDI*.

Yepes, M. (2024, 5 August). *Innovación y talento: guía de la escena local de tecnología y startups en México*. Entrepreneur. https://www.entrepreneur.com/es/emprendedores/innovacion-y-talento-guia-de-la-escena-local-de/478030

Publicaciones recientes de la CEPAL
ECLAC recent publications

www.cepal.org/publicaciones

Informes Anuales/*Annual Reports*
También disponibles para años anteriores/*Issues for previous years also available*

Estudio Económico de América Latina y el Caribe, 2025
Economic Survey of Latin America and the Caribbean, 2025

La Inversión Extranjera Directa en América Latina y el Caribe, 2025
Foreign Direct Investment in Latin America and the Caribbean, 2025

Anuario Estadístico de América Latina y el Caribe, 2024
Statistical Yearbook for Latin America and the Caribbean, 2024

Perspectivas del Comercio Internacional de América Latina y el Caribe, 2024
International Trade Outlook for Latin America and the Caribbean, 2024

Panorama Social de América Latina y el Caribe, 2024
Social Panorama of Latin America and the Caribbean, 2024

Balance Preliminar de las Economías de América Latina y el Caribe, 2024
Preliminary Overview of the Economies of Latin America and the Caribbean, 2024

Panorama de las Políticas de Desarrollo Productivo en América Latina y el Caribe, 2025
Panorama of Productive Development Policies in Latin America and the Caribbean, 2025

El Pensamiento de la CEPAL/*ECLAC Thinking*

Repensar el desarrollo en América Latina y el Caribe: contribuciones de la Comisión Económica para América Latina y el Caribe (CEPAL) en su 75° aniversario

América Latina y el Caribe ante las trampas del desarrollo: transformaciones indispensables y cómo gestionarlas
Development Traps in Latin America and the Caribbean: Vital Transformations and How to Manage Them

Cooperar o perecer: el dilema de la comunidad mundial. Tomo I: Los años de creación (1941-1960)

Libros y Documentos Institucionales
Institutional Books and Documents

Capacidades institucionales técnicas, operativas, políticas y prospectivas (TOPP) para la gestión de las transformaciones: fundamentos para un nuevo paradigma
Technical, operational, political and prospective (TOPP) institutional capabilities for managing transformations: underpinnings of a new paradigm

América Latina y el Caribe a 30 años de la Cumbre Mundial sobre Desarrollo Social: hacia un pacto mundial por el desarrollo social inclusivo
Latin America and the Caribbean 30 Years on from the World Summit for Social Development: Towards a Global Pact for Inclusive Social Development

Panorama Fiscal de América Latina y el Caribe, 2025: impulsar la inversión para el crecimiento y el desarrollo sostenible
Fiscal Panorama of Latin America and the Caribbean, 2025: boosting investment for growth and sustainable development

Libros de la CEPAL/*ECLAC Books*

Endeudarse para cuidar: género y desigualdad en la Argentina

Sistemas de pensiones no contributivos en América Latina y el Caribe: avanzar en solidaridad con sostenibilidad
Non-contributory pension systems in Latin America and the Caribbean: towards solidarity with sustainability

Estado abierto y gestión pública: el papel del sector académico

Versiones accesibles/*Accessible versions*

Perspectivas del Comercio Internacional de América Latina y el Caribe, 2024. Resumen ejecutivo. Versión accesible
International Trade Outlook for Latin America and the Caribbean, 2024. Executive summary. Accessible version

Estudio Económico de América Latina y el Caribe, 2024. Resumen ejecutivo. Versión accesible
Economic Survey of Latin America and the Caribbean, 2024. Executive summary. Accessible version

Metodologías de la CEPAL
ECLAC Methodologies

Observatorio Demográfico
Demographic Observatory

Revista CEPAL/*CEPAL Review*

Notas de Población

Series de la CEPAL
ECLAC Series

Documentos de Proyectos
Project Documents

Coediciones/*Co-editions*

Catálogo de Publicaciones 2024-2025

Printed and bound by CPI Group (UK) Ltd, Croydon, CR0 4YY
09/11/2026
14999543-0003